A Hedonist's guide to
# London

EDITED BY Fleur Britten

# A HEDONIST'S GUIDE TO LONDON
2nd Edition

MANAGING DIRECTOR — Tremayne Carew Pole
MARKETING DIRECTOR — Sara Townsend
SERIES EDITOR — Catherine Blake
DESIGN — Katy Platt
MAPS — Richard Hale & Amber Sheers
REPRO — Dorchester Typesetting
PRINTER — Leo Paper
PUBLISHER — Filmer Ltd

SLEEP by Talib Choudhry
EAT by Lucas Hollweg and Kate Spicer
DRINK (Bars) by Nick Hackworth and Simon Kurs
DRINK (Pubs) by Jennifer Coyle and Ollie Wright
SNACK by Helen Brown and Ruby Warrington
PARTY by Fleur Britten and Julia Rebaudo
CULTURE by Fleur Britten and Freire Barnes
SHOP by Daisy Finer and Fleur Britten
PLAY by Fleur Britten and Helen Brown
INFO by Fleur Britten

Photography — Ed Lane Fox, Leila Miller, Tremayne Carew Pole, John Spaull,
Danir Fabijana, Visit London, Mark Whitfield, John Trampner, Jason Lowe, Eddie
MacDonald, Stephen McLaren, Angell
Additional research — Anita Bhagwandas

Email — info@hg2.com
Website — www.hg2.com

Published in the United Kingdom in June 2008 by
Filmer Ltd
47 Filmer Road
London SW6 7JJ

ISBN — 978-1-905428-23-6

# Hg2 London

## CONTENTS

# How to…

A *Hedonist's guide to London* is broken down into easy to use sections: Sleep, Eat, Drink, Snack, Party, Culture, Shop, Play, and Info. In each section you'll find detailed reviews and photographs. At the front of the book is an introduction to the city and an overview map, followed by introductions to the five main areas and more detailed maps. On each of these maps the places we have featured are laid out by section, highlighted on the map with a symbol and a number. To find out about a particular place simply turn to the relevant section, where all entries are listed alphabetically. Alternatively, browse through a specific section (e.g. Eat) until you find a restaurant you like the look of. Surrounding your choice will be a coloured box – each colour refers to a particular area of the city. Simply turn to the relevant map to find the location.

# Updates

Hg2 have developed a network of journalists in each city to review the best hotels, restaurants, bars, clubs, etc., and to keep track of the latest developments – new places open up all the time, while others simply fade away or just go out of style. To access our free updates as well as the content of each guide, simply log onto our website www.Hg2.com and register. We welcome your help. If you have any comments or recommendations, please feel free to email us at info@hg2.com.

# Book your hotel on Hg2.com

We believe that the key to a great city break is choosing the right hotel. Our unique site now enables you to browse through our selection of hotels, using the interactive maps to give you a good feel for the area as well as the nearby restaurants, bars, sights, etc., before you the area as well as the nearby restaurants, bars, sights, etc., before you book. Hg2 has formed partnerships with the hotels featured in our guide to bring them to readers at the lowest possible price. Our site now incorporates special offers from selected hotels, as well as a diary of interesting events taking place, 'Inspire Me'.

# The concept

A *Hedonist's guide to…* is designed to appeal to quirky, urbane and the incredibly stylish traveller. The kind of person interested in gourmet food, elegant hotels, hip clubs and seriously chic bars – someone who feels the need to explore, shop, and pamper themselves away from the crowds.

We give you an insider's knowledge of London, we want you to feel like a in-the-know local, and to take you to the most fashionable and hippest places in town to rub shoulders with the scenesters and glitterati alike.

Work so often rules our life, and weekends away are few and far between; when we do manage to break away we want to have as much fun and to relax as much as possible with the minimum amount of stress. This guide is all about maximizing time. The photographs of every place we feature help you to make a quick choice and fit in with your own style.

Unlike many other people we pride ourselves on our independence and our integrity. We eat in all the restaurants, drink in all the bars, and go wild in the nightclubs – all totally incognito. We charge no one for the privilege for appearing in the guide, and every place is reviewed and included at our discretion.

Cities are best enjoyed by soaking up the atmosphere: wander the streets, indulge in some retail therapy, re-energize yourself with a massage and then get ready to eat and party yourself into a stupor.

# London

Virgin visitors to London might expect to find it teeming with red buses, black cabs and bobbies on the beat, variously dotted around the Monopoly board, where trips to Buckingham Palace and Big Ben are followed by fish and chips and a nice cup of tea. In fact, these tourist icons live on in London, remaining as rare constants in a city that embraces progress. Though, yes, Old Kent Road really is still on the lowest rung of the property ladder, and Mayfair the highest.

Most Londoners are quietly proud of their Britishness, and, provided it continues to generate tabloid headlines while holding no real power, the monarchy remains popular. While London's historical VIPs — Shakespeare, Dickens, Newton, Darwin, etc — lend the city wisdom and influence, it is the people on the ground past and present that afford London its individuality — the Dickensian waifs and strays, the East End gangsters and pearly kings and queens, those naughty punks, goths, mods and rockers, and a multi-ethnic influx of immigrants — Polish and other Eastern Europeans, Afro-Caribbeans, Africans, Asians etc. In fact, as many as one-third of Londoners are now not British-born, largely due to the government's pro-immigration policy, and out of a total of 12 million in Greater London (some 609 square miles), its non-white population is the largest of any European city (it's also the most populous). And thanks to a tidy little tax set-up for non-domiciles, London's super-rich scene is now characterized by international bankers, Russian oligarchs, and Chinese and Indian entrepreneurs. Some Londoners complain these 'non-doms' are pushing up property and art prices (admittedly dizzying) while not contributing to the public purse; others happily welcome some of the world's best brains and biggest bank accounts.

Like New York, London is less of a melting pot, more a mosaic of cultures free to retain their own identity, mostly as a result of the (albeit controversial) policy for multiculturalism (the criticism being that it has created a cultural apartheid). But while London can seem unfriendly, insular and competitive, all over are village communities, from the quaint Englishness of Primrose Hill to the curry-pushing enclave of Brick Lane. Where Christianity once dominated, London is now a pluralist society with huge communities of Hindus (the largest outside India), Jews, Muslims, Sikhs, Buddhists and a seemingly endless supply of Hare Krishna converts recruiting up and down Oxford Street.

London is a global city – ie, along with New York, Tokyo and Paris (so go the textbooks), it has a direct effect on global affairs, culturally, politically and socio-economically; it's also the world's leading financial centre. As you'd expect from a country with the world's sixth largest GDP, money is king in its capital. London consistently hits the top five in The Most Expensive City charts.

But world-class status brings world-class quality: a new breed of superchefs means London is no longer burning its food, its art and fashion are coveted world-over (London is one of the world's four fashion capitals), its music scene continues to rock the world with ever-evolving sounds from glitch to grime, while contemporary architecture maintains an iconic skyline. Building booms for the Millennium and the 2012 Olympics brings yet more attractions. Creativity sits easy within this corporate powerhouse as London thrives on the clash of opposites – the Establishment versus the underground, tradition versus experiment, the homegrown versus the imported. London's liberal, progressive outlook makes for a modern, dynamic metropolis happy to adopt a new set of icons – namely, the London Eye, 'Chelski' Football Club and chicken tikka masala (though perhaps that was more to do with our own erstwhile cooking talents).

9

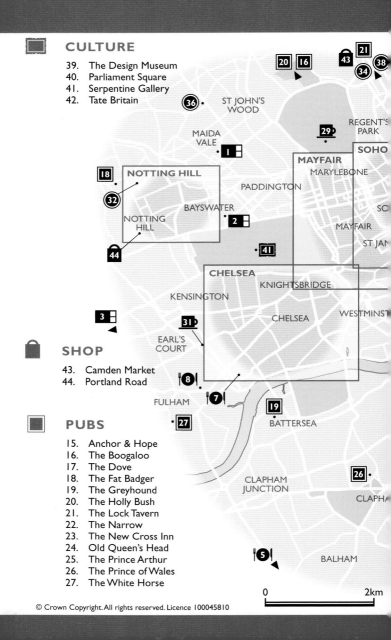

## CULTURE

39. The Design Museum
40. Parliament Square
41. Serpentine Gallery
42. Tate Britain

## SHOP

43. Camden Market
44. Portland Road

## PUBS

15. Anchor & Hope
16. The Boogaloo
17. The Dove
18. The Fat Badger
19. The Greyhound
20. The Holly Bush
21. The Lock Tavern
22. The Narrow
23. The New Cross Inn
24. Old Queen's Head
25. The Prince Arthur
26. The Prince of Wales
27. The White Horse

0        2km

ST JOHN'S WOOD

REGENT'S PARK

MAIDA VALE

SOHO

MAYFAIR

MARYLEBONE

PADDINGTON

SO

NOTTING HILL

BAYSWATER

MAYFAIR

NOTTING HILL

ST JAM

CHELSEA

KNIGHTSBRIDGE

KENSINGTON

CHELSEA

WESTMINST

EARL'S COURT

FULHAM

BATTERSEA

CLAPHAM JUNCTION

CLAPHA

BALHAM

# London city map

## PARTY

32. 12 Acklam Road
33. Bardens Boudoir
34. Barfly
35. Jazz Café
36. The Luminaire
37. Plan B
38. Proud Camden

## EAT

4. Acorn House
5. Chez Bruce
6. Cinnamon Club
7. La Famiglia
8. Marco
9. Viet Grill

## SNACK

28. Bincho Yakitori
29. The Garden Café
30. S&M Café
31. The Troubadour Café

## DRINK

10. A10 Russian Bar
11. Barrio North
12. Bistrotheque
13. Buffalo Bar
14. St Pancras Champagne Bar

## SLEEP

1. Colonnade Town House
2. The Hempel
3. High Road House

# Central London

Where is the centre of London? What exactly comprises central London? Frankly, there are several versions of the truth, not least thanks to estate agents' licence ('an exceptionally well-appointed property in the heart of central London' is often none of the above). Central London essentially constitutes the City of Westminster, and is hemmed in by the river (south), the City (London's financial centre; east), Regent's Park (north) and Park Lane (west). If you were to follow a road sign that read, 'Central London, 20 miles' for precisely 20 miles, you'd eventually find yourself at Charing Cross Station: it is from here that all mileages to London are measured (it's not the geographical centre, simply fuzzy British logic).

London's dark heart is known as the West End – an imprecise zone that is neither west nor an end, but that buzzes with pleasure-seekers (note though that the pace of life is fast and tourists are often on the receiving end of pavement rage for walking too slowly). It includes the consumer frenzy of high-streety Oxford Street and Regent Street, the rather more exclusive Bond Street, Covent Garden's theatreland and seedy Soho. Covent Garden (once 'Convent's Garden' where monks grew vegetables and which until recently had a huge fruit and veg market), right, is now an entertainment and shopping destination with theatres and street performers galore, hip clothes shops, and lots of dawdling tourists unfeasibly fascinated by those silver-frosted living statues.

Soho, a historic network of narrow streets, harbours numerous wanton scenes (gay, sex, nightlife – sometimes all at once), the creative industries (advertising, TV and film) and an extended family of colourful characters that exist outside convention and inside its pubs. Also in the West End are Leicester Square (aka Cinema Central and Tourist Hell – a pedestrianized square full of naff nightclubs, rip-off restaurants, cut-price ticket booths and preying pickpockets) and Piccadilly Circus (London's Time

Square, with vast neon advertising hoardings, a statue of Anteros, the Greek god of requited love, often mistaken for his – possibly more appropriate – brother Eros, god of love and lust, and lots of traffic; people even say 'Oooh, it was just like Piccadilly Circus' to mean extremely busy). Avoid both. Just north of Leicester Square is London's compact but authentic Chinatown – the main drag is Gerrard Street with ersatz oriental gates, phone box pagodas, and ornamental lions, dragons and lanterns.

Beyond the West End, the capital is back to business. The legal quarter lies just east in Holborn, and has done since medieval times when barristers worked and lodged in public houses, so-called the Four Inns of Court (Lincoln's Inn, Gray's Inn, Inner Temple and Middle Temple – the latter two were owned by the Knights Templar and are now the haunt of Da Vinci code-crackers; all now mark geographical areas).

To the north are Bloomsbury and Fitzrovia. Bloomsbury is considered London's intellectual land, home to the University of London, The British Museum and, in the early 20th century, the Bloomsbury Group, an elite circle of artists and writers, including Virginia Woolf, EM Forster and John Maynard Keynes. Blue plaques punctuate Bloomsbury's elegant Georgian terraces to commemorate other brainy residents – Dickens, WB Yeats and Edgar Allen Poe. Just west of Bloomsbury, to the west of Tottenham Court Road (the golden mile of electrical bargains), is Fitzrovia (aka Noho, as in North of Soho), which has become a zone for TV and post-production companies, and also includes a little-known Spanish quarter.

0    250m    500m

Underground
Station

## EAT

9.  L'Atelier du Joel Robuchon
10.  Barrafina
11.  Hakkasan
12.  J. Sheekey
13  Yauatcha

## SHOP

Broadwick Street
Brewer Street
Earlham Street
Floral Street
41.  Hamley's
42.  Liberty
Monmouth Street
Neal Street
Shorts Gardens

## SNACK

20.  Balans
21.  Dehesa
22.  Maison Bertaux
23.  National Café
24.  Villandry
25.  Wahaca

## DRINK

14.  Bloomsbury Bowling
15.  Electric Birdcage
16.  Shochu Lounge
17.  Vanilla Bar

# Mayfair and North

Flanking the south of the West End is the political powerhouse of Westminster, the royal seat in Victoria, and Mayfair. Monopoly's premier property zone, Mayfair remains a des res for old money and new (particularly Russians and Arabs), understandably charmed by its palatial properties, the quaint bistros and bars of Shepherd Market, and its proximity to London's best auction houses, commercial art galleries and Bond Street boutiques. It's only fitting that such privilege is cushioned by a generous buffer of royal parkland – St James's Park, Green Park and Hyde Park.

North of Mayfair is Marylebone, at once a villagey residential area, a destination for medical excellence with Harley Street's numerous private dental and cosmetic clinics, and a stronghold of independent endeavour with boutiques, coffee shops and eateries.

North London proper starts at King's Cross (beyond this map). In Victorian times it was an industrial area serviced by Euston, King's Cross and St Pancras stations, but its redbrick warehouses were eventually abandoned by all but prowling prostitutes and junkies. King's Cross is now undergoing a major urban regeneration spearheaded by the arrival of uber-architect Norman Foster's Eurostar rail link at St Pancras Station, opened late 2007.

To its north-west is Camden, a training-ground for London teenagers riding out their angry goth phase, and a stomping-ground for subversives of all ages (punks, emos, crusties; Doc Martens remain the boots of choice); shopping for bootleg CDs and vintage clothes at Camden market is a rite of passage for any young Londoner. Tapping into the glamour of rebellion, a hedonistic clique of indie rock stars – the Camden Caners – recently made Camden cool again, and big investments in hip hangouts followed. Just west is the vastly prettier and posher Primrose Hill – a picturesque hilltop park with views over

London, sandwiched between London Zoo and its own village. Its cosy gastropubs, expensive Victorian townhouses and celebrity scene have made it a fashionable destination, though now loaded bankers have bought into it, forcing up property prices and, some say, pushing out its soul. On Camden's east is Islington, a buzzy, young area lined with independent boutiques, bars and restaurants – like its neighbour Hoxton, its fine Georgian houses are largely populated by trendy-leftie professionals, but its nightlife has become such a mecca that at week-ends, it can seem like one big stag party.

The neighbourhoods of Holloway, Archway, Highbury, Stoke Newington and Kentish Town sit just north of Islington and Camden and are large-ly residential – rent is cheaper, horizons are rugged with industrial wastelands, and there are plentiful pockets of ethnicity – just the edge to attract a cool, creative crowd.

But it is the venerable villages of Highgate and Hampstead, on either side of Hampstead Heath's rolling hills, that lend North London its intellectual and artistic associations. Famous Hampstead inhabitants have included Sigmund Freud, Robert Louis Stevenson, John Constable and George Orwell. Highgate – the highest point in London – has been home to Samuel Taylor Coleridge, JB Priestley and Yehudi Menuhin, while in Highgate Cemetery are buried Karl Marx, Douglas Adams and George Eliot. One of the area's biggest communities is Jewish, most concentrated around Golders Green. Its cemetery is the final resting-place of famous Jewish people including Marc Bolan, Peter Sellers and Sigmund Freud. Many live in North London's most expen-sive areas including 'Millionaires' Row' – The Bishops Avenue near Highgate. Increasingly also a lair also for London Arabs, it's rather like Hollywood's Bel-Air, with faux Grecian temples here, mock Tudor mansions there and one-upmanship all around.

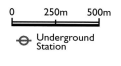

**Underground Station**

## PARTY

29. Mahiki

## SHOP

    Bond Street
    Bruton Street
    Conduit Street
32. Dover Street Market
33. Fortnum & Mason
34. Gray's Antique Markets
    Jermyn Street
    Marylebone High Street
    Savile Row
35. Selfridges
    South Molton Street

## SNACK

26. Claridge's
27. Inn the Park
28. Sketch Parlour

## DRINK

24. Claridge's Bar
25. Duke's Hotel Bar

# Chelsea and South

Kensington, Chelsea and Fulham remain the territory of the Sloane, that upper-middle-class horsey type identified in the 1980s and named after one of their favourite haunts, Sloane Square. Extending from Sloane Square is the King's Road where the Swinging Sixties – and Mick Jagger, Twiggy and Mary Quant – once swung, and where punks roamed in the 1970s, lured by Vivienne Westwood and Malcolm McLaren's emporium called (for controversy's sake) SEX. These days, the youthquake has passed and the scene is rather more Chelsea Pensioners (those scarlet-uniformed war veterans who retire to the Chelsea Royal Hospital) and Sloanes (not dissimilar to their 1980s counterparts, if now more posh-chav in appearance – stripey blonde hair and lots of slap) who can afford to live in the area's beautiful townhouses.

Some of Britain's most expensive real estate is in nearby Belgravia – grand, stuccoed houses all painted cream gloss, many inhabited by international embassies. Next door, Knightsbridge – certainly no knockdown neighbourhood, having at the time of going to press claimed the world record at £6,000 per square foot – is home to Harrods, the designer boutiques of Sloane Street, and affluent Arabs. Just west is South Kensington, also posh and pricey but with the added gravitas of 'Albertopolis', a loose campus of national museums and colleges commissioned by Prince Albert in the 1850s.

Most of South London lies south of the river (beyond the map). Known as 'Saarf London' because of its working-class majority, it's arguably the underdog in terms of wealth and status. Fans maintain that inhabitants are salt-of-the-earth, hard-working types and not the bourgeois snobs of the north (NB: petty north–south rivalry endures). Critics – usually North Londoners – say it's an ugly, unsafe suburban sprawl with terrible transport links. In reality, it's this and more – its lag stems from pre-bridge medieval times when North London was developed and South London languished – few historic monuments were built here. However, the South Bank is London's most important contemporary culture centre, and is lined with galleries, concert halls and theatres.

Just beyond the riverbank, Waterloo, Southwark, Borough and Bermondsey have all seen recent gentrification of old industrial-age factories. Further south, Elephant and Castle, Vauxhall and New Cross (an area that includes Old Kent Road, Monopoly's cheapest street) are more 'earthy', with gloomy tower blocks and grim shopping centres. Some delight in these last bastions of pre-gentrification – New Cross, the scene of the latest youthquake, is being hailed as South London's Shoreditch; non-believers call it all plain inner-city decay. Upstream are Battersea and Clapham, residential neighbourhoods with plenty of live-ly hangouts to service its young (and conventional) graduate communi-ty. With Battersea Park (and its boating lake, zoo and river views) and Clapham Common (with its summer concerts), the quality of life is good and the reason why many good-time South Africans and Australians settle here.

Brixton, Camberwell and Peckham are the antidote to the safe, squeaky grad scene. Here you will find Jamaican communities in Brixton, West Africans in Peckham, and a mixture in Camberwell; these areas are also popular with the liberal, middle-class and politically cor-rect social-worker cliche who wants to unite with their brothers and sisters, preferably in a communal squat over a Camberwell Carrot (a fat spliff). Music is instrumental to the area, especially Brixton, whose black- and dance-music scenes attract both diehard and try-hard club-bers. Brixton is not all so mellow, however – the area is charged with attitude, and an increasing Yardie presence, a high incidence of gun, drug and street crime, and a history of race riots lend a tough edge. Camberwell and Peckham, with the nearby Camberwell College of Arts, share a more easy-going, artistic feel, though all – run-down and rough yet dynamic and diverse – provoke extreme reactions either way. Rather like the north–south divide in fact.

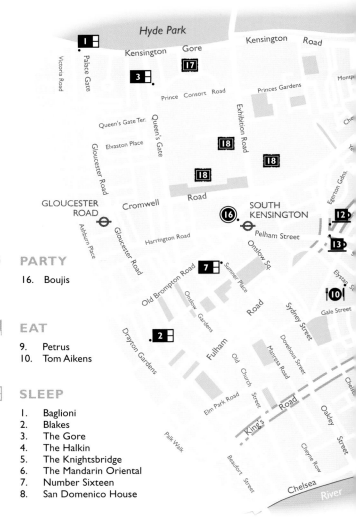

## DRINK

11.  Blue Bar

Hyde Park

Kensington Gore

Kensington Road

**SLEEP**

## PARTY

16.  Boujis

## EAT

9.  Petrus
10.  Tom Aikens

## SLEEP

1.  Baglioni
2.  Blakes
3.  The Gore
4.  The Halkin
5.  The Knightsbridge
6.  The Mandarin Oriental
7.  Number Sixteen
8.  San Domenico House

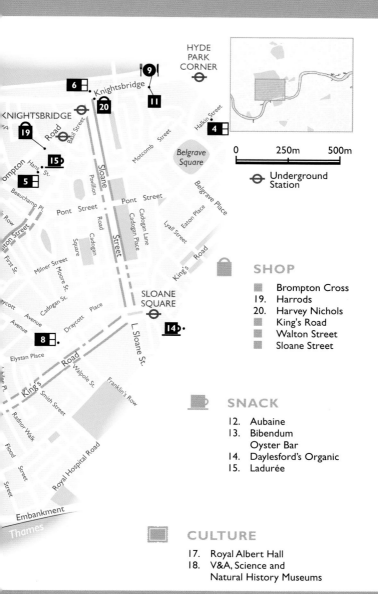

# Chelsea and South local map

HYDE PARK CORNER

KNIGHTSBRIDGE

Knightsbridge

Brompton Road

Basil Street

Sloane Street

Hans St.

Beauchamp Pl.

Pavillion Road

Pont Street

Cadogan Square

Milner Street

Moore St.

Cadogan St.

First St.

Draycott Avenue

Draycott Place

Elystan Place

King's Road

Smith Street

Radnor Walk

Miller Pl.

Walpole St.

Franklin's Row

Flood Street

Street

Embankment

Thames

Morcomb Street

Belgrave Square

Belgrave Place

Eaton Place

Lyall Street

Cadogan Lane

Cadogan Place

King's Road

SLOANE SQUARE

L. Sloane St.

Royal Hospital Road

Halkin Street

| 0 | 250m | 500m |

Underground Station

## SHOP

Brompton Cross
19. Harrods
20. Harvey Nichols
King's Road
Walton Street
Sloane Street

## SNACK

12. Aubaine
13. Bibendum
 Oyster Bar
14. Daylesford's Organic
15. Ladurée

## CULTURE

17. Royal Albert Hall
18. V&A, Science and
 Natural History Museums

# Notting Hill and West

There's a particular breed of West Londoners – posh, conservative (and Conservative) and English – whose reputation prevails over the entire area, so much so that the expression 'that's so West London' (often used by the more hip, possibly chippy, Hoxtonites) has come to describe a look that is pretty, safe and moneyed. The heartbeat of this bourgeoisie radiates from Notting Hill, where stuccoed mansions provide the kind of comfort to which these Londoners are accustomed. In truth there are other power tribes in Notting Hill: in the 1950s, West Indian immigrants took root here and local Caribbean culture continues to be a proud part of street life. The annual Notting Hill Carnival in August – started in the 1960s to promote harmony between the immigrant communities and the English majority – is still Caribbean in flavour, with steel drum bands and exotically dressed dancers on floats. The privileged throw parties on their decked terraces overlooking the riffraff – rather less integrationist but, frankly, London's biggest street party needs all the space it can get.

In the 1960s Notting Hill was a haven for bohemians and many still live here, now with their grown-up posh-hippy offspring. Other settlers – from Morocco, Spain, Portugal and Greece – have added a welcome Mediterranean flavour with vibrant bistros and colourful food markets, but in many ways Notting Hill remains awfully English – hence a good location for a Hollywood romcom about a Hollywood star who falls in love with an archetypal bumbling British chap (Hugh Grant, who else?). And the film? *Notting Hill*, of course. That location manager had a gift of a job – Notting Hill's middle-class bohemia makes for a perfectly picturesque set thanks to the romance of Portobello Road, a cute, characterful lane lined with candy-coloured cottages, and buzzing with antiques shops and its famous street market. Just west (beyond this map), Holland Park is a grown-up, more affluent version of Notting Hill, minus the ethnic diversity. The steady encroachment of bland-tasted bankers into both areas has seen the high-end global brands move in, and individuality increasingly driven out.

Further west, the BBC's TV studios take out a large proportion of Shepherd's Bush; the rest a home for Polish, East African and West Indian communities (and lots of Brits). Its neighbour, Hammersmith, is right on the river with historic pubs aplenty; both are a mix of expensive townhouses and sorry social housing.

Plenty of other ethnic enclaves characterize West London – Bayswater's hookah cafés and shwarma shops service a lively Lebanese, Egyptian and Algerian community; St John's Wood is a wealthy Jewish district (also home to EMI's Abbey Road recording studio and that famous zebra crossing,  hence a place of pilgrimage for Beatles fans), while Earl's Court has become a refuge for backpacking antipodeans, and Kilburn for the Irish.

West London also has a rich royal legacy – Britain's kings and queens have historically looked west for their parks and palaces. Hyde Park, acquired by Henry VIII as a hunting ground, spreads westwards from Marble Arch to Kensington. At the west end of Hyde Park is Kensington Palace, once home to the Prince and Princess of Wales (Charles moved to St James's after his divorce from Diana); further out is Hampton Court, Henry VIII's Tudor palace on the Thames, and Richmond Park, London's largest open space with 2,350 acres, and a royal park since the 13th century. Windsor Castle, the Queen's weekend retreat, is 20 miles west in the Berkshire countryside. No wonder the posh chose this royal corridor to take up residence.

WESTBOURN
Gt. Western Road
Tavistock Crescent
Aldridge Rd. Villas
Tavistock Road
St. Luke's Rd.
All Saint's Rd.
Lancaster Road
Westbourne Park Road
Ledbury Road
Ta
 8
Talbot Road
6  5
Kensington Park Road
Portobello Road
Colville Terrace
9
Ladbroke Grove
Westbourne Grove
Chepstow Vil
Portobello Road
Pembri
Kensington Park Road
2
Ladbroke Grove
Ladbroke Square
Ladbroke Road
Holland Park Avenue

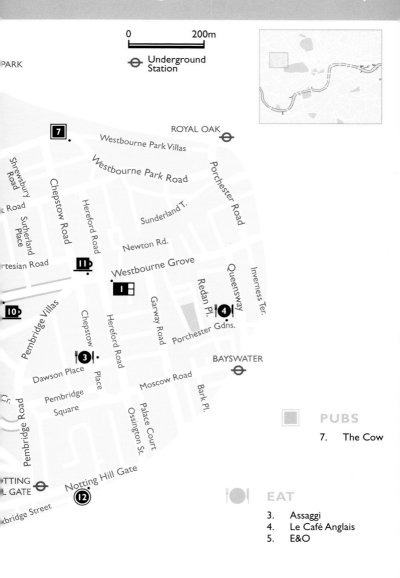

0    200m

⊖ Underground
   Station

PARK

ROYAL OAK ⊖

Westbourne Park Villas

**7**

Westbourne Park Road

Shrewsbury Road

Porchester Road

Chepstow Road

Hereford Road

Road

Sutherland Place

Sunderland T.

Newton Rd.

tesian Road

**11**

Westbourne Grove

**1**

Queensway

Redan Pl.

Inverness Ter.

**10**

Pembridge Villas

Garway Road

**4**

Porchester Gdns.

Chepstow Place

Hereford Road

**3**

BAYSWATER ⊖

Dawson Place

Moscow Road

Bark Pl.

Cr.

Pembridge Square

Pembridge Road

Palace Court

Ossington St.

TTING
L GATE ⊖

Notting Hill Gate

**12**

bridge Street

PUBS

7.    The Cow

EAT

3.    Assaggi
4.    Le Café Anglais
5.    E&O

# The City and East

All eyes have gazed on the dynamic east in the last few years, with the self-consciously cool, arty camp gravitating towards Shoreditch, Hoxton and Hackney, and ever more stratospheric skyscrapers being built in Canary Wharf.

London's eastern promise begins in Clerkenwell, where abandoned warehouses, old French Huguenot residences and ex-watchmakers' workshops have been converted into loft accommodation, photographic studios, media offices, style bars, gastropubs and night clubs. Just south is Fleet Street, forever the namesake of British journalism, and although all the papers have now dispersed, some of the original buildings and legendary pubs frequented by legendary hacks still remain. Just east, the City of London contains the 'square mile' of London's financial quarter. During the week, it's eyes down, full throttle in hive-like endeavour where the Stock Exchange is the queen bee; by the weekend, it's a ghost town. Alongside the City's contemporary architecture (famously, the Gherkin and Lloyds of London, pictured right) are some of the oldest parts of London — scores of 17th-century Wren-designed churches (including St Paul's Cathedral), the medieval Tower of London and relics of Roman walls.

Hoxton and its neighbours Shoreditch and Hackney are collectively London's HQ of cool (at least its residents smugly claim as much, with their experimental haircuts and clashing thrift chic). In the early 1990s, it was a wasteland of disused industrial structures and rundown council estates. Impoverished artists moved in, bringing with them cachet and counterculture, and other creatives soon followed (notably the dot-com entrepreneurs). Cheap rents also lured an influx of immigrants — Bangladeshis populate Brick Lane (now famed for its curry houses); the Vietnamese settled around Kingsland Road and Afro-Caribbeans in Hackney. Then came gentrification and the chains, yet more chains, and the bridge and tunnellers — on a Saturday night it can feel more like Leicester Square. As money continues to pour into East End night culture, with private members' clubs and glossy, over-designed bars, the avant garde marches on to ever more remote sites of graffiti-ed, gritty urbanity – Dalston, Stoke Newington and Hackney Marshes. Meanwhile, the artistic community has come of age, attracting bankers with bonuses to blow at the burgeoning commercial art gallery scene of Hackney's Vyner Street and Herald Street. The East's crown of cool endures, albeit now ripe for parody with all those tragic

try-hards. But the real tragedy is that the original working-class East Enders – or Cockneys, born within earshot of Bow Bells – have been displaced by soaring property prices paid for by middle-class 'Mockneys'. To that, they probably retort, 'What a load of pony and trap.'

Further east is the City's younger brother, Canary Wharf (beyond this map) – a recent financial development built on old docklands that includes three of London's tallest buildings: the totemic office blocks of One Canada Square, and HSBC and Citigroup Towers. The entire area is designed with one thing in mind – maximizing profits, minimizing distraction – so there's not much to see. Just next door is the infamous Millennium Dome, the Labour Party's colossal white elephant, which is now a concert venue, The O2 Arena, while further east is Greenwich and the chance to walk the line of longitude that marks GMT (evidence that London really is centre of the universe). Greenwich is also London's maritime zone and home to the Old Royal Naval College and the famous 19th-century tea clipper, the *Cutty Sark*. And with the preparations for the London Olympics to be held in Stratford (just east of Hackney) in 2012, there's yet more urban regeneration, human traffic and focus to come to East London.

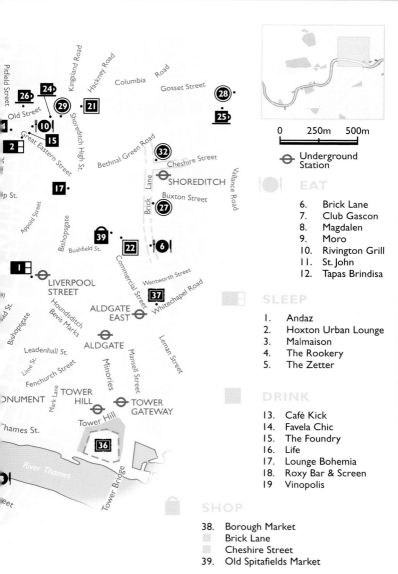

Kingsland Road

Hackney Road

Columbia Road

Gosset Street

Pitfield Street

Old Street

**26**

**24**

**29**

**21**

**28**

**25**

Shoreditch High St.

**10**

**15**

**2**

Great Eastern Street

Bethnal Green Road

**32**

Cheshire Street

## SHOREDITCH

Brick Lane

Vallance Road

**17**

p St.

Buxton Street

**27**

Appold Street

Bishopsgate

Bushfield St.

**39**

**22**

**6**

Commercial Street

**1**

Wentworth Street

## LIVERPOOL STREET

Houndsditch

Bevis Marks

**37**

Whitechapel Road

## ALDGATE EAST

Bishopsgate

Leadenhall St.

## ALDGATE

Lime St.

Fenchurch Street

Mansell Street

Minories

Leman Street

MONUMENT

Mark Lane

## TOWER HILL

## TOWER GATEWAY

Thames St.

Tower Hill

**36**

River Thames

Tower Bridge

leet

0    250m    500m

Underground Station

## EAT

6. Brick Lane
7. Club Gascon
8. Magdalen
9. Moro
10. Rivington Grill
11. St. John
12. Tapas Brindisa

## SLEEP

1. Andaz
2. Hoxton Urban Lounge
3. Malmaison
4. The Rookery
5. The Zetter

## DRINK

13. Café Kick
14. Favela Chic
15. The Foundry
16. Life
17. Lounge Bohemia
18. Roxy Bar & Screen
19 Vinopolis

## SHOP

38. Borough Market
    Brick Lane
    Cheshire Street
39. Old Spitafields Market

# sleep...

In eclectic, eccentric London, sleek design hotels rub shoulders with chandelier-strewn *grandes dames*, bijou boutique residences and a plethora of global chains that offer comfortable but homogenous lodgings with a corporate bias (needless to say, the latter don't get much of a look-in here). Some of London's oldest hotels are also the most beautiful and atmospheric. Claridge's, Brown's and The Ritz conjure up a glamorous, old-world feel reminiscent of empire and PG Wodehouse's Jeeves and Wooster. Each has proudly preserved the quintessentially British tradition of afternoon tea: their tea salons are destinations in their own right. The grand hotels constantly vie for poll position, with ongoing renovation (in many cases literally re-gilding the lily), competitive service (offering personal butlers, e-butlers even, and striving for the highest staff-to-guest ratio) and discreet modernization (WiFi here, bluetooth there, all concealed behind a façade of tradition); all are seemingly out to win the title for the biggest, tallest, longest, most expensive presidential suite. The upshot is excellent service in the plushest of surroundings – at a price (London's hotels were recently declared the most expensive in Europe).

Intimate boutique hotels range from the ultra-modern (The Hempel, The Baglioni) to those bursting with period charm (Hazlitt's, Miller's Residence). But the notion of a 'boutique' hotel is as much about sensibility as it is about size, as Soho Hotel, part of husband-and-wife duo Tim and Kit Kemp's ever-expanding empire has proved. It may have 91 rooms, but it also bears all the boutique hallmarks, thanks to the Kemps' quirky and charming English-style design. Meanwhile, as the concept of luxury is ever de-valued by the ubiquity of Frette bed linen, pillow menus and Molton Brown toiletries, the top hotels are developing a gap in the luxury market: the personal touch – in décor (with, for example, Marilyn Monroe's shoes in one room of San Domenico House) and service (Andaz has banished hand-tucked-behind-the-back formality entirely).

Another emerging trend is for self-contained apartments with 24-hour room service – perfect for private types who'd need a disguise just to get down the hotel corridor, or indeed who'd prefer to walk it naked. Apartments are available at The Hempel, but No. 5 Maddox Street, which pitches itself as a 'hotel alternative', offers the best value, location and flexibility in terms of length of stay.

London's design hotels (The Sanderson, St Martin's Lane, Andaz) – unfairly renowned for employing models for staff and (therefore) for lofty service – all clamour for the holy trinity of the hotel industry: the hottest restaurant, the coolest bar and the hippest guests. Not that the hip hotel bar is exclusive to contemporary hotels: the classics alike know a good branding exercise when they see one. London's hotel bars are often more beautifully designed, and attract more beautiful people, than the rooms themselves – see and be seen at The Langham's Artesian Bar, Claridge's Bar, Soho Hotel's Refuel and The Sanderson's Long Bar. But to really generate a scene, the haute hotels are starting to throw wild parties, for example at St Martin's Lane (with the arrival of members' club Bungalow 8), Haymarket Hotel, right, (with their drag-queen pool parties), and Claridge's and Andaz (with regular sceney parties). Londoners themselves have

not been beyond temptation at four in the morning when they can't remember where they live and there's the promise of a fry-up breakfast in a crisp king-size bed. Benders in hotels are good for business.

The rates quoted here range from the price of a standard double in low season to a one-bedroom suite in high season (from May to September; Christmas and Easter are also peak times).

**Our top ten hotels in London are:**
1. Claridge's
2. Mandarin Oriental
3. Haymarket Hotel
4. The Lanesborough
5. The Connaught
6. The Ritz
7. The Sanderson
8. Brown's
9. Hazlitt's
10. Miller's Residence

**Our top five hotels for style are:**
1. The Sanderson
2. Claridge's
3. Miller's Residence
4. High Road House
5. The Connaught

**Our top five hotels for atmosphere are:**
1. Claridge's
2. Andaz
3. The Sanderson
4. Haymarket Hotel
5. Hoxton Urban Lodge

**Our top five hotels for location are:**
1. The Ritz
2. Mandarin Oriental
3. Brown's
4. The Lanesborough
5. The Knightsbridge Hotel

## Andaz, 40 Liverpool Street, EC2

Tel: 020 7618 5000  www.andaz.com
Rates: £160–720

Woah! Where's the front desk? Where's the concierge? You're really offering bedtime stories? Andaz – the first of a brand new Hyatt chain – is getting brave with its concept. What was until 2007 The Great Eastern Hotel has done away with convention: removing all physical barriers, things are meant

to be a bit more personal (andaz meaning personal style in Hindi). And inventive – hence short-term ideas like the 'reader-in-residence', drag-queen room service and beach parties in the foyer. For all that, it's still a grand old station hotel: behind the Victorian redbrick façade lies a sleek, modern lobby, vast atrium and exposed glass lift shafts, which sit alongside original 1880s staircases and stained-glass windows. The 267 five-star rooms (including 25 suites) feature clean lines, dark woods, cream tones, chrome accents. Its seven bars and restaurants include Aurora, a modern European restaurant with a beautiful stained-glass dome; the buzzy Eastway brasserie; the excellent Catch seafood restaurant; and the Champagne Bar. But back to that innovation: Andaz is keen that everything is all-inclusive, so extras such as laundry, movies and a non-alcoholic mini-bar are free. Perhaps that's because they now have nothing to hide behind when guests balk at big bills.

**Style 9, Atmosphere 9, Location 7**

## Baglioni, 60 Hyde Park Gate, Kensington, SW7

Tel: 020 7368 5700  www.baglionihotellondon.com
Rates: £260–385

Like Fellini's celluloid heroines who smoulder in the wall-mounted moody stills, the Italian-owned Baglioni hotel is dark, sexy and alluring. Sixty-six five-star rooms (50 of which are suites) are housed in an imposing five-storey Victorian building that belies the glitzy opulence within; the reception area, with its polished dark-wood floors, gold-leaf walls and Murano glass chande-liers, sets a sultry tone for the rest of the hotel. The bedrooms are distinctly mas-culine with sleek, modern furniture and a palette of black and gold with flashes of scarlet. Super-

soft Frette bed linen and mood lighting add a feminine edge. In-room gad-getry is suitably slick – including Bang & Olufsen phones, Gaggia espresso machines and Philips LCD TVs (through which you can access 150 free movies and 1,500 music tracks) Downstairs, the mini-spa, gym, bar and restaurant are all added attractions, though can involve expensive add-ons. That said, the typical guest is unlikely to be phased – Kensington is the area of choice for visiting sheikhs, diplomats and minor European royals. Perhaps the bulletproof windows in the Presidential Suite were a prudent extrava-gance.

**Style 8, Atmosphere 8, Location 7**

## Blakes, 33 Roland Gardens, South Kensington, SW7

Tel: 020 7370 6701  www.blakeshotels.com
Rates: £265–565

Arguably the original boutique hotel, Blakes was the theatrical first venture of Anouska Hempel (aka Lady Weinberg, the wife of leading city financier Sir Mark Weinberg) and reflects her background as both fashion designer and actress. Opened in the early 1980s, the five-star Victorian townhouse hotel is a temple to the heady excesses of the time – heavily swagged, themed rooms have a sumptuous, boudoir feel with *trompe-l'oeil* murals and fantastical beds bedecked in exotic silks. They are perhaps a little *de trop* for more contemporary tastes but impressive nonetheless and a lot of fun. Fans of minimalism should instead beat a path to The

Hempel (see page 46) in Bayswater, Anouska's painterly masterpiece in a staggering 32 shades of white. Downstairs, the décor is dark, dramatic and sexy, particularly in the oriental-themed restaurant. The superbly executed international menu has attracted a glamorous crowd for over 20 years. It seems that here conspicuous consumption has never gone out of fashion.

**Style 7, Atmosphere 7, Location 7**

### Brown's, 33 Albemarle Street, Mayfair, W1
Tel: 020 7493 6020  www.brownshotel.com
Rates: £235–899

Opened in 1837 by James Brown, butler to the poet Lord Byron, this was London's first luxury hotel and has been a haunt for the rich and famous ever since. Following a £24 million refurbishment, Brown's was reopened in winter 2005 by hotel supremo Sir Rocco Forte and his *interiorista* sister, Olga Polizzi. Her redesign of the 11 adjoining townhouses in Mayfair is an update rather than a reinvention – The Grill restaurant still has its dark wood panelling, intricate Jacobean plaster ceiling and famous carving trolley, but has been refreshed with moss-green leather banquettes and sparkling

1930s-style lanterns. The English Tea Room (where old money mixes with the chattering class-es) and lobby are similarly tra-ditional-with-a-twist. However, Polizzi has com-pletely modern-ized the 117 five-star guest rooms (including 29 suites), chucking out the chintz in favour of a subtle mixture of Art Deco, contemporary furniture and original British artworks (such as graphic Bridget Riley prints); limestone or marble bathrooms are luxurious. The basement spa and Donovan Bar (a homage to the famous fashion photographer) are glamorous new additions that are always picture-perfect not least thanks to their well-heeled regulars.

**Style 8, Atmosphere 8, Location 9**

### Charlotte Street Hotel, 15 Charlotte Street, Fitzrovia, W1
Tel: 020 7806 2000   www.charlottestreethotel.co.uk
Rates: £225–388

As with its sisters, Covent Garden and Soho Hotels, the crowd here is a heady mix of people from the film, music and advertising worlds. Owners Tim and Kit Kemp (London's most glamorous hoteliers) have leant their contemporary English stamp to the décor – bold patterns in soft colours, all safely short of chintz – but here with a Bloomsbury Set theme (inspired by its proximity to the haunts of this elite literary circle). The cosy drawing rooms feature original paintings by Vanessa Bell and Duncan Grant, and

vibrant murals in the busy brasserie are painted in the style of early 20th-century frescos. Each of the 52 five-star rooms also features an original piece of Bloomsbury artwork or handmade furniture. Fabric-clad walls and simple, pleated canopies above the bed lend a soft but not overtly feminine feel; sleep spray and Tivoli radios by the bed are a thoughtful touch; the oak and granite bathrooms all have mini-colour TVs, deep bathtubs and walk-in showers. The popular Saturday-night film club includes dinner in the brasserie and a classic film (think *Breakfast at Tiffany's*) in the sexy red-leather basement cinema. Bloomsbury-style post-film critiques in the bar are optional.

**Style 9, Atmosphere 9, Location 8**

### Claridge's, Brook Street, Mayfair, W1
Tel: 020 7629 8860   www.savoy-group.com
Rates: £279–1,185

With a guest register that includes Queen Elizabeth II, Winston Churchill and Jackie Onassis, Claridge's is London's most-loved luxury hotel. And with its welcoming committee of whatever-madam-desires doormen, international flags flying and attendant paparazzi, arriving does feel rather like something of an arrival. That it was the hotel of choice for many a royal exile during World War II is testament to its majesty. The jewel in the hotel's crown is the stunning Art Deco lobby, topped by a vast Dale Chihuly chandelier made of 300 hand-blown glass pieces. New York-based designer Thierry Despont was responsible for renovating the building in 1999 and wisely chose to restore and update its 1930s styling. Many of the hotel's 203

five-star rooms have an Art Deco theme while others take their inspiration from the opulence of pre-revolutionary France; boldly tiled marble and chrome bathrooms are exceptionally spacious. Its added extras are equally superlative: chef Gordon Ramsay's restaurant is arguably London's best (and most expensive; see EAT), its salon *the* place for afternoon tea, and its David Collins-designed cocktail bar the venue of choice for Kate Moss' infamously debauched 30th birthday bash.

**Style 9, Atmosphere 10, Location 9**

## The Colonnade Town House, 2 Warrington Crescent, Maida Vale, W9

Tel: 020 7286 1052  www.theetoncollection.com
Rates: £135–250

This charming 19th-century townhouse lies in the gorgeous residential area of Little Venice where canals are lined with colourful narrowboats. Its unusually shaped 1920s elevator (used to transport stretchers when the building was a hospital) is a quirky historical throwback, while the softly lit tapas bar is a thoroughly modern innovation. The hotel played host to Sigmund Freud in 1938 and JFK in 1962 – both have suites named after them. The 43 four-star rooms (seven of which are suites) are full of period charm, featuring four-poster beds, rich fabrics and antiques. Many also have small terraces with canal views. Frette bed linens, bowls of apples and Penhaligon toiletries in the reasonably sized bathrooms are nice extras. A note of caution: avoid the two basement bedrooms, which reverberate with

rumblings from the Underground. This is not the place to stay if you want to be in the heart of the action, but the slightly offbeat location (which is in fact only a 15-minute tube journey from Oxford Circus) means that the luxurious rooms are very reasonably priced.

**Style 8, Atmosphere 7, Location 6**

### The Connaught, Carlos Place, Mayfair, W1
Tel: 020 7499 7070   www.the-connaught.co.uk
Rates £349–£1,400

For over a hundred years the five-star Connaught has been synonymous with royalty, glamour and celebrity – a fact which made the insanely decadent Marc Jacobs bash in February 2007 the perfect way to mark the hotel's closure for a multi-million pound refurb. A crack team of craftsmen and

41

architects (including British interior designer Guy Oliver) was then drafted in to revive period details and sympathetically integrate 21st-century comforts. The 88 guest rooms skillfully balance pale period colours, damask silks and antique furnishings with new bespoke pieces, abstract paintings and discreet technology. Beds are dressed in Italian linen and caramel cashmere blankets, while the white marble bathrooms boast both cast-iron tubs and separate showers; the most luxurious feature flat-screen TVs and sound systems. Downstairs, the jewel-coloured Coburg Bar (a reference to the hotel's original name) has been strewn with crystal chandeliers, velvet armchairs and Julian Opie paintings: the perfect place to sip an appletini after a hard day's shopping in nearby Mount Street, which, like the rest of this pretty pocket of Mayfair, is enjoying a renewed buzz.

**Style 9, Atmosphere 8, Location 9**

### Covent Garden Hotel, 10 Monmouth Street, WC2
Tel: 020 7806 1000 www.coventgardenhotel.co.uk
Rates: £285–375

A former 1880s hospital, this hip hotel is now a home-away-from-home for a mélange of fashion mavens, film directors and A-listers (Liv Tyler once

checked into the stunning two-floor loft suite for three months). Another Kemp hotel, its interior has been designed in signature 'contemporary English' style. Next to the bustling lobby (all polished wood floors and lavish floral curtains) is the low-key brasserie where theatregoers and media darlings come in waves throughout the day. A sweeping stone staircase leads up to the sumptuous drawing room and library – pleasantly quiet places where guests can sit by the log fires and admire the vivid upholstery fabrics.

Mix-and-match fabrics have also been used to wonderful effect in the 58 individually designed five-star bedrooms and suites. Frette sheets, padded headboards and ridiculously plump armchairs make for an intimate, cosy feel. Granite and mahogany bathrooms are similarly luxurious. These super-stylish yet super-comfortable rooms have ensured that the notoriously fickle cool crowd have stuck around for over a decade.

**Style 9, Atmosphere 9, Location 9**

## The Gore, 190 Queen's Gate, South Kensington, SW7
Tel: 020 7584 6601 www.gorehotel.com
Rates: £149–440

Something of a Kensington institution, the four-star Gore is enjoying a renaissance thanks to a recent £2.5 million refurbishment. The interior of the rambling Victorian townhouse is the antithesis of so many bland, contemporary hotels; with antiques and curios at every turn, and over 5,000 pictures  lining the walls, it has the air of an eccentric country house. Its 50 rooms are sumptuous and theatrical – think mirrored headboards, embroidered linens and dramatic silk swags. Perhaps the campest of all is the Venus room where the star attraction is a four-poster bed that once belonged to Judy Garland (numerous celebrities performing at the nearby Royal Albert Hall have chosen to sleep in it since). Although The Gore is stuffed with antiques, it has a decidedly unstuffy, upbeat atmosphere. Chef David Newstead is delivering satisfyingly simple comfort food in the restaurant, while the rakish Bar 190 (all deep red walls, dark woods and chocolate leather) attracts a glamorous crowd who party until 3am.

**Style 8, Atmosphere 8, Location 8**

### The Halkin, 5 Halkin Street, Belgravia, SW1

Tel: 020 7333 1000  www.halkin.como.bz

Rates: £225–385

It may have an ornate Georgian façade, but the interior of this elegant, five-star hotel is sublimely understated. Armani-uniformed staff glide around an angular white marble lobby, beyond which are curved charcoal corridors and 41 muted bedrooms in soft, earthy tones with strong black accents. There's a prevailing sense of stealth wealth and the emphasis here is on luxurious functionality – high-tech bedside control panels operate everything

from the lights to the Do Not Disturb sign; capacious marble bathrooms have exceptionally deep tubs and a generous smattering of Bulgari products. The nearby Shambhala Urban Escape (that's a gym and spa, in English) at The Halkin's much larger sister hotel, The Metropolitan (Old Park Lane, W1; 020 7447 1000), is also at your disposal. The hotel restaurant, Nahm – London's only Michelin-starred Thai – is famed for its elaborate dishes containing up to 20 ingredients. Excellent for 'event' dining and for lovers of spicy food, but for Armani-like simplicity, guests might prefer the Japanese fare (and star-spotting) at Nobu in The Metropolitan instead.

### Style 8, Atmosphere 6, Location 8

### Haymarket Hotel, 1 Suffolk Place, Trafalgar Square, SW1

Tel: 020 7470 4000  www.firmdale.com

Rates: £250–1,750

Opened in 2007, this 55-room five-star hotel contains all the Kemp

ingredients which have proved so popular in their sister hotels (Charlotte Street, Covent Garden et al), plus a few added attractions. Super-plush guest rooms are English-eccentric in feel, bathrooms are kitted out in granite and oak and the thoughtfully designed communal areas feature quirky artworks by a host of contemporary artists. But it's the glamorous 18ft swimming pool (cleverly illuminated with coloured lighting) and adjacent bar that take centre stage. The fun, buzzy atmosphere reaches a crescendo on Friday nights when The Globe Girls (drag queens who are anything but a drag) perform cabaret acts for the amusement of revellers. It's a more genteel affair upstairs in the Brumus bar and restaurant which serves Italian fare throughout the day. The hotel's super-central location (literally a stone's throw from Piccadilly Circus and Trafalgar Square) is either a huge plus or pain depending on your sensibilities. But if the commotion of the capital gets too much you can always take a stroll through nearby St James's Park.

**Style 9, Atmosphere 9, Location 9**

### Hazlitt's Hotel, 6 Frith Street, Soho, W1
Tel: 020 7434 1771  www.hazlittshotel.com
Rates: £149–300

Set in a trio of townhouses built in 1718, Hazlitt's is located in the frenzied centre of Soho, and is named after a former resident, the celebrated early 19th-century essayist William Hazlitt. The Georgian property was converted into a four-star hotel 20-odd years ago and furnished in charming period style, with plush antiques and rich paintings that complement the

45

ornate, high ceilings and beautiful (now defunct) fireplaces. Each of the 23 rooms is named after Hazlitt's friends and con-quests, who includ-ed Jonathan Swift and Lady Frances Hewitt. There are numerous atmos-pheric nooks for reading one of the many signed books left behind by visiting authors in homage to the essayist. With its discreet Frith Street entrance, the rooms are also highly prized by celebrities seeking privacy. The downside? There is no lift, air-conditioning or restaurant on site (room service is available), although its excellent location means that there are innumerable eateries nearby. Just be sure to ask for a room that doesn't overlook the street if you require perfect silence to aid slumber.

**Style 9, Atmosphere 7, Location 9**

### The Hempel, 31–35 Craven Hill Gardens, Bayswater, W2

Tel: 020 7298 9000   www.the-hempel.co.uk
Rates: £175–835

Opened in 1997 by Anouska Hempel, this five-star hotel is a temple to mini-malist design. The discreet, easily missed 'H' outside the portico-ed front door sets the tone – a sparse, white reception (all polished Italian plaster and Portland stone) is flanked at either end by long, low fires with flickering blue flames. Walls are devoid of ornament and only a handful of decorative touches break the simple lines – a roughly carved Indian door used as a table, artfully arranged groups of orchids. Each of its 36 rooms and six self-contained apartments are similarly spare. Beds are set on platforms or sus-pended from ceilings; bathtubs are hewn from blocks of black granite or pale limestone. That's not to say that rooms are monastic – Frette bed linen,

plump armchairs and Diptyque candles are comforting additions. So too are its large garden and the excellent fusion food served up in the basement restaurant I-Thai. The problem faced by era-defining design hotels is that nothing dates faster than modern design. That said, The Hempel has a sump-tuous simplicity and tranquillity that appeals to a sizeable loyal fanbase.

**Style 7, Atmosphere 6, Location 7**

### High Road House, 162 Chiswick High Road, W4
Tel: 020 8742 1717  www.highroadhouse.co.uk
Rates: £140–160

The idea behind HRH (aka Soho House Chiswick) is don't try and get home from this leafy West London suburb after a big night – just stay over. Opened in 2007 by Soho House's creator Nick Jones, the HRH crowd is

slightly older but just as media-savvy – people who've been there, designed the T-shirt and moved out to suburbia; non-members can gain instant access by staying in one of the 14 small but reasonably priced guest rooms. Design guru Ilse Crawford's judicious use of fresh colours and eclectic furniture has resulted in rooms both restful and characterful. Bathrooms have decent-sized showers (no baths) and a generous sprinkling of Cowshed products. Downstairs, the thirtysomething hipsters party like it's 1999 on Friday and Saturday nights after dumping the kids with nanny; Sundays begin with a bleary-eyed brunch accompanied by their little darlings. The location – a short stroll from Kew Gardens and a 20-minute drive to Heathrow – makes it a good West London base if the centre of town has little appeal.

**Style 9, Atmosphere 8, Location 6**

### The Hoxton Urban Lodge, 81 Great Eastern Street, EC2
Tel: 020 7550 1000  www.hoxtonhotels.com
Rates: £1–189

Put simply, The Hoxton Urban Lodge aims to offer a boutique experience on a high-street budget. In 2006, the suits behind the Pret a Manger chain

applied the same money-spinning philosophy to hospitality that transformed the humble sandwich. So far, so unappealing? Don't be put off: the results are surprisingly upmarket. Look past the explosion of 'eclectic' design motifs (mock-baronial fireplaces, ugly papier-mâché bird light fittings) cluttering the huge lobby and you'll find that The Hoxton is a jolly nice place to stay. Rooms are undeniably cosy: red fabric lamps cast a warm glow over simple, curvy furniture, Frette bed linens and flat-screen TVs, and while bathrooms are devoid of actual tubs, slate-tiled power showers feel suitably stylish. The absence of mini-bars is a minor quibble but the lobby bar's comprehensive cocktail list should adequately quench thirst; besides, the whole point is that Hoxton is on your doorstep. That and the Ryan Air-style '£1 sale' (five rooms sold each night in low season for a quid) – you'll be lucky, but with rooms available at £59 every night of the year a stay at The Hoxton is still undeniably bargainous.

**Style 7, Atmosphere 9, Location 8**

## The Knightsbridge Hotel, 10 Beaufort Gardens, SW3
Tel: 020 7584 6300  www.knightsbridgehotel.com
Rates: £210–595

Situated in a quiet tree-lined street in Knightsbridge, this beautiful town-house hotel is a stone's throw away from the chichi shops of Sloane Street. As part of the Kemp portfolio, the high-style hoteliers have tried to marry

design and affordability: considering its excellent and expensive location, this five-star hotel is reasonably priced and still provides all the Kemp classics – modern English décor, granite and oak bathrooms (with showers only) and Frette linens. Most of the 44 rooms have large windows overlooking the leafy street below – be sure to request one that does. Downstairs, the tasteful African-themed drawing room and pastel-hued library both have wood-burning sandstone fireplaces and quirky original artworks. In Kemp tradition, there is also an honesty bar, where guests can mix a drink to their liking and simply make a note of how many they've had. Whether the clientele of fur-clad ladies who waft through reception will be able to muster the energy for such a knees-up after a hard day's shopping is questionable, however.

**Style 9, Atmosphere 6, Location 9**

## The Lanesborough, Hyde Park Corner, SW1

Tel: 020 7259 5599  www.lanesborough.com
Rates: £335–845

With the double privilege of overlooking both Green Park and Hyde Park, The Lanesborough was built as a grand private residence in 1719, only to become St George's Hospital 50 years later. In the 1990s it was converted into a five-star hotel and restored to its original grandeur – halls are decked

with hand-woven carpet, magnificent oil paintings and antique silk armchairs, while the elegant Withdrawing Room and Library Bar capture the essence of a traditional gentlemen's club. Renowned chef Nick Bell oversees an Italian menu in the Tihany-designed Apsley's Restaurant, and its afternoon tea comes highly praised by The UK Tea Council. All 49 rooms and 46 suites are large and opulent (rosewood panelling, canopied beds and marble bathrooms), with subtly integrated high-tech trickery – a panel concealed in each bedside table controls virtually everything in the room, and also summons the 24-hour butler who will 'do anything so long as it's legal'. The fact that the £5,000-a-night Royal Suite is seldom unoccupied speaks volumes about the hotel's clientele (royalty, CEOs, A-listers), although every guest is privy to the same unparalleled hospitality.

**Style 9, Atmosphere 8, Location 9**

## The Langham, 1 Portland Place, Oxford Circus, W1

Tel: 020 7636 1000  www.langhamhotels.com
Rates: £179–505

When The Langham opened in 1865 it was the first luxury hotel to offer the combination of hot and cold running water and a hydraulic lift. After it was bombed in World War II, the building was used as office space by the BBC, until the early 1990s when Hilton International took it over and refurbished it (the BBC's radio HQ, Broadcasting House, is still over the road). However, this is not just another conveyor-belt chain hotel. The stone façade

mimics a Florentine palace (think gargoyles, cupolas and columns), while the public rooms reflect the power and majesty of the British Empire at its height (huge chandeliers, a palm-lined dining hall, elegant wallpaper re-created from the original design). Its 474 five-star guest rooms are less opulent but nonetheless tastefully furnished with pale French provincial furniture and striped or floral fabrics. And then, in 2007, David Collins – the man all London establishments seem to call when ready for a fix – paid a

visit, leaving in his wake The Landau restaurant (in the capable hands of Roux-trained chef Andrew Turner), and Artesian Bar (above), where Art Deco meets Orientalism meets masterful mixology meets the masters and mistresses of the media universe.

**Style 7, Atmosphere 6, Location 8**

## Malmaison, 18–21 Charterhouse Square, Clerkenwell, EC1

Tel: 020 7012 3700  www.malmaison-london.com
Rates: £125–£295

The thing about McMaison, oops, Malmaison is that as a British chain in 11 cities, you know what you're getting – a good thing to some people, not to others. But for all its homogeneity, what the 'Mal' sets out to do – namely, affordable chic – it does well. Like all the other casts of the national

mould, its 97 rooms feature minimalist design with 'moody' spotlighting, plus entry-level luxuries of Egyptian cotton bed linen, fluffy robes and techy toys (the hotel has a free DVD and CD library for in-room entertainment). Its biggest danger is its safety: monochromed this, slate-floored that, and lilac, dove and earth tones sitting politely in muted harmony – to 'rock' it up, there are antique Napoleon and Malmaison portraits (Malmaison being his grand residence outside Paris – the chain's original reference point for 'iconic style'). For that, just look out of the window: housed within the shell of a red-brick Victorian nurses' residence for St Bartholomew's Hospital, it overlooks a private park in the quaintly cobbled square – be sure ask for a square-facing room.

**Style 7, Atmosphere 7, Location 7**

## Mandarin Oriental Hyde Park, 66 Knightsbridge, SW1

Tel: 020 7235 2000  www.mandarinoriental.com
Rates: £275–1,500

The old, palatial Hyde Park Hotel (where Queen Elizabeth II learned to ballroom-dance) was given a staggering £57 million makeover in 1999, reopening its doors as the five-star Mandarin Oriental. The marble-clad, chandelier-bedecked interior is still impressively Victorian in feel and HRH would surely approve of the still-sparkling ballroom. Many of the 200 richly decorated rooms (Irish linen sheets, goosedown pillows, fresh orchids) have fine views of the park and original paintings on the walls (at a combined value of over £5 million); marble bathrooms have vast baths and separate glass-

walled power showers. The Michelin-starred restaurant Foliage and the stylish, modernist Mandarin Bar (which houses London's largest humidor and hotel wine cellar) attract a sophisticated, older crowd, while the immaculately appointed basement spa is among the best in the UK (see PLAY). £57 million well spent, it seems.

**Style 8, Atmosphere 8, Location 10**

## Miller's Residence, 111a Westbourne Grove, Notting Hill, W2

Tel: 020 7243 1024  www.millersuk.com
Rates: £150–230

This quirky, 18th-century-style B&B is run by antiques enthusiast and author Martin Miller; that he also lives here gives the four-star hotel its name, and, yes, it is his collection of antiques and *objets d'art* that decorates it. Behind

an anonymous red door lies a candlelit staircase, which leads up to a theatrical 40ft drawing room. Upholstered in rich red velvets and overflowing with antiques, it has the air of an old curiosity shop. Visitors are welcomed by a roaring wood fire and are free to help themselves to a drink from the gregarious owner's well-stocked bar. On the upper two floors are six rooms and two suites (both with kitchens, lounges and dining tables) named after English romantic poets including Byron, Keats and Wordsworth. Each has an appropriate verse by the poet on the door and opulent décor reflecting his life – the Byron room, for example, is hung with landscapes of Venice, where the poet famously swam the Grand Canal. Miller's resonates with character and old-world charm – the perfect choice for romantics seeking refuge from 21st-century life.

**Style 9, Atmosphere 8, Location 8**

## Myhotel Bloomsbury, 11–13 Bayley St, Bloomsbury, WC1
Tel: 020 7667 6000  www.myhotels.co.uk
Rates: £189–500

When it opened in 1999, Myhotel's minimalist white walls and feng shui philosophy were the talk of the town. Now, as the pendulum swings ever closer to maximalism, flashes of bright colour and softer textures have been introduced to temper the monasticism. Its four-star rooms are tasteful, tranquil and bright, if on the small side, while clever design in the compact, white-tiled bathrooms (filled with Aveda products) helps to create space. On the ground floor, Mybar is fitted out with modern design classics (Saarinen Tulip tables, Tom Dixon lights); the basement library houses arty

tomes, complementary refreshments and two workstations – popular with the high proportion of corporate clients here. There is also a 'well-being centre' (ie, a gym and treatment room) and Mysnug, a cosy area that screens black-and-white movies. A second branch is in Chelsea (35 Ixworth Place, SW3; 020 7225 7500). Both hotels ask guests to complete a form before arrival to help personalize their stay (feather or foam pillows, classical or pop music, etc) and rooms are customized accordingly. This clever gimmick helps Myhotel to feel like your hotel as soon you arrive.

**Style 7, Atmosphere 7, Location 7**

### No. 5 Maddox Street, 5 Maddox Street, Mayfair, W1
Tel: 020 7647 0200  www.no5maddoxst.com
Rates: £215–720

No. 5 Maddox Street is a discreet Mayfair hideaway that combines the luxury of 24-hour room service with the privacy and space of an apartment. Located just off Regent Street, it has 12 five-star one-, two- and three-bedroom suites with private kitchen facilities. All have understated design schemes (neutral tones, bamboo flooring, faux sable throws) and a stock of

groceries ranging from 'good' (organic pasta) to 'bad' (peanut butter) to 'baddest' (Ben & Jerry's ice-cream). Also provided are kimono robes for lounging around in and rentable Muji bikes for exploring the city. Many suites have decked balconies while two have planted terraces which offer sanctuary from the busy city below. As the only public spaces are the tiny (but tasteful) reception and steep, five-floor stairwell (there's no lift), it's best to think of it as your personal pied-à-terre.

**Style 7, Atmosphere 5, Location 9**

## Number Sixteen, 16 Sumner Place, South Kensington, SW7

Tel: 020 7589 5232  www.numbersixteenhotel.co.uk
Rates: £200–270

As part of the burgeoning empire of hip boutique hoteliers Tim and Kit Kemp, this small but beautifully furnished five-star hotel is essentially an

ultra-stylish take on a traditional B&B. Forming part of a row of gleaming white Victorian townhouses in the heart of South Kensington, Number Sixteen provides an excellent base for exploring the nearby museums and independent boutiques. Impeccably decorated, the two ground-floor drawing rooms are light and bright with a liberal sprinkling of modern art. All 42 rooms have crisp Frette linens, exquisitely hand-embroidered bedspreads and granite bathrooms. The hotel's unique selling point is an airy conservatory and a pretty, tree-filled garden which serves food throughout the day. Most of the bedrooms overlook the garden and a handful have private courtyards with direct access to it.

**Style 8, Atmosphere 6, Location 8**

## Portobello Hotel, 22 Stanley Gardens, W11

Tel: 020 7727 2777   www.portobello-hotel.co.uk

Rates: £190–310

The décor may be whimsical and chintzy, but this privately owned bolthole has been servicing all manner of wild celebrities for over 35 years. A persist-

ent rumour that Johnny Depp filled the Victorian bath in room 116 with champagne for Kate Moss, only to have a maid inadvertently drain it, is just one of the many stories feeding the mythology of Portobello Hotel. The 24 smallish four-star rooms have a bohemian feel – each brimming with flowing drapes and eclectic antiques. Many have free-standing bathtubs in open alcoves next to sumptuous four-poster or circular beds. This hotel is the distilled essence of Notting Hill – insouciantly stylish with a sexy edge. After a heavy night, guests can refuel with breakfast in bed – his'n'hers trays serve porridge and a fry-up for him, muesli and a passion fruit salad for her. The restaurant is tiny, but nearby Julie's is under the same ownership, scene-filled and worth a visit. Assuming you can be bothered to get out of bed, that is.

### Style 8, Atmosphere 8, Location 8

## The Ritz, 150 Piccadilly, W1

Tel: 020 7493 8181   www.theritzlondon.com

Rates: £270–995

Architecturally, this French chateau-style building is the grandest of London's grand hotels. Since returning to private ownership in 1995, over £25 million has been spent returning the glitz to The Ritz (née 1906). The restaurant, with its frescoed ceiling, garlanded chandeliers, marble walls, and views over Green

Park and the hotel's Italian Garden, is often cited as one of the most beautiful in the world. The 95 five-star rooms and 38 suites are impressively large and high-ceilinged, and are all decorated with rich fabrics, 24ct gold leaf and antique Louis XIV-style furniture; bathrooms are particularly sizeable. Taking tea in The Palm Court is an institution in itself and must be booked weeks in advance (the hotel is firmly on the tourist trail). The Ritz prides itself on swift service and boasts a ratio of two staff to every guest room, though a high proportion seem to spend their time intercepting scruffy interlopers in the lobby – the hotel appears to view itself as a venerable old lady to be treated with respect, subtly subverting the hotel-guest power dynamic.

**Style 9, Atmosphere 8, Location 10**

## The Rookery, 12 Peter's Lane, Clerkenwell, EC1
Tel: 020 7336 0931   www.rookeryhotel.com
Rates: £132–265

The brainchild of Peter McKay and Douglas Blain (who also own Hazlitt's in Soho), The Rookery has a similar historic charm following extensive restoration (though the associations here are rather less intellectual – it was once a brothel). Polished wood panelling, stone-flagged floors, open fires and antique furniture give the four-star hotel a period drama atmosphere. Each of the 33 rooms are beautifully decorated (carved wooden headboards, plush furnishings and claw-footed baths) and are all named after people who have lived in the building over the last 250 years. The Rook's Nest, the most sumptuous of the hotel's three suites, has a 12m (40ft) ceiling, magnificent

views across London's rooftops from St Paul's to the Old Bailey, and a bathtub in the corner of the bedroom. For added indulgence, have breakfast in bed or in the conservatory, with its small but pretty patio garden.

**Style 9, Atmosphere 7, Location 8**

### St Martin's Lane, 45 St Martin's Lane, Covent Garden, WC2
Tel: 020 7300 5500   www.stmartinslane.com
Rates: £205–680

Opened in 1999, the five-star St Martin's Lane is slightly older – and less exclusive – in feel than its sister hotel The Sanderson, but is equally stylish. Entered through towering yellow glass revolving doors (the tallest in London), the lobby is a soaring, dramatic space. Giant chess pieces, gilt

chairs and molar-teeth stools (all by designer Philippe Starck) are scattered across the open space, while recessed niches are painted a welcoming deep yellow. Flashes of mood-altering colour are a recurring theme at St Martin's – The Light Bar has four separate colour-saturated areas, and each of the 204 bedrooms has an interactive light installation, allowing guests to bathe the space in a spectrum of colours at the flick of a switch. While not afraid of making bold statements, Starck has been careful not to overdesign: there are pristine white beds, Lucite chairs and onyx desktops with floor-to-ceiling windows overlooking busy Covent Garden. If that induces agoraphobia, there's plenty to stay in for – including excellent caipirinhas at the modernist Rum Bar, fusion food at its restaurant Asia de Cuba and celeb-spotting as they spill out of its new private members' club Bungalow 8.

**Style 9, Atmosphere 8, Location 8**

## San Domenico House, 29 Draycott Place, SW3
Tel: 020 7581 5757 www.sandomenicohouse.com
Rates: £235–310

The notion that the fashion tribe is a flighty bunch is only partly true. While handbags and hemlines change with dizzying frequency, other lifestyle choices are more constant. Fashion editors are curiously loyal to their hotel of choice

 – provided they retain the three Cs (cachet, comfort and convenience). Effortlessly ticking all of these boxes, San Domenico House plays host to key members of the international press during London Fashion Week, including American Vogue editrix Anna Wintour. So what sets it apart from the others? Exclusivity (there are just 16 rooms making this a truly boutique hotel) and oodles of romantic charm.

Many of the individually themed rooms feature four-poster beds, 19th-century furniture, paintings and *toile de Jouy* fabrics, plus unique touches such as Louis Vuitton trunks in one room, a pair of Marilyn Monroe's shoes displayed in another. Crucially, the roomy commodes are large enough to accommodate the most expansive of travelling wardrobes and should visitors have an unforeseen fashion emergency the upscale shops of Sloane Square are but seconds away in a chauffeur-driven car.

**Style 9, Atmosphere 8, Location 8**

## The Sanderson, 50 Berners Street, Fitzrovia, W1
Tel: 020 7300 1400  www.sandersonlondon.com
Rates: £240–800

When the partnership between hotelier Ian 'Studio 54' Schrager and design guru Philippe Starck produced The Sanderson in 2000, the media swooned, celebrities rocked up and aesthetes applauded. Inside a grey 1950s office block (a former Sanderson wallpaper factory, hence the name), Starck has created a witty, modern 'dreamscape' with floaty drapes and eclectic statement pieces – Cocteau-esque furniture, Louis XIV settees and carved African armchairs, set against a pure white canvas. The Long Bar, a 24m (80ft) glowing onyx rectangle, and its Malaysian restaurant Suka attract

bright young things and rich businessmen who mingle with a complicit sense of quid pro quo. A courtyard garden is open to the sky for most of the year while the cloud-like Agua spa is another oasis of calm. Moodily lit mauve corridors lead onto 91 five-star rooms, all without any internal walls –

bathrooms are encased in a clear glass box and levels of privacy controlled with electronically operated white silk drapes. Studio 54 would surely approve.

**Style 9, Atmosphere 9, Location 8**

## The Soho Hotel, 4 Richmond Mews, Soho, W1
Tel: 020 7559 3000   www.firmdale.com
Rates: £250–450

The five-star Soho was opened to much fanfare in autumn 2005 by Tim and Kit Kemp, the glamorous hoteliers fast monopolizing the industry in London. Although their largest offering (with 91 rooms), it still has a boutique feel thanks to warm and witty pastels and homely florals. Despite

being in the centre of Soho, the hotel is set back in a quiet cul-de-sac. The ground-floor drawing rooms and library offer comfort and seclusion, while the bar/restaurant, Refuel, is packed with dressed-down media types. Purpose-built on the site of a former car park, rooms are well proportioned and suffused with light; large granite and oak bathrooms boast generous baskets of products from English perfumer Miller Harris. Unsurprisingly, Soho's film crowd have embraced the hotel and Hollywood executives have taken to block-booking the six top-floor apartments – the £2,500-a-night Terrace Suite, with views as far as Canary Wharf, was lauded as the world's most glamorous hotel suite.

**Style 9, Atmosphere 9, Location 9**

## The Zetter, 86–88 Clerkenwell Road, EC1

Tel: 020 7324 4444  www.thezetter.com
Rates: £160–389

When restaurateurs Mark Sainsbury and Michael Benyan opened the four-star Zetter in 2004, their aim was to offer comfort and style without the usual hefty London price tag. Mission accomplished: the 59 rooms are at once effortlessly stylish and reasonably priced. Housed in a converted Victorian warehouse in the heart of Clerkenwell, the hotel retains many original 19th-century features, counterbalanced by a contemporary-meets-kitsch décor. Flashes of vintage wallpaper, chintzy carpet and classic 1960s furniture sing out in a predominantly calm design scheme. The busy, glass-fronted restaurant serves rustic Italian fare and takes up most of the ground floor in a deliberate (and successful) attempt to attract passing trade. Retire to the high-camp retro cocktail lounge, Atrium, for post-dinner drinks,

then sink into bed with one of the Penguin Classic novels provided. Not sleepy? Then from the comfort of your room you can surf the web, rock out to one of the 4,000 music tracks available or flick the lighting panel to 'porno pink'. Enough said.

## Style 8, Atmosphere 8, Location 7

# eat...

The days when eating out in London meant enduring overcooked meat and boiled-to-oblivion vegetables are, for the most part, long gone. You may, if you look hard enough, find better French cuisine in Paris and more authentic *dim sum* in Hong Kong, but for the sheer breadth of dining experiences on offer, London now leads the way. Prices are increasingly high, but then, so too is quality (it's really only around the obvious tourist traps of the West End that restaurants charge astronomical prices for truly appalling food).

As for trends, high-end modern French remains eternally popular (much of it championed by Britain's three-Michelin star superchef and restaurateur Gordon Ramsay), although there has also been a welcome return to simplicity, with the likes of Galvin offering upmarket reinventions of Gallic bistro classics. There is some exceptional Italian (notably at Locanda Locatelli and Assaggi), some thrilling new-Indian (at the Cinnamon Club), and some pretty good Spanish (at Barrafina and Brindisa). In fact, whether you want contemporary oriental, modern British, North African or just plain cosmopolitan, you'll find it somewhere in London – and increasingly, three times a day as the fashionable power breakfast is added to the menu (try The Wolseley, Automat and Cecconi's).

One of the current buzzwords is grazing, which means a choice of smaller tasting courses in place of the standard three – there are few cuisines that haven't been given the tapas treatment. There's also a trend towards 'diffusion' restaurants, with top chefs (read: brands) such as Gordon Ramsay and Tom Aikens branching out with pubs, bistros and even a fish and chip shop. Tom's Place, with its commitment to eco-friendly fishing, marks another foodie moment: the 'environmoment' (see also Acorn House).

But perhaps most excitingly, a British renaissance is afoot. Championed by the likes of Magdalen (right), Rivington Grill and St John, it makes a virtue of the unpretentious, and while it sometimes borrows from France, Italy and Spain, its heart – and ingredients – are firmly rooted in home soil.

Some well-known names have been omitted from these pages. Where are those hardy perennials The Ivy, Le Gavroche, Le Caprice? The answer is, first, we thought you might know about them already. But, secondly, we've also tried to recommend places where you don't necessarily have to book months in advance to get a table. So Sheekey's, for example, is owned by the same group as The Ivy, and is just as exciting, but a reservation is easier to come by. In most cases, booking ahead is still essential, but it is always worth calling at the last minute to check for cancellations. Third, we've conceded – turn to page 102–103 for a round-up.

London restaurants tend not to have extended annual closing periods; with the exception of Christmas Day and possibly Easter Sunday, many are open year round. But if you want to eat on a public holiday, it's a good idea to call to check they're open.

Restaurants are rated here in three categories: food (quality of the cooking and presentation), service (efficiency and warmth) and atmosphere. The price has been calculated on the cost of three courses for one with half a bottle of wine.

An optional service charge (12.5% is generally the norm) is usually added to the final total. If you're paying by credit card, make sure you aren't paying the charge twice – unless, of course, you want to.

**Our top ten restaurants in London are:**
1. Gordon Ramsay at Claridge's
2. The Wolseley
3. Petrus
4. St John
5. Locanda Locatelli
6. J Sheekey
7. Tom Aikens
8. Chez Bruce
9. Scotts
10. E&O

**Our top five restaurants for food are:**
1. Petrus
2. Tom Aikens
3. St John
4. Locanda Locatelli
5. Gordon Ramsay at Claridge's

**Our top five restaurants for service are:**
1. Gordon Ramsay at Claridge's
2. Petrus
3. Texture
4. J Sheekey
5. Chez Bruce

**Our top five restaurants for atmosphere are:**
1. The Wolseley
2. Nobu Berkeley
3. Sketch
4. E&O
5. Scotts

## Acorn House, 69 Swinton Street, King's Cross, WC1
Tel: 020 7812 1842  www.acornhouserestaurant.com
Open: 8am–10pm Mon–Sat                                    £45
**European**

Do judge a restaurant on its box of matches. Acorn House's contains not a single match but a pack of seed sticks – the message here, from probably London's greenest restaurant, is that smoking is out, Mother Nature is in.

One day perhaps all restaurants will operate by the eco/ethical order, but for now Acorn House is out there. Opened in winter 2006 by the team behind Jamie Oliver's Fifteen restaurant (minus Oliver), all food is locally sourced (they've even got English 'champagne'), all kitchen waste is recycled or composted, plus there's green electricity, community projects… Take it that no stone is left unturned. But what about the food? Described as 'Modern London' (ie, British and European, plus gluten- and sugar-free options), it's overseen by the Roux-trained, ex-Fifteen/River Café chef Arthur Potts Dawson: risottos, roasts and grills made with high-quality ingredients and no fuss. Actually, another restaurant is hard on Acorn House's heels, with solar power and everything: only its new Hoxton outpost Water House (10 Orsman Road, N1; 020 7033 0123).

**Food 7, Service 8, Atmosphere 7**

## Assaggi, 39 Chepstow Place, Bayswater, W2

Tel: 020 7792 9033
Open: 12.30–2.30pm, 7.30–11pm Mon–Fri; 1–2.30pm, 7.30–11pm Sat     £53
**Italian**

This low-key room above a pub in Bayswater isn't the first place you'd expect to find one of London's best-loved dining experiences. There are

barely more than a dozen tables and the ochre walls punctuated by monochrome squares of modern art are definitely not to everyone's taste. But ask the capital's foodies where they most like to eat and Assaggi comes up time and again. The reason? Sardinian chef Nino Sassu's cooking is simple and restrained. It's all about Italian classics – immaculately judged calves' liver, perhaps, or a pared down plate of *spaghetti alio e olio* – made with top quality ingredients and served with genuine passion. Front of house is run by Pietro Fraccari, who greets first-timers like old friends; Assaggi has fans in high places so you may well recognize the people at the table next to you. But the hum of conversation, the laughter of contented diners and the blissfully simple food should provide all the kicks you need.

**Food 9, Service 7, Atmosphere 7**

## L'Atelier de Joel Robuchon, 13 West Street, Covent Garden, WC2

Tel: 020 7010 8600   www.joel-robuchon.com
Open: daily, noon–3pm, 5.30–11pm (10.30pm Sun)     £60
**French**

The superchef is becoming a global brand: working the same formula already applied to Paris, Tokyo, New York, Vegas and Hong Kong comes L'Atelier de Joel Robuchon, where guests seat at a (deeply sexy) illuminated counter as tapas-style French dishes with Italian and Spanish influences are prepared by the chef in front of them (hence *l'atelier*, or workshop). Of course, 'chef' is unlikely to be Robuchon himself, on account of his other commitments, but

 since he's the world's most Michelin-starred chef, London is evidently pleased to have him – or rather his brand. The concept might lack the stars or culinary acrobatics of his more prestigious sisters, but it still provides a spellbinding insight into Robuchon's magic, and can be good value, if you have the discipline to stick to the set menus; largely though, it's expensive, not least since portions are decidedly *nouvelle*. Upstairs, La Cuisine is a more formal affair: the food more intricate, the setting more intimate, the bill more immoderate, but is low on charm. For that you need to skip upstairs again to Le Bar where a dramatic fireplace, seductive cocktails and more await.

**Food 9, Service 8, Atmosphere 7**

**Automat, 33 Dover Street, Mayfair, W1**
Tel: 020 7499 3033   www.automat-london.com                              £42
Open: 7am–11am, noon–midnight Mon–Fri; 11am–4pm, 6–11pm Sat/Sun
**American**

There's no doubting Automat's A-list aspirations. This upmarket take on an

American diner is the brainchild of Carlos Almada, the restaurateur behind New York's 1990s fashionista favourite Man Ray. Almada has always cultivated a starry following, and when Automat opened in 2005 there was no

shortage of famous faces to wish him well; Alexander McQueen held a party here before the doors even opened. The celeb count has fallen off a bit since, but the place still draws an attractive crowd, all happily chowing down on upscale comfort food (there's lobster and fish cakes as well as mac'n'cheese and chicken noodle soup). Add in a buzzy brasserie vibe, sparky staff and a kitchen that works seamlessly from breakfast to dinner, and this Mayfair slice of the Big Apple has considerable appeal. Most seating is out back in a bright cafeteria-like room with an open kitchen, but if you want to get intimate, book a booth in the 'dining car', where dark leather seats and a polished wooden ceiling give the luxurious feel of a 1920s railway carriage. First-class passengers might like to reserve seats in the fine-dining room.

**Food 7, Service 7, Atmosphere 8**

### Barrafina, 54 Frith Street, Soho, W1
Tel: 020 7813 8016  www.barrafina.co.uk
Open: noon–3pm, 5pm–11pm, Mon–Sat                                    £37
**Spanish**

Sam and Eddie Hart's original restaurant Fino (33 Charlotte Street, W1; 020 7813 8010) was a shoo-in for the title of best Spanish in town. Now, though, it just feels like a warm-up for the main event. That being Barrafina: everything about the restaurant – which the brothers opened in 2007 – is bang on, from the food to the concept to the décor. Modelled on the iconic

Barcelona tapas joint Cal Pep, there's an L-shaped metal bar with just 23 stools and an open kitchen, where chefs furiously chop and cook. The zippy menu is heavy on grilled seafood – clams, langoustines, and giant prawns – plus tuna tartare, fabulous Spanish ham and pitch-perfect renditions of tapas-bar staples such as *croquetas* and egg *tortillas*. It's a turn-up-and-wait number – sometimes even for 30 minutes – but cold beer from Seville and the smell of pristine shellfish being given a dose of flame and garlic mean it's hardly an onerous experience, and at peak times the place attracts queues of voracious media folk. In summer, battle it out for one of the eight al fresco tables and watch the *beau monde* go by.

**Food 9, Service 8, Atmosphere 8**

## Bentley's Oyster Bar, 11–15 Swallow Street, Piccadilly, W1

Tel: 020 7734 4756  www.bentleys.org
Open: daily, noon–midnight (10pm Sun)                                   £44
**Seafood**

This London institution first opened in 1916 to serve oysters and Black Velvet (champagne with Guinness), so it seems only fitting that, in 2005, after a decade of decline, it was born again under the enthusiastic steward-ship of Irishman Richard Corrigan. The short menu is fishy through and through from the best oysters in town (both rock oysters and sublime Colchester natives in season – September to March) to a stellar fish pie, piscine soups and simple Dover sole. Corrigan is a chef with a robustly

hearty approach to eating, and his Irish roots shine through in the homemade and sweetly delicious dark soda bread. There's a more formal fine-dining restaurant upstairs, but the ground-floor oyster bar, done out with red leather banquettes and oyster-shell lampshades (what else?), is the place to be – and in our view one of the most convivial lunch spots in London. The meeting, greeting and seating is done by Jon Spiteri, a restaurant manager with a natty line in suits and thick-rimmed Joe 90 glasses. If you turn up on spec, you might just get a seat at the bar, but book ahead if you want a table.

**Food 8, Service 8, Atmosphere 8**

## Brick Lane and around, E1
**Bangladeshi/Indian/Pakistani**

Running through the heart of London's Bangladeshi community, Brick Lane is, on the face of it, a pretty good place to go looking for curry. The street is home to a seemingly endless array of Indian restaurants, all gaudily lit in the hope of attracting passing punters, and when business is slack, touts are sent out onto the pavement to entice diners inside. If all you're after is something hot and spicy to round off a night on the beers, then you can take your pick – the food tastes much the same in all of them, due to the widespread use of generic sauces. But don't expect anything particularly good or authentic. For that, you have to head off the main drag to New Tayyabs (83 Fieldgate Street, E1; 020 7247 9543), where the excellent North Indian and

Pakistani grills and *karahi* (wok) dishes constantly play to a packed house. A little further afield is the Lahore Kebab House (2–4 Umberston Street, E1; 020 7488 2551), an extremely basic Pakistani canteen serving some of the East End's best curries and kebabs – all at ludicrously low prices.

## Le Café Anglais, 8 Porchester Gardens, Bayswater, W2
Tel: 020 7221 1415  www.lecafeanglais.co.uk
Open: daily, noon–3pm, 6.30–11pm            £40
**French**

It's worth riding out the shame of stepping into Whiteleys shopping centre (aka chav central) to enter the new world of the Roux-trained British chef Rowley Leigh – he who in 1987 gave London the agenda-setting restaurant Kensington Place (don't bother – he's left). Actually Le Café Anglais is not

such a new world, but a homage to yesteryear – French yesteryear. There are plenty of historical references for foodie nerds to decipher, plenty of old-fashioned dishes to bewilder the young (eggs *en gelée*, anyone?) and a kitchen-full of acclaimed, creative ambition cooked up with plenty of complex, grown-up flavours (game, anchovies, kippers etc). That, and a French-heavy wine list, is served up by friendly if at times confused staff in a pleasingly spacious Art Deco salon, filled with light and crispness and plenty of elder statesmen, from eminent political writers to aging lothario pop stars, many of whom count themselves as friends of one of the industry's most likeable men. Not that there's a huge amount of competition.

**Food 8, Service 6, Atmosphere 8**

## Cecconi's, Burlington Gardens, Mayfair, W1

Tel: 020 7434 1500  www.cecconis.co.uk
Open: daily, 7am (8am Sat/Sun)–12.45am (11.30pm Sun)          £44
**Italian**

This Mayfair Italian has been through many changes in the last two decades. From being the favoured haunt of the rich and royal during the 1980s, its fashionable credentials went rapidly downhill when the original owner, Enzo Cecconi, sold up in 1999. Now though, Cecconi's is riding high again under the ownership of Nick Jones (the brains behind the hip Soho House members' clubs in London and New York, and the Electric; see SNACK). The all-day menu – courtesy of chef Andrea Cavaliere – offers decent Italian classics, from lobster spaghetti to *osso bucco*, plus a range of Venetian-style

*cichetti* (tapas) at the bar, and fresh juices at breakfast time. But the food isn't really the point. This is a restaurant where the beautiful people go and its proximity to the designer boutiques of Bond Street and art galleries of Cork Street ensures it vibrates with a glitzy cross-generational Eurocentric crowd. The décor – designed by interiors guru Ilse Crawford – is glitzy too: striped black-and-white marble floors, mirrored walls, great bright green leather chairs. It's a vast improvement on its former greige and brown incarnation.

**Food 7, Service 7, Atmosphere 8**

### Chez Bruce, 2 Bellevue Road, Wandsworth, SW17
Tel: 020 8672 0114   www.chezbruce.co.uk
Open: daily, noon (12.30pm Sat/Sun)–2pm (2.30pm Sat, 3pm Sun), 6.30pm
(7pm Sun)–10.30pm (10pm Sun)                                      £50
**French**

It's hardly a hot ticket for celeb spotters, and even the sunniest optimist couldn't describe it as central, but Bruce Poole's restaurant in Wandsworth has diners flocking from across the capital. Poole has been here since 1995 and his French-meets-Mediterranean food – honest, hearty and high-end in equal measure – is hard to fault. The menu changes daily to make the most

of seasonality and freshness, with regular highs that include a fantastic *foie gras parfait*. Front of house, there's crisp linen, spot-on service, and a smart but informal atmosphere that makes Chez Bruce feel more like a neigh-bourhood brasserie than the Michelin-starred dining room that it is – the only downside is that some tables can be a little cramped. Add one of London's best cheese boards and a brilliant wine list from the restaurant's youthful Canadian sommelier, Terry Threlfall, and Chez Bruce is close to perfect. Sit at the front, and the view out across Wandsworth Common might even make you forget you're in London.

**Food 9, Service 9, Atmosphere 7**

## Cinnamon Club, The Old Westminster Library, 30–32 Great Smith Street, Westminster, SW1

Tel: 020 7222 2555  www.cinnamonclub.com
Open: 7.30–10am, noon–2.45pm, 6–10.45pm Mon–Fri; 6–10.45pm Sat    £55
**Indian**

If you fancy brushing up on your knowledge of the British political elite, you could consider hanging out at this pioneering contemporary Indian restaurant in Westminster. Housed in a converted library, the dining room's distin-

guished yet clubbable atmosphere (a blend of spice-coloured walls, pukka starched table cloths and general bonhomie) attracts MPs and journos from the nearby Houses of Parliament, as well as the sort of celebs who'd rather keep a low profile. The real draw, though, is Vivek Singh's food, which diverges deliciously from the curry-house norm. Singh mixes inspirations from across the subcontinent with European influences to create a surprising and sophisticated hybrid. Early birds can turn up for breakfast (the full English, as well as Anglo–Indian treats such as kedgeree – spiced rice and fish); night owls might prefer the groovy downstairs bar with white rubber floors, leather walls and colourful

Bollywood movies playing behind glass panels. Be warned that the Indian-themed cocktails don't always deliver on their exotic promise.

**Food 8, Service 7, Atmosphere 7**

## Club Gascon, 57 West Smithfield, EC1

Tel: 020 7796 0600   www.clubgascon.com
Open: noon–2pm, 7–10pm Mon–Fri (Fri–10.30pm); 7–10.30pm Sat        £65
**French**

Housed in a former Lyon's Coffee House on the edge of Smithfield meat market, Pascal Aussignac's restaurant is a temple to Gascon gastronomy. The mind-blowing menu puts a modern spin on the robust cooking of southwest France, which has been reinvented as tapas-sized dishes designed for sharing

(roughly five or six dishes per person make up a full meal). The place has become a mecca for *foie gras* fans, offering no fewer than 10 variations. *A la carte* prices are high, but the good-value tasting menu is a great introduction to Aussignac's food. The elegant room and good French wine list make it a popular spot for business lunches, but in the evenings true gastronauts take over. If you don't want the full blowout, there's a wine and tapas bar next door and a deli/café on the other side of the market (Comptoir Gascon, 61–63 Charterhouse Street, EC1; 020 7608 0851) selling Gascon delicacies to take away. The same team is behind Le Cercle in Chelsea (1 Wilbraham Place, SW1; 020 7901 9999), a more modern space with a more modern crowd.

**Food 9, Service 7, Atmosphere 7**

### E&O, 14 Blenheim Crescent, Notting Hill, W11
Tel: 020 7229 5454  www.eando.nu
Open: daily, noon–3pm (4pm Sat/Sun), 6–11pm                    £40
**Pan-Asian**

E&O (the initials stand for Eastern and Oriental) is the restaurant that first ignited the trend for pan-Asian dining in London and, several years on, Will Ricker's smart Notting Hill hangout is still the place that does it best. The

menu runs the gamut from *dim sum*, *tempura* and *sashimi* to fragrant soups and salads, all stunningly presented and with tantalizing layers of flavour. Oversized lampshades and muted colours give the dining room a chic contemporary feel, while model-turned-waiter staff and a supporting cast of Notting Hillites mean there are few better places to edge in on west London's monied scene. There might be more suits in evidence these days, but early visits from the likes of Nicole Kidman (who once named it her favourite restaurant in town), Elton John and Madonna have ensured that E&O remains

see-and-be-seen central for famous faces and locals alike. If you can't make it to Notting Hill, check out E&O's sister restaurant, Eight Over Eight, in Chelsea (392 King's Road, SW3; 020 7349 9934). Same beautiful food, different beautiful people.

**Food 8, Service 8, Atmosphere 9**

### La Famiglia, 7 Langton Street, Chelsea, SW10
Tel: 020 7351 0761  www.lafamiglia.co.uk
Open: daily, noon–2.45pm, 7–11.15pm                    £45
**Italian**

Run by father-and-daughter team Alvaro and Marietta Maccioni, this veteran Chelsea restaurant feels like a throwback to a different age of London dining. The blue-and-white tiled rooms, the white-coated waiters – it has all changed very little since the place first opened in 1976. Not that it matters. As Alvaro says, 'the best decoration is the dish on your plate' – and the loyal clientele of old-school Chelsea-ites and fashionable glitterati obviously agrees. The Tuscan menu stretches to a dozen or so classic pasta dishes (including a memorable *pappardelle* with wild boar *ragu*), and there are simple fish dishes and grilled vegetables, plus some superb bits of meat – the *bisteca alla Fiorentina* is the best this side of Florence. Risotti are another Alvaro passion, and there's a different special each week, as well as a legendary straw-

berry risotto in season. Note: on sunny days, arrive early to grab a table in the courtyard garden. It's first come, first served, and the prime people-watching spots fill up fast.

**Food 8, Service 8, Atmosphere 7**

### Galvin, 6 Baker Street, Marylebone, W1
Tel: 020 7935 4007   www.galvinrestaurants.com
Open: daily, noon–2.30pm, 6–11pm Mon–Sat; noon–9.30pm Sun          £53
**French**

Baker Street used to be a bit of a gastro-wasteland, but the arrival of Galvin in 2005 has put it squarely on the culinary map. Along with Racine (239 Brompton Road SW3; 020 7584 4477), this Gallic-inspired '*bistro de luxe*' has become a standard-bearer for London's bourgeois French restaurant revival,

bringing supercharged brasserie fare to the capital. It's a family affair, run by the Galvin brothers, Chris and Jeff, who have over 40 years of cheffing experience between them, and have left some pretty high-profile kitchens to launch their own (Chris was head chef at the Wolseley, see page 100; Jeff cooked at L'Escargot in Soho). Even the black-and-white photographs on the wall are by their sister Sarah. The L-shaped dining room – all wood panelling and leather benches – makes a nostalgic nod to the old-school brasseries of France, without descending into pastiche. Unfortunately, the same can't always be said of the French waiting staff. Still, if you want unpretentious food, served in an equally unpretentious setting, Galvin hits all the right notes. For a room with a view, there is now Galvin at Windows, at the top of the Hilton (22 Park Lane, W1; 020 7208 4021).

**Food 8, Service 7, Atmosphere 7**

### Gordon Ramsay at Claridge's, 55 Brook Street, Mayfair, W1
Tel: 020 7499 0099   www.gordonramsay.com
Open: daily, noon–2.45pm (3.15pm Sat–Sun), 5.45–11pm (10.30pm Sun)   £90
**French**

This isn't the headquarters of Gordon Ramsay's culinary empire – that honour goes to his Michelin three-star establishment in Chelsea – but unless you've put your name down at birth, getting a table at Royal Hospital Road

can be near impossible. It's not exactly easy at Claridge's, either, but the odds are definitely more in your favour – and if you strike lucky, there are few more glamorous places to eat. The fabulously restored 1930s dining room, filled with dramatic three-tiered chandeliers and plump purple chairs, is made all the more fabulous by its sparkly dusting of famous faces. Service is as smooth as one of Ramsay's truffled white bean *veloutes*, and few experts could tell the haute French food of his right-hand man, Mark Sargeant, from the work of the maestro himself. If feeling brave, check the availability of the chef's table, which gives a ringside view of the kitchen. If, however, Claridge's can't accommodate you anywhere, don't despair. Ramsay is monopolizing the industry: plenty more chances (albeit diluted) at Maze (10 Grosvenor Square, W1; 020 7107 0000), The Narrow (see PUBS), and his latest acquisition, Foxtrot, right back we started on Royal Hospital Road (Number 79; 020 7352 4448).

**Food 9, Service 9, Atmosphere 8**

### Hakkasan, 8 Hanway Place, Fitzrovia, W1
Tel: 020 7927 7000
Open: daily, noon–3pm (5pm Sat/Sun), 6pm–midnight (11pm Sun)          £80
**Chinese**

London's alpha crowd can be a fickle bunch, but more than five years after it opened, this 'Chinese Nobu' is still packing them in. Hidden down a back-street off Tottenham Court Road, the location may be a little downbeat, but inside, the seductively decorated dining room is glamour all the way. Lattice

screens, exotic flowers, slate walls and low lighting conspire to make you feel as if you've entered the inner sanctum of a sybaritic, imperial Chinese palace – and the exquisite Michelin-starred food backs it up. Lunchtime *dim sum* is as delicate as it is delectable, while evening dishes such as five spice braised pork and a house special of cod cooked in champagne and honey show how subtle Chinese food can be. Even the cocktails are mindblowingly good. Of course, it all comes with a pretty glamorous price tag, and while the food is arguably worth it, the strict two-hour time limit on tables and sometimes less than gracious service can make the bill a little less easy to swallow.

**Food 9, Service 7, Atmosphere 9**

### J Sheekey, 28–32 St Martin's Court, Covent Garden, WC2
Tel: 020 7240 2565  www.j-sheekey.co.uk                    £48
Open: noon–3pm, 5.30pm–midnight Mon–Sat; noon–3.30pm 6–11pm Sun
**Fish/Seafood**

Sheekey's (nobody calls it 'J Sheekey') is part of the same group that owns the legendary Ivy, but to those in the know this is by far the better restaurant. Located down an alleyway between St Martin's Lane and Charing Cross Road, it is every bit as glamorous in its own way as its more famous sibling – and high-profile diners are spared the indignity of being snapped by preying paparazzi as they leave. The mirrored windows in Sheekey's Dickensian façade do a fine job of preserving the identities of those inside, and the series of elegant wood-panelled rooms makes it a great spot for intimate dinners. On the food front, the simple fish-based menu (including

perennial favourites such as potted shrimps and skate in brown butter) is everything you could wish for – right down to the sort of traditional puddings that reduce grown-up British schoolboys to tears of nostalgic joy. Best of all, it is way easier to get a table at Sheekey's than at The Ivy. But then you didn't want to go there anyway, did you?

**Food 9, Service 8, Atmosphere 8**

---

**Locanda Locatelli, 8 Seymour Street, Marylebone, W1**
Tel: 020 7935 9088   www.locandalocatelli.com
Open: daily, noon–3pm (3.30pm Sun), 7–11pm (10pm Sun)          £55
**Italian**

There has been a fashionable buzz about Giorgio Locatelli's new-wave

Italian ever since it opened back in 2002 and it's still up there as one of the capital's culinary hotspots. Locatelli is Britain's finest Italian chef, with a knack for taking fabulous ingredients and lifting them to almost poetic heights. His simple brilliance is sometimes lost on those more used to the overt fireworks of French cuisine, but at its best – in the likes of veal shank ravioli or quail risotto – his food is nothing short of genius. Even better, you get to eat in David Collins' Euro-smart interior, one of the most understatedly luxurious dining rooms in town, with lighting so flattering it would make even Jackie Stallone look good. Waiters are super-informed, happily pointing diners in the direction of new experiences, and it's not uncommon for Giorgio himself to do a spot of meeting and greeting later in the evening. Getting a table isn't easy. But persevere – for food this good, it's worth it.

**Food 9, Service 8, Atmosphere 8**

## Magdalen, 152 Tooley Street, London Bridge, SE1
Tel: 020 7403 1342  www.magdalenrestaurant.co.uk
Open: noon–2.30pm, Mon–Fri; 6–10.20pm, Mon–Sat                    £42
**British**

London has a growing cohort of British revival restaurants, but Magdalen is undoubtedly one of the best. The two-story corner site – just a turnip's

throw from the buzzing farmers' market at Borough – is done out in that gents' club mix of dried ox-blood walls and dark wood bistro chairs that has become the ubiquitous uniform of born-again Brit eateries. Then again, perhaps Brit isn't quite the word. The food here is a deliciously, peasanty amalgam of seasonal ideas from English, Italian and southwestern French cooking, similar to that championed by nearby gastropub, The Anchor & Hope (see PUBS). In practice, that means droolsome meat dishes of braised hare or slow-cooked lamb shoulder, plus potted crab, skate and caper salad, or cuttlefish with chickpeas and gremolata. It's pretty much a family outfit, the kitchen run by James Faulks (ex of, surprise, surprise, The Anchor & Hope, as well as Heston Blumenthal's Fat Duck), with his father Roger and wife Emma, who does the puddings. A handful of tables are kept for walk-ins, but it's best to book – the place is justifiably popular.

**Food 8, Service 8, Atmosphere 7**

## Marco, Stamford Bridge, Fulham Road, SW6
Tel: 020 7915 2929  www.marcorestaurant.co.uk
Open: noon–2.30pm, 6–10.30pm Tues–Sat                                    £50
**European**

Set into the defensive wall of Chelsea FC's home ground, Marco Pierre White's latest restaurant is prime chomping ground for foodie football fans. There's even the occasional sighting of off-duty players from Roman Abramovich's world-beating team (or maybe that's what puts potential diners off). The room – designed by society decorator Tara Bernerd – has a sultry nightclub feel, with yellow bar stools, black walls and a glittering gold

central column that seems to be crying out for a gigantic pole-dance. It's worth booking on Fridays and Saturdays, although the location means it can be painfully quiet during the week. This is a shame because the food is winningly good. White was Britain's first three-star Michelin chef and the menu – cooked by his long-term collaborator Matthew Brown – is a reminder of the easy-access edibility that originally put him on the map (his Italian restaurant, Luciano, comes highly recommended: 72 St James's Street, SW1;

020 7408 1440). A la carte, there are classic fish dishes, braises, steaks, superior shepherd's pie and oxtail and kidney pudding, plus MPW signatures such as braised pig trotter with morelles. Match-day diners get the likes of salt-beef stoveys, sherry trifle and first-class fish and chips. The restaurant was also the winner of *Wallpaper** magazine's best cocktail award. Football, food and fire in the belly – what more could a boy ask for?

**Food 9, Service 8, Atmosphere 5**

## Momo, 25 Heddon Street, Mayfair, W1

Tel: 020 7434 4040  www.momoresto.com

Open: noon–2.30pm, 6.30–11.30pm (11pm Sun). Closed Sunday lunch.    £48

**Moroccan**

Mourad Mazouz's '*restaurant familial*' has been open for over a decade now. Not that you'd know it. Only a year or so ago Madonna booked the restaurant for Guy Ritchie's birthday bash – proof that this North African diner has lost none of its rock'n'roll appeal. The menu is a mix of traditional *cous-*

*cous* dishes and *tagines*, and modern Maghrebi-influenced cuisine, and it's as good as anything you'll find in Marrakech. But at Momo you also get eye-candy staff, a pulsating atmosphere, a hip and hypnotic 'arabesque' soundtrack – not to mention a fabulous interior (with carved wood screens, brass lanterns and louche, low-level seating) that hints at orient excess without looking like the Disney set for *Ali Baba and the 40 Thieves*. The trendy Kemia bar in the basement is members-only (although you can have a drink there before your meal and you can book for live music on Monday and Tuesday evenings) while the Mo

Tea Rooms next door offers pastries, mint tea and the chance to buy your very own *tagine*.

**Food 6, Service 7, Atmosphere 8**

## Moro, 34–36 Exmouth Market, Clerkenwell, EC1

Tel: 020 7833 8336   www.moro.co.uk

Open: 12.30–2.30pm, 7–10.30pm (tapas all day). Closed Sundays.       £40

**Spanish/Moroccan**

Until husband-and-wife team Sam and Samantha Clark opened their Andalusian-inspired restaurant in 1997, Exmouth Market was off the radar as far as most food lovers were concerned. These days, people travel from across town to sample their food. And you can't blame them. Influenced by

the two Sams' travels through southern Spain and North Africa, it is as mouth-watering as it is inventive. The deceptive simplicity is matched by the no-frills dining room – there are bare wooden floors, tightly packed tables and a zinc-topped bar along one side for tapas and sherry (there are 13 available by the glass), plus an open kitchen where the Clarks are kept busy over the charcoal grill and wood-fired oven (the bread here is sublime). Despite their success, the pair remain charmingly unassuming – something that has obviously rubbed off on the front of house. Service, though not always the most efficient, is friendly to a fault, ensuring that a meal at Moro is always a relaxed experience.

**Food 8, Service 7, Atmosphere 8**

## Nobu Berkeley, 15 Berkeley Street, Mayfair, W1

Tel: 020 7290 9222  www.noburestaurants.com
Open: noon–2.15pm, 6–11pm Mon–Fri (midnight Thur/Fri); 6pm–midnight
Sat/Sun (10pm Sun). Bar open until 2am. £80
**Japanese**

For anyone who has eaten at Nobu Matsuhisa's other restaurants around
the world, the food here will hold few surprises. It's the same phenomenally
good – and phenomenally expensive – Japanese–Peruvian fusion that has
won the chain A-list fans from LA to Tokyo. Nobu Berkeley has a more
youthful vibe than its older, Park Lane sibling (Nobu London, 19 Old Park
Lane; 020 7447 4747): diners congregate in the downstairs bar, where drinks

are served by Amazonian waitresses in little black dresses and vertiginous
heels. Upstairs, there's seating for 200, as well as a separate *hibachi* table and
sushi bar. It should be desperately glamorous, but at times the bare wooden
tables and raucous crowd make it seem more like an upmarket canteen.
Still, judging by the number of flash cars parked in the street outside, the
capital's bright young things aren't going to let the decibel level get in the
way of a good time.

### Food 8, Service 7, Atmosphere 9

## La Petite Maison, 53–54 Brook's Mews, Mayfair, W1

Tel: 020 7495 4774  www.lpmlondon.co.uk
Open: noon–2.15pm, 6–10.45pm Mon–Sat £55
**French**

You might wonder how the market-fresh seasonal delights of Niçoise cuisine would translate to Bond Street, but it does so successfully in this mini-me of the original LPM in – yes – Nice, much loved by the great, the good, the gourmands and the frightfully rich (take heed). The chefs come ready trained in the Niçoise style of southern French and Ligurian cooking (less of the French fuss, more of the Italian simplicity); the décor is light and simple, the atmosphere relaxed. But two words elevate this place from good to great – roast chicken. That is, the roast *poulet de Bresse*, the aristocracy of the chicken world: bred in Bresse (of course), it's so rich, complex, tender, and popular that few make it out of the country. Call ahead to pre-book your order (served whole with a chunk of bread soaked in its delicious juices, and a fat slab of *foie gras*) because everyone else seems to know how good it is, and they do run out. That, mixed with a thorough inspection of its rosés and, in summer, dining alfresco, will surely bring an Azur glint to the jaded Londoner's eye.

**Food 8, Service 7, Atmosphere 7**

---

**Petrus, The Berkeley, Wilton Place, Knightsbridge, SW1**
Tel: 020 7235 1200   www.gordonramsay.com
Open: noon–2.30pm, 6–10.45pm. Closed Sat lunch and Sun.                    £90
**French**

You'd be hard-pressed to find anyone with a bad word to say about this posh hotel dining room in Knightsbridge. From the exquisite food and

immaculate service to the comfortable opulence of the claret-purple interior, Petrus is pretty much spot on. Like so many of the capital's top restaurants, it's part of the Gordon Ramsay empire (see The Narrow; PUBS, and Gordon Ramsay at Claridge's, page 80), but the credit here goes to chef Marcus Wareing, a prodigious talent whose modern French cooking at times makes you want to cry with gratitude. If you go for one of the tasting menus, you get endless extra little *amuse-bouches*, pre-desserts and *petit fours*, and as you'd expect from a place that's named after one of Bordeaux's best chateaux, there's an exceptional wine list, including no fewer than 30 vintages of the restaurant's namesake. Among the more curious elements of the décor are two large abacuses. It's not clear whether they're to help you tot up how much you've spent, although most conclude that, whatever it costs, it is worth it.

**Food 10, Service 9, Atmosphere 7**

### The Providores & Tapa Room, 109 Marylebone High St, W1
Tel: 020 7935 6175   www.theprovidores.co.uk
Providores: daily, noon–2.45pm, 6–10.30pm (10pm Sun)                    £52
Tapa Room: 9am–11.30am, noon–10.30pm Mon–Fri; 10am–3pm, 4–10pm
Sat/Sun                                                                 £33
**Eclectic**

Don't let the name mislead you: this isn't a Spanish restaurant. The chef, Peter Gordon, is from New Zealand, and the word 'tapa' refers to the Pacific tribal cloth that decorates one wall of his ground-floor café. Gordon was one of the first chefs to bring Australasian fusion food to Britain and this upstairs-downstairs establishment in Marylebone is a reminder of what made it so exciting. The Tapa Room is a diner-style space with a globetrotting array of grazing dishes, as well as delicious cakes and breakfasts, all served at high communal tables and casual banquettes. The first floor

Providores, meanwhile, showcases the full inventive scope of Gordon's cooking, with its marriage of oriental, middle-eastern and Pacific flavours. Simple white décor reflects the fact that the food is the star – although the fantastic Kiwi wine list merits a visit in its own right.

**Food 8, Service 6, Atmosphere 6**

## Rivington Grill, 28–30 Rivington Street, Shoreditch, EC2
Tel: 020 7729 7053   www.rivingtongrill.co.uk
Open: daily, 8am–3pm (4pm Sat/Sun), 6–11pm (10.30pm Sun)          £47
**British**

The idea of Mayfair prestige parachuting into Shoreditch might have had staunch East Enders shaking their heads in disapproval. But when chef director Mark Hix of Caprice Holdings (The Ivy and co) opened up Rivington Grill, the local YBA community couldn't resist the gravitational pull. Was it the nostalgic kitchen-table menu (chops with bubble and squeak, steak and chips, plus all sorts on toast – Welsh rarebit, potted shrimps, eggs Benedict)? Was it the sympathetic clean-up job on a converted warehouse – whitewashed walls, stripped wooded floors, white linens? Perhaps the presence of 'team colours' on the wall (in the form of artists Tim Noble and Sue Webster's neon, reading 'Fucking Beautiful' backwards)? Perhaps the deli,

selling gourmet delights appetizing enough to remind that artistic temperament to stock the larder? Or perhaps the lengthy bar, a re-fuelling station for so many of them. Or indeed its lack of competition. It's certainly not its tasty breakfasts (boiled duck eggs with soldiers, porridge, posh fry-ups). Mornings are not hip in Shoreditch.

**Food 8, Service 6, Atmosphere 8**

### St John, 26 St John Street, Clerkenwell, EC1

Tel: 020 7251 0848  www.stjohnrestaurant.com
Open: noon–3pm, 6–11pm. Closed Sat lunch and Sun. £48
**British**

Fergus Henderson's stark, white former smokehouse of a restaurant – now over a decade old – has become a celebrated gastro landmark. Henderson

is an advocate of 'nose-to-tail eating' – using the bits of animal that most other folk leave behind – and his extraordinarily austere style of modern British cooking manages to conjure winning flavours from even the most obscure bits of offal. If you suddenly feel the urge to eat pig's spleen, rook chicks or bone marrow salad, this is the place for you (and even if you don't, there's usually less outré fare on offer). Also worth seeking out is the restaurant's bustling younger sister, St John Bread and Wine in Spitalfields (94–96 Commercial Street, E1; 020 7247 8724), which has a line-up of (marginally) less unconventional dishes that is updated throughout the day. The City-fringe location makes it a popular choice with adventurous suits and local creatives alike.

**Food 9, Service 7, Atmosphere 6**

## Sake No Hana, 23 St James's Street, Mayfair, SW1
Tel: 020 7925 8988
Open: noon–3pm, 6pm–midnight Mon–Sat £80
**Japanese**

Having glamorized the noodle bar (Wagamama) and Cantonese cooking (Hakkasan and Yauatcha), restaurateur Alan Yau has now put his stamp on

posh Japanese. When it opened, Sake No Hana (meaning 'sake flower') was being touted as the new Nobu and it certainly has the right clientele. Yau's partner is the Aeroflot heir Evgeny Lebedev, making it a favoured haunt for Russian oligarchs, their high-maintenance arm-candy and their money-buys-class attitude. The room, which soars upward like a modernist Japanese forest of blond wood and bamboo, oozes a cold luxury, while the staff are so glam it's hard to tell who's dining and who's serving. As the name suggests, sake is the thing to drink (in any case, the only wine on the menu is champagne, starting at £30 for a glass of Krug; cf money/class) and there are 60 varieties, chosen by sake sommelier Stuart Hudson. Alongside sushi, sashimi and home-style braises, the menu is studded with the sort of prestige ingredients – wagyu beef (£70 a pop) and white truffle rice – that get plutocratic pulses racing. Alas, quality varies from mediocre to merely good and it all comes without much explanation which can be baffling. If you're going to take pot luck, make sure your wallet can handle it.

**Food 6, Service 6, Atmosphere 4**

### Scott's, 20 Mount Street, Mayfair, W1
Tel: 020 7495 7309  www.scotts-restaurant.com
Open: daily, noon–10.30pm (10pm Sun)                                    £45
**Fish/Seafood**

Once the most glamorous oyster bar in town – Ian Fleming reputedly had his first Martini shaken not stirred here – Scotts was opened by a passionate Scottish fishmonger in 1860, and was talk of the town for the next 100 years. Until, that is, the IRA bombed it in 1975, killing one and heralding the start of its dark decades when only curmudgeonly old buffers went there. A recent buyout by owners of The Ivy, Caprice Holdings, has sandblasted the

barnacles off this London institution, commissioning art works from YBAs Tracey Emin, Gary Hume and Michael Landy, and inviting Future Systems to design a 'crustacean display' (one for the CV, surely) which forms the centerpiece of its island oyster bar (a useful set-up for spying on the likes of Elton John and Jack Nicholson). But Scott's doesn't need to name-drop – its fresh, fresh fish does the talking (almost): there's an ample choice of native oysters as well as a simple, people-pleasing menu of exquisite fish, meat and game. No barnacles were harmed in the return of this classic.

**Food 7, Service 9, Atmosphere 8**

---

### Sketch: Gallery and Glade, 9 Conduit Street, Mayfair, W1

Tel: 08707 774488   www.sketch.uk.com

| | |
|---|---|
| Gallery open:  7–11pm. Closed Sundays. | £65 |
| Glade open: noon–3pm. Closed Sundays. | £35 |

**Eclectic**

---

When this extraordinary gastro-complex opened in 2003, it was the £125-a-head Library and Reading Room fine-dining restaurant that captured the headlines. But you can eat incredibly well at Sketch for far less. At night, the downstairs Gallery – a contemporary art space by day – becomes one of the hippest brasseries in town, its white modernity softened with Louis-something chairs and curvaceous patterned screens. The inventive menu

(from French superchef Pierre Gagnaire) ranges from neo-comfort food (gnocchi 'with the flavours of Costa Rica') to expectation-defying genius (salad of raw seafood with acorn-fed ham and cheese). Everyone from supermodels to septuagenarians eats here (the charismatic owner Mourad Mazouz says he hates his customers to be predictable) and it invariably makes for a fun time. At midnight, the tables are lowered, the chilled DJs crank up the sound system, and the party kicks off. For food that is both simpler and cheaper, check out Glade, a members' club by night, dining room by day – although the jury's still out on its modernist-meets-sylvan décor.

**Food 8, Service 7, Atmosphere 9**

### Tapas Brindisa, 18–20 Southwark Street, Borough, SE1

Tel: 020 7357 8880   www.brindisa.com                                                  £33

Open: 11am–3pm, 5–11pm Mon–Thurs; 9am–4pm, 5.30–11pm Fri–Sat

**Spanish**

This buzzy and unpretentious tapas bar (a spin-off from Brindisa's popular shop at neighbouring Borough food market) is all about letting fabulous Spanish ingredients speak for themselves, and is packed out night after night by a young crowd who value honest food over glitzy surroundings. Iberian classics such as manchego cheese with quince jelly and exemplary charcuterie (including the legendary acorn-fed *pata negra* ham) are augmented by

the likes of salt-cod fritters, garlic grilled chicken, and goat's cheese with blossom honey – a winning combination. In terms of both taste and expectation, Brindisa is a far cry from Britain's lacklustre tapas-bar norm, thanks to the gifted hands of chef José Manuel Pizarro. Turn up and wait for a stool at the bar (with some almonds and a glass of Manzanilla) or book ahead for one of the casual café tables.

**Food 7, Service 7, Atmosphere 7**

## Texture, 34 Portman Square, Mayfair, W1

Tel: 020 7224 0028  www.texture-restaurant.co.uk
Open: noon–2.30pm, 6.30–11pm, Tues–Sat                                    £60
**European**

There can't be many restaurants where you get to sample the crunch of crispy cod skin (think luxury pork scratching) with your preprandial champagne. But textural treats are Texture's USP. If it sounds gimmicky, it's not. Co-owners chef Agnar Sverrisson and sommelier Xavier Rousset met at Raymond Blanc's legendary Manoir Aux Quat' Saisons, and they've put together arguably the best modern European place in town. Sverrisson is big on contrasting textures: cod from his native Iceland might be teamed with chorizo, coco beans and avocado, while Jerusalem artichokes come pickled, roasted and raw. The result is some very, very good food. Add Rousset's

inspired wine selections, housed in a modernist glass cube at the back of the room, and a great front-of-house team and you have one of London's current foodie highlights. It all comes in a space that mixes grandeur (there's a fabulous plaster ceiling) with easy-going modernity – and if you can get a lunchtime table, the tasting dishes costs a mere £8.50 each.

### Food 8, Service 9, Atmosphere 7

## Tom Aikens, 43 Elystan Street, Chelsea, SW3

Tel: 020 7584 2003  www.tomaikens.co.uk
Open: noon–2.30pm, 7–11pm. Closed Sat and Sun.                         £90
**French**

Aikens opened this sleek restaurant in 2003 and has been winning awards pretty much constantly ever since. On the menu: brilliant French-inspired food of global reach. At first glance, it appears simple, listing dishes under

their principal ingredient – Pigeon, Veal, Raspberry, Cheese. But appearances can be deceptive. 'Piglet', for instance, translates as roast suckling pig with pork lasagne, baby squid and caramelized onions. Dark furniture and wooden screens in the windows create a fashionable frame for Aikens' culinary efforts, although given the high-end cooking, both the service and the setting manage to feel remarkably unstarchy. There's also a fantastic wine list, put together by sommelier Gearoid Devaney; as one diner puts it: 'It's an adventure playground for oenophiles.' In recent years Aikens has branched out from fine-dining to open Tom's Kitchen, a relaxed brasserie cheffed by his identical twin Robert (27 Cale Street, SW3; 020 7349 0202), and his latest venture, Tom's Place (pun intended), a modernist fish and chip shop, where all the catch comes from sustainable sources (1 Cale Street, SW3; 020 7351 1806).

**Food 9, Service 8, Atmosphere 7**

## Viet Grill, 58 Kingsland Road, Hackney, E2
Tel: 020 7739 6686  www.vietgrill.co.uk
Open: noon–3pm, 5.30–11pm (11.30pm Fri/Sat) Mon–Sat; noon–10.30pm
Sun                                                                                      £30
**Vietnamese**

Hackney's Kingsland Road (or 'Little Hanoi') is to Vietnamese food what Brick Lane is to curry. Here you'll find an array of Vietnamese-run restaurants and cafés, most of which serve decent enough grub (try Au Lac at 104, Viet Hoa at 74 or Song Que at 134), although some can be severely lacking in atmosphere. However, for the best food – and certainly the most

lively ambience – head for Viet Grill, the new big sis of the also excellent Cay Tre (301 Old Street, EC1; 020 7729 8662). Food is authentic, fragrant and delicious, with a wonderfully named house special of *cha ca la vong* – marinated fish, stir-fried with dill and fennel – plus Indochine beef (like sweetly aromatic *carpaccio*) and a brilliant version of the classic Vietnamese noodle soup *pho* (pronounced like the French 'feu'). The room is rather utilitarian and canteen-like – as is the way in Little Hanoi – but the sweet, black-clad Vietnamese staff harbour none of the grandeur of your average EAT entry. It's a good – and not all that prodigal – idea to sample several of the dishes, though a bowl of *pho* perfectly lines the stomach before burrowing deep into the East End in search of an all-night happening.

**Food 8, Service 8, Atmosphere 7**

### Wild Honey, 12 St George Street, Mayfair, W1
Tel: 020 7758 9160   www.wildhoneyrestaurant.co.uk
Open: noon–2.30pm, 5.30–10.30pm Mon–Sat; 12.30–3.30pm, 5.30–9.30pm Sun                                                                £50
**European**

This is the second collaboration between chef Anthony Demetre and front-of-house Will Smith, a dynamic duo that's fast gaining a reputation for relaxed dining rooms and outstanding food (they also own the excellent

Arbutus in Soho: 63 Frith Street, W1; 020 7734 4545). Wild Honey won a Michelin star in 2008 and with good reason: it's everything a restaurant should be. Formerly Drones members' club, the room has retained the stout wood-panelled walls and comfortable booths that made it an exclusive London haunt, but these days, the tables are filled by a buzzy mix of posh suits and jeans and T-shirts. The food is simply brilliant: understated seasonal combinations that are precise but never prissy (compliments to the chef for the wild honey ice cream with honeycomb). You can buy small carafes of wine so it's easy to have something different with every course. It isn't even expensive: a three-course pre-theatre menu is only £17.95. Just one problem: you might struggle to get a table.

**Food 9, Service 7, Atmosphere 8**

## The Wolseley, 160 Piccadilly, Mayfair, W1

Tel: 020 7499 6996  www.thewolseley.com
Open: daily, 7am (8am Sat/Sun)–midnight (11pm Sun)                    £46
**European**

Everyone says it: the Wolseley has stolen The Ivy's crown as the top place in London to see and be seen. And it's true that no meal here is complete without an *amuse-bouche* of discreet star-spotting. The glittering restaurant – open from breakfast to dinner – is the creation of Christopher Corbin and Jeremy King, founders of The Ivy and Le Caprice, and many of their former regulars have followed. The pair is big on the personal approach and you'll usually find one or the other working the room. There's a menu of

crowd-pleasing continental favourites (from oysters with chorizo to Wiener schnitzel); and the magnificent pillared space (originally a luxury car showroom) has been remodelled to look like a grand mittel-European café. Peak times in the restaurant tend to get booked up, but there's also a separate tearoom and bar, and the café menu is served from 7am until midnight; if you can't get a table for lunch or dinner, pop in for tea and patisseries instead.

**Food 8, Service 7, Atmosphere 9**

## Yauatcha, 15 Broadwick Street, Soho, W1

Tel: 020 7494 8888
Open: noon–11.30pm Mon–Sat; noon–10.30pm Sun
Tearoom: daily, 9am–11pm (10.30pm Sun)                                    £41
**Chinese**

There's no missing this stunningly modern Chinese restaurant (originally the brainchild of restaurateur Alan Yau – he sold it along with Hakkasan early 2008 but the name has stuck). At night, the opaque glass walls glow blue out of the darkness, drawing in diners like a moth trap. Occupying the lower floors of a Richard Rogers building on the corner of Berwick Street, Yauatcha is high concept in every sense, from Christian Liaigre's minimalist interior (a sparse white tearoom on the ground floor and atmospheric basement dining room with a star-spangled ceiling and fishtank bar) through to the staff uniforms (very *Crouching Tiger…*). The food, too, has a concept –

namely that you can eat *dim sum* from morning to night (traditionally they are only served at lunchtime). And what *dim sum*; compared with nearby Chinatown, the food here is both vibrant and surprising. Upstairs, the tearoom brews 50 varieties of chai, and there are exquisite cakes (European, rather than oriental) laid out like a collection of Lilliputian hats.

**Food 8, Service 7, Atmosphere 8**

## THE BEST OF THE REST

**Aubergine** A foodie's favourite, serving brave French food in a pretty, cosy setting (1 Park Walk, Chelsea, SW10; 020 7352 3449)

**Le Caprice** A modern European menu perennially served to socialites and lovers in this dark Art Deco dining room (Arlington House, Arlington Street, SW1; 020 7629 2239)

**Le Gavroche** Opened in 1967 by the Roux brothers, it was London's first three-starred Michelin restaurant; now under Michel Roux Junior (43 Upper Brook Street, Mayfair, W1; 020 7408 0881)

**Gordon Ramsay at Royal Hospital Road** Ramsay's flagship with a French menu and three Michelin stars. Good luck getting a table (68 Royal Hospital Road, Chelsea, SW3; 020 7352 4441)

**Hereford Road**  Tom Pemberton's British revival neighbourhood restaurant in Notting Hill is simple, innovative and delicious (3 Hereford Road, W2; 020 7727 1144)

**The Ivy**  An institution since 1917, its waiting list and attendant paparazzi are almost as famed as its modern Brit–Euro food (1–5 West Street, Covent Garden, WC2; 020 7836 4751)

**Randall & Aubin**  No-reservations buzzy seafood joint perfect for Champagne and langoustines with chips and garlic butter (16 Brewer St, W1; 020 7287 4447)

**St Alban**  The chi-chi Mediterranean offering from the Wolseley's Chris Corbin and Jeremy King – a favourite with the society crowd (4–12 Regent St, SW1; 020 7499 8558)

**Zuma**  Glamorous, gastronomic Japanese restaurant and cocktail bar loved by bankers and their WAGs (5 Raphael Street, Knightsbridge, SW1; 020 7584 1010)

# drink... (bars)

What makes a good bar? In his autobiography *My Last Breath*, legendary Spanish film director Luis Buñuel offered the following prescription: 'The bar… is an exercise in solitude. Above all else, it must be quiet, dark, very comfortable – and, contrary to modern mores, have no music of any kind, no matter how faint. In sum there should be no more than a dozen tables, and a clientele that doesn't like to talk.' It is quite possible that the entire 609 square miles of Greater London doesn't contain a single bar that would have met with his exacting standards – an indictment, perhaps, of his misanthropy, but also of the reality of lifestyle conditions in a modern megalopolis. On peak nights (Thursdays, Fridays and Saturdays), people, people and more people making vast amounts of noise form a compulsory accompaniment to your drink. On other nights it would have been the modern menace of piped-in music and attention-seeking décor that would have irritated the surrealist Spaniard. But he's dead, so who cares what he thinks…

In the opinion of lots of other people, London's bar scene took off from a standing start in the 1990s. Back then, it was all about the Met Bar and the Atlantic, two paparazzi-patrolled institutions that set the glam tone and sig-nalled New Britain's aspirations of upward mobility – to get ruinously drunk (a British constant, impervious to fashions), not on warm pints down the local but instead on caipirinhas and cosmopolitans, preferably within hazy eyesight of a

Z-list celebrity. Since then, 'style' bars – from swanky hotel bars where bankers flash their cash to cooler-than-thou DJ bars – have spread virus-like throughout the capital. If barhopping time is limited, then Soho and Mayfair should constitute your primary zone of investigation. Soho's vibe is informal, populist and often raucous, especially on Friday nights when local workers celebrate the end of the week and their inalienable right to drink 10 pints as quickly as possible and collapse of 'exhaustion'. Mayfair offers more distinguished (and expensive) drinking opportunities. The perennial splendours of Claridge's form a backdrop against which money (new and old) mingles with celebrities across the alphabetical spectrum; Dukes Bar is equally civilized, provided the de-civilizing effects of alcohol are discounted.

For London's arty 'alternative' scene head to East London which, since the early 1990s, has suffered rampant gentrification and the concomitant influx of hordes of young trendies, spawning an economy fuelled solely by art galleries, bars, clubs and hairdressers. That 'alternative scene' (loitering musicians, artists and the fashionably unemployed) has steadily migrated further eastwards from Hoxton Square to Kingsland Road, to escape the encroaching establishment and 'bridge and tunnel' army. Sample Russia's drinking habits in A10 (left), Czech beer at Lounge Bohemia and curious cabaret acts at sceney Bistrotheque.

For really modern drinking, the current thing is 'cocktail grazing' (pinched from the foodie trend for 'grazing menus'. Essentially offering a more dignified take on working your way from left to right through a bar, Artesian at The Langham Hotel offers tours through daiquiris, rum and whisky cocktails etc, while Lounge Bohemia has the Lab Test, a test-tube rack of six shots. Of course tastings are no new thing at vineyards, and neither are they at the wine theme park, Vinopolis. As if bingeing Brits need any encouragement... Talking of which, the recent arrival of later drinking licences did not encourage the hoped-for continental attitude of I-don't-need-to-get-wasted culture; as that British constant, consumption rages on.

## A10 Russian Bar, 267 Kingsland Road, Dalston, E1

Tel: 020 7684 3616

Open: 7pm–3am Sun–Weds; 8pm–5am Thurs–Sat

Among Those Who Know, the Russian bar is already an institution – though new visitors might be hard-pressed to explain why. From the outside it resembles a seedy massage parlour, and things are hardly more exquisite inside. A shrine to communist kitsch, Russian flags plaster every wall and

pendants bearing Lenin's face stare down from the ceiling onto the retro mirrored dance-floor. The bar area itself is an object lesson in soviet utilitarianism and little more than a counter area where drinks – draught beer, bottles and spirits – are served by appropriately surly Slavic staff. But come 10pm from Wednesday to Sunday the place explodes with scruffy fervour, and along with the equally shabby-chic Melange further up the street (281 Kingsland Road, E2), the Russian bar is now the venue of choice for some of the capital's finest underground parties. Like a true modern-day drinking den, the bar stays open devilishly late, and the electro bass and bleeps keep coming till dawn. Brace yourself.

## Barrio North, 45 Essex Road, Islington, N1

Tel: 020 7688 2882  www.barrionorth.com

Open: daily, noon–midnight (3am Fri/Sat)

For all its upmarket boutiques and shiny restaurants, Islington's Upper Street suffers from a severe dearth of decent, no-stag-nights-please bars. Thankfully, the same cannot be said of nearby Essex Road, one of London's new drink-

ing hotspots. Barrio (Spanish for neighbourhood) glorifies the Hispanic ghettos of Harlem and Miami – because low socio-economic status is, like, sooo exotic! – and, rather like Favela Chic in Hoxton (suspiciously like, in fact; see page 114), uses reclaimed allsorts to create a kaleidoscopic décor of colourful mosaics, mismatching sofas, and even a stripped-out vintage caravan, which the owners bought from eBay. Like any self-respecting ghetto, there's eye-catching graffiti, while the barmen, well versed in all things Latino, mix a mean Mojito. While weekdays see an influx of older business crowds thirsty for cocktails, on the weekends it's the turn of younger revellers, who descend to enjoy DJs spinning latin-infused house. At which point, there's no option but to lose those Anglo-Saxon inhibitions and start knocking back shots of Cachaça (a Brazilian spirit made from sugarcane) like a true Latino.

## Bistrotheque, 23–27 Wadeson Street, Hackney, E2

Tel: 020 8983 7900  www.bistrotheque.com
Open: daily, 6pm (1pm Sun)–midnight. Food served until 10.30pm.

Playing hard to get has become a highly developed tactic in the East End: art galleries, bars and restaurants try hard to avoid looking like they're, well, trying too hard – like they don't really need your custom in any case. Based on appearances alone, Bistrotheque has perfected this art. Located on an unremarkable Hackney side street filled with identical industrial buildings, Bistrotheque – with impressive self-confidence – eschews any signage or exterior decoration that might distinguish it from anonymity. First-time visitors thus run the risk of being no-time visitors, passing by obliviously. Coming from Cambridge Heath Road, it's the first entrance on the left – a discreet concrete courtyard. Inside you'll find a great restaurant – the best

in the area – and a cool, comfortable and tasteful bar, with a nicely spare colour scheme and not-too-loud music. Given its far-flung location the crowd is 'genuine' New East End – fashion types, artists or those with some connection to the many local art galleries (such as you'll find on the parallel road, Vyner Street). The scene is completed by the occasional staging of modern cabaret and burlesque where, amusingly, not trying hard goes out the window.

### Bloomsbury Bowling, Tavistock Hotel, Bedford Way, WC1
Tel: 020 7691 2610  www.bloomsburybowling.com
Open: daily, noon–1am (3am Thurs–Sat)

Once the preserve of the proletariat and impoverished students, ten-pin bowling is enjoying something of a boutique moment in London. Bloomsbury Bowling, like its neighbour, All Star Lanes (Victoria House,

Bloomsbury Place; 020 7025 2676), is retro-fabulous, with Chesterfield sofas, an old jukebox and kitsch 1950s carpets. The eight lanes have been shipped over

from the States and installed in what was once the car park of the Tavistock Hotel (recently rendered redundant thanks largely to Red Ken's congestion charge scheme, which caused a tail-off in hotel guests arriving by car). Much less luxurious than All Star Lanes, the Bloomsbury has captured the seedier side of what late-night bowling should be all about. The concrete in-ramp at the entrance, with its incongruously deposited cheap carpet, is a taster to the low-rent interior beneath. Here, two karaoke booths and a screening room provide entertainment for those disinterested in strikes and spares, while a DJ and a horseshoe-shaped bar straight from New York's legendary Lucky Lanes provide the hippest bowlers in Britain with good, cheap reason to stay all night.

## Blue Bar, The Berkeley, Wilton Place, Knightsbridge, SW1
Tel: 020 7235 6000   www.the-berkeley.co.uk
Open: 4pm–1am Mon–Fri; 3pm–1am Sat; 4pm–11pm Sun

The five-star Berkeley Hotel's in-house bar is – like it says on the packet – all blue. Not just any old blue, mind, but a rather fine Lutyens blue – which won't mean much unless you happen to know the favourite colour of the late, great Edwardian architect Edwin Lutyens (whose original carved pan-

elling decorates the walls). OK, so it's a lavender blue, as prescribed by David Collins, interior designer to the stars and famed for breathing modernity into classics (see Claridge's Bar, page 111). Behind Venetian glass doors is sophistication in a salon – a mix of modern and antique, with outrageously laidback occasional chairs in – what else – Lutyens blue leather. The extensive selection of

109

champagnes, whiskies and classic cocktails lubricate a stylish post-work crowd into relaxing after a hard day's power-broking; the tapas-style bar menu keeps the svelte figures trim while a well-stocked humidor keeps the oligarchs chomping on their Double Coronas into the early hours of the morning. With seating for only 50 you know you're going to be in exclusive company.

## Buffalo Bar, 259 Upper Street, Islington, N1
Tel: 020 7359 6191  www.buffalobar.co.uk
Open: 8.30pm–2am Sun–Thurs; 9pm–4am Fri–Sat

Like its namesake, the bar is not known for its good looks. Desperately lo-fi and unstuffy, the draw of this baked-earth hued cellar is its ear-to-the-ground music programming (it's even produced its own compilation album). From art punk to noisy garage to acoustic 1960s harmonies, half of the fun

is the unpredictability of what heard-it-here-first unsigned band might play next. The Monday salsa night and dance lessons seem a little incongruous in what is predominantly a live music venue, but the eclectic spectrum of the Buffalo's acts and nights holds a mirror to London's diversity – this beast is not afraid to experiment. For that there's an energy here that money couldn't buy (this venue sits resolutely in the non-commercial camp) and an enticingly friendly atmosphere. A disparate crowd spans the 'youf' subcultures, often seen clutching their demo tape to deliver to the promoters. Definitely more 'dive' than 'diva'.

## Café Kick, 43 Exmouth Market, Clerkenwell, EC1

Tel: 020 7837 8077   www.cafekick.co.uk

Open: daily, noon–11pm (10.30pm Sun)

Even those with no competitive urge will be drawn in by the infectious spirit of Clerkenwell's table football bar. It's an intimate set-up – three tables by the door are constantly surrounded by players and those waiting their turn,

and the Latin beat whips the atmosphere into a frenzy of football fever. A global selection of beers and cheap but well-mixed cocktails keep the players motivated – winner stays on so for maxing your staying power, balance a few strong drinks with a couple of plates of their tapas. It's charmingly shabby, but then again, it's what Exmouth Market's all about (ie, more interested in getting the fun than getting London's Chicest Street Award). It's an incredibly welcoming and inclusive place for a laidback if somewhat frenetic beer, where you're likely to bond with total strangers in a love–hate relationship over a game of Baby Foot.

NB there's also Bar Kick (127 Shoreditch High Street, E1; 020 7739 8700), which hosts monthly tournaments and shows live TV sports.

## Claridge's Bar, Brook Street, Mayfair, W1

Tel: 020 7629 8860   www.claridges.co.uk

Open: noon–2am Mon–Sat; noon–midnight Sun

There are, of course, people whose engines only run on champagne. And of those, there are many who insist on only drinking it at Claridge's – otherwise, frankly, why bother? For the elegant Art Deco bar of arguably London's top hotel is considered by many to be matchless as a bastion of

refinement. And after the recent, sublimely modern facelift courtesy of designer darling David Collins, Claridge's lead has moved up a gear. So now, in addition to the hotel's straightforward pluto-cratic regulars, the super-famous A-list has arrived. On the plus side (if you like that kind of thing), the occasional film/pop/art star does pop in to take a break, no doubt, from the tedium of their pala-tial suites. On the minus side are groups who sit around waiting for said stars.

However, if you couldn't give a fig about such things and have unlimited means, then it's an extremely pleasant way of fuelling the economy – per-haps on a dollop of beluga caviar, an expertly mixed cocktail or maybe some of their rarest vintage champagne. Or all of the above.

## Dukes Hotel Bar, 35 St James's Place, Mayfair, SW1
Tel. 0871 332 5127  www.dukeshotel.co.uk
Open: daily, noon–11pm

For the last word in elegant, liquid suicide, head far away from the herd and down to Dukes Hotel, a charming old-school establishment, tucked away in its own courtyard off St James's. There, amid the traditional wood-panelled and tastefully decorated surroundings of its bar, you will find Alexandro, head barman and mixer of reputedly the best Martinis in London. At your pleasure Alexandro will wheel out his Martini trolley to your table, prepare his paraphernalia and ask you 'Gin or Vodka, Sir [or Madam]?' The answer is academic, for either path is a route to swift and sure inebriation. Ernest Hemingway, recalling the effect of his first two Martinis, claimed, 'They made me civilized'. If being civilized equates to being oblivious to the hideousness of one's fellow man, then one must concur. After a couple of quick Dukes

Hotel Martinis, the typically odd Mayfair crowd that frequents the bar – at once wealthy, tawdry and slightly disreputable – fades into the background, the conservatively patterned wallpaper and tasteful old school prints blur, and one is left only semiconscious, clutching a large bill and in urgent need of paracetamol.

## Electric Birdcage, 11 Haymarket, Piccadilly, SW1
Tel: 020 7839 2424  www.electricbirdcage.com
Open: noon–4am Mon–Fri; 5pm–4am Sat. Closed Sundays.

If Lewis Caroll had turned his hand to interior design, rather than writing, then this deliciously absurd bar may have been the result. Tables are shaped like tree roots, chairs like huge hands, while three huge iron birdcage chan-

deliers dangle from a fluorescent pink ceiling (actually, for all this we have designer Shaun Clarkson – of The Pigalle, and Profile bar – to thank/blame). Fortunately the clientele are not all so flamboyant – alongside the predictable mix of super fashionable, super wealthy types inevitably drawn to such an environment, there's a fair smattering of well-dressed professionals sipping cocktails at the black marble bar, or chowing down on *dim sum* in the adjacent restaurant. A destination – an event even – in itself, and truly a trip worth taking through the looking glass (unavoidable after just a few of its high-camp, high-sugar, high-inducing cocktails).

## Favela Chic, 91–93 Great Eastern Street, Hoxton, EC2
Tel: 020 7613 5228   www.favelachic.com
Open: 6pm–1am (2am Fri–Sat). Closed Mondays.

Named after and styled on the favelas of Rio, there is the ready accusation that Hoxton has romanticized poverty at its most rudely commercial. Actually, blame the French since it's in fact an outpost of Favela Chic in Paris. However, once seduced by the carnival spirit – and several toxic

caipirinhas down – all is forgiven, or involuntarily forgotten. Within a setting that is artfully scuffed up with peeling pastel paint, shabby sofas and random arrangements of planks of wood nailed onto the walls, is a bar/restaurant/club in one. Latin sounds predominate and latin laidbackness rules – things are gentle and easygoing on weekdays and hot up from Thursdays with live music, fiestas and DJs spinning inspired selections to a sexy, inebriated crowd. If you're planning on eating here, be warned – the relaxed and kooky Brazilian vibe means that things aren't necessarily done in any great hurry. But again, somehow all is forgiven.

## The Foundry, 84–86 Great Eastern Street, Hoxton, EC2
Tel: 020 7739 6900  www.foundry.tv
Open: 4.30–11pm Tues–Fri; 2–11pm Sat; 2–10.30pm Sun

Hoxton has long since shed its old mantle as a rough, tough, white working-class neighbourhood, but not all the art-related invaders who came in the early 1990s were smooth yuppies in disguise. Proof, if it were needed, is to be found at the Foundry, a happily down-at-heel bar/pub/gallery/perform-

ance venue run by artist and McDemo's co-founder Tracey Moberly. Here a crowd of artists, writers and other non-conformists hang out – drinking the cheap beer, and listening to open-mic sessions by the likes of The Worm Lady – a local poet in her late 60s who writes rhyme exclusively about the garden worm (a subject of surprising depth and subtlety). If that fails to impress, the Libertines used to be the regular live entertainment – except obviously they're not there anymore. But you get the point. In the terrifying basement some equally terrifying art tends to get shown, often with a pleasingly ado-lescent anti-capitalist theme. An essential stop on any East End tour, though not for anyone for whom a complicated cocktail and a clean environment is a prerequisite for a good time.

## Life, 2–4 Old Street, Clerkenwell, EC1
Tel: 020 7250 3737  www.life-oldst.com
Open: daily, 5pm–2am

Don't be fooled by the underwhelming appearance that greets you on entering this Japanese basement bar. A closer look reveals a carefully consid-

ered aesthetic that artfully combines 1960s Tokyo (think mid-century wood-
en furniture) with the stripped-down concrete and exposed piping so

beloved of Shoreditch hangouts. It's a true fusion of east
meets west – much like the
customers themselves who
range from the thirtysomething
ad men and media creatives of
nearby Clerkenwell, to Japanese
teenagers in loose skaterwear.
Upstairs, a stark, brick-lined
restaurant continues this fusion
theme with dishes including
seared '*aburi*' eel sushi with
Camembert, but down here it's
sake that is the main draw. It's
available in four varieties all
served at the requisite 98.4°F,
but you should also opt for the
lethally moreish sake cocktails.
Charmingly, no one really
speaks much English, but their
grasp of market forces is unaffected: there's a Japanese art shop right next
to the bar for shopping under the influence and waking up surprisingly light
of pocket, heavy with Hello Kitty.

## Lounge Bohemia, 1E Great Eastern Street, Hoxton, EC2

Tel: 07720 707000  www.loungebohemia.com
Open: 6pm–midnight Mon–Sat; 6–11pm Sun

Hoxtonites like to think they're bohemian, so it's fitting that one of
Hoxton's newest bars pays homage to the original Bohemia (in what is now
the Czech Republic). Tucked between a kebab shop and a newsagent at the
less fashionable end of Great Eastern Street, this cavernous basement space
is (or was) a well-kept secret. Even if you know where it is, it's fiendishly dif-
ficult to find, thus happily avoiding the passing trade of weekend boozers
and brawlers who have invaded the area in recent years. Instead a steady,
never torrential, stream of hip locals come to sip hard-to-find Czech lagers

and snack on traditional Czech canapés as chilled jazz reverberates around the alcoved space. Careful design touches deftly reinforce the Czech theme – from the 1960s communist décor to Art Deco lamps and early Modernist wallpaper. Even the drinks menus are artefacts in their own right, fashioned from old Slavic novels. Visit once and you'll wish it were your local – just don't broadcast it.

## Montgomery Place, 31 Kensington Park Road, W11

Tel: 020 7792 3921   www.montgomeryplace.co.uk
Open:  5pm–midnight Mon–Fri; 2pm–midnight Sat–Sun

The first rule of running a great bar is knowing the demands of your clientele, and Montgomery Place is as well–heeled and sophisticated as the affluent Notting Hill professionals who frequent it. As a result, the dimly lit space

is busy almost every night, filled with excited chatter and flowing drink. There are no gimmicks, nor attempts to be edgy; instead this is a high-end neighbourhood bar that harks back to the golden era of New York saloons, drawing its influences from the legendary Harry's Bar and El Floridita. Comfort and understated luxury are paramount – think the lounge scene from the movie Swingers. Much care has also been taken with the comprehensive drinks menu, and behind the bar the shelves heave with every spirit, aperitif and digestif imaginable, while the wine list blossoms with fine vintages from Europe and the new world. In fact, it's fair to say that Hemingway would have loved it (especially the masterfully–mixed Hemingway Special cocktail said to have been invented for him) – though he, like everyone else, would be wise to book a table in advance if he wanted to visit.

## Roxy Bar and Screen, 128–132 Borough High Street, London Bridge, SE1

Tel: 020 7407 4057  www.roxybarandscreen.com

Open: 5pm–midnight Mon/Tues; 5pm–1am Weds/Thurs; noon–1.30am Fri; noon–2.30am Sat; noon–midnight Sun

Turn up expecting a crowd of beret-wearing Truffaut fanatics, and you might be disappointed. The Roxy is London's first cine-bar – that's a watering hole with the added pleasure of a professional cinema set-up as well – but unlike the concept, which is as pretentious as a convention on German expressionist film, there are few airs and graces here. In fact, it's all rather cosy and understated: dark red velvet drapes line the walls, while a hotchpotch of

furniture (weathered Chesterfields, flea-market tables, beaten-up cinema seats) are scattered in front of a 4m screen. Surely the best part of a film is immediately afterwards, discussing its merits over a glass of wine – at The Roxy, you need not even leave your seat. Films run from Sunday to Wednesday, spanning recent releases, cult classics and shorts. There is a tempting selection of *mezze*-style dishes to keep the munchies at bay, and the close proximity to Borough Market has obviously influenced the menu. Not a dodgy hotdog in sight.

## Shochu Lounge, 31 Charlotte Street, Fitzrovia, W1

Tel: 020 7580 6464  www.shochulounge.com
Open: 5pm–midnight Mon, Sat; noon–midnight Tues–Fri; 6pm–midnight Sun

Feudal Japan is brought to the heart of London's medialand, courtesy of Rainer Becker, the restaurateur behind Zuma and Roka. As you may have deduced, shochu shots are the bar's signature drink: vodka-like spirits infused with herbs and fruits, said (by whom is debatable) to be medicinal.

What's unde-niable is that they're dan-gerously addictive. Try a Hello Kitty (shochu, rasp-berries, rose, lemon and sparkling water) while lounging in the bar's seductive rus-tic setting, replete with low tables and vast wooden vats (apparently used for brewing shochu), and you won't want to leave. Hunger is not a problem either. The Lounge is located directly below Roka, so you can order any of the ludicrously tasty sushi without even having to trouble yourself from your plush red seat. As befits the location, it's frequently packed with PRs, graphic designers and music industry types all rinsing their expense accounts. And come the weekend, you'll likely bump into a D-list celeb hoping to be papped: Britain's own feudal system, if you like.

## St Pancras Champagne Bar, St Pancras International, Pancras Road, NW1

Tel: 020 7843 4250  www.stpancras.com/drink
Open: daily, 10am–midnight

London might already have its fair share of champagne bars, but how many can match the magnificent environs of St Pancras station, with its high-vaulted Victorian arches, and the romance and spectacle of seeing sleek, high-speed trains slink away as you sip on a glass of perfectly chilled bubbly? The newly restored St Pancras station is a figurehead for the King's Cross regen-

eration, and there's no doubting its success as you sit at this glass cube of a bar, flicking through a menu boasting more than 70 bins, ranging from affordable to vintage Krug. At more than 90m in length, it's claimed this is Europe's longest champagne bar, with seating for 110 along a series of banquettes, all pleasingly lit by Art Deco lamps. Predictably, it's frequented by well-heeled commuters who have doubtless just stepped off the Eurostar, but thanks to the unique surrounds and the enticing all-day menu (breakfast starts at 8am, while afternoon tea with a glass of Pommery is a perfectly civilized post-lunch option), this railway bar is truly a glamorous destination in its own right. Toot toot!

## Vanilla, 31 Great Titchfield Street, Oxford Circus, W1

Tel: 020 3008 7763   www.vanillalondon.com

Open: 9am–midnight Mon–Fri; 6pm–midnight Sat. Closed Sundays.

When Stanley Kubrick was envisaging the retro-futuristic aesthetic of *2001: A Space Odyssey*, it's fair to say that he probably didn't imagine it was a look that would ever become popular on terra firma. Yet it has – in Fitzrovia, at least. After descending a darkened staircase, the senses are truly assaulted by a room which is almost entirely pure snow-white, and blindingly so. LED

mood lighting further add to the blaze, casting a neon glow over the distinctive Panton chairs while crystal chandeliers shimmer above. Vanilla is the brain-child of Mattheiu Destandau

and Xenios Voniatis – two men who have form when it comes to high-concept, highly exclusive ventures. Destandau was formerly a manager at Firevault, an exotic restaurant housed in a designer fireplace showroom, while Voniatis hails from Milk and Honey, the New York members' club. Together they have contrived a bar-cum-restaurant-cum-lounge that is pure sci-fi. Indeed, everything here screams OTT, in-your-face luxury, including the drinks menu, which includes a top selection of wines, champagnes and cock-tails. Then again, for the crowd of visiting Eurocash, media stalwarts and clued-up fashionistas, money really is no object if it buys this kind of show.

## Vinopolis, 8 Stoney Street, Borough Market, SE1

Tel: 0870 241 4040   www.vinopolis.co.uk

Open: noon–10pm Mon, Thurs, Fri; 11am–9pm Sat; noon–6pm Sun. Closed Tuesdays and Wednesdays.

Not many have tried to combine drinking and education in one go – but Vinopolis have made a business of it. The large, distinctively late 1990s-looking complex (bare brickwork, wooden flooring – that sanitized industrial aesthetic) lies beneath the arches of a Victorian railway viaduct, smack in the

heart of the newly chic Bankside. Catering for the ever-widening wine market, Vinopolis offers a range of wine tours and packages for those keen to progress beyond the 'I'll have the Liebfraumilch please' stage of affairs. As a visitor, however, you should be doing better things with your time than tasting wine – such as drinking the stuff, which you can do in Wine Wharf, Brew Wharf or Bar Blue – the three drinking establishments here. Brew Wharf is lubricated by a micro-brewery – for those who want to bypass wine completely, while Bar Blue is an upmarket wine/cocktail bar. Best, however, to head to Wine Wharf, since when in Rome… There you'll find over 300 different wines, ports, sherries, manzanillas and brandies – and if you manage a glass of each one you can award yourself a diploma in intoxication.

## BEST OF THE REST

**Artesian at The Langham**  David Collins's stunning Chinese-goes-Deco space in this five-star grand hotel, with a fine line in fine rums (1c Portland Place, Oxford Circus, W1; 020 7636 1000; see SLEEP).

**Big Chill House**  From the dudes behind the Big Chill Festival is a DJ bar with live music, three floors and a smoking terrace (257 Pentonville Road, Kings Cross, N1; 020 7427 2540).

**Cecconi's Bar**  Take a seat at the marble island bar at this classic Italian restaurant for American cocktails served by gentlemanly white-tuxedoed waiters (5 Burlington Gardens, Mayfair, W1; 020 7434 1500; see EAT).

**E&O Bar**  A visual feast of minimal Japanese décor, elegant cocktails, *dim sum* bar food and a moneyed, starry crowd (14 Blenheim Crescent, Notting Hill, W11; 0871 971 6506; see EAT).

**The Haymarket Hotel Swimming Pool & Bar**  Nothing adds sexiness to a cocktail bar quite like a dramatic, pink-lit swimming pool; expect five-star hotel quality and Kemp-style quirky yet slick décor (1 Suffolk Place, Piccadilly, SW1; 020 7470 4000; see SLEEP).

**Lounge Lover**  Surreal, high-camp cocktail bar artfully adorned with taxidermy, curios and bric-a-brac (1 Whitby Street, Bethnal Green, E2; 020 7012 1234).

**Nobu Berkeley Bar**  Glossy, David Collins-designed bar at Nobu Matsuhisa's Japanese fusion restaurant: sake cocktails, big bills and the socially ambitious (15 Berkeley Street, Mayfair, W1; 020 7290 9222; see EAT).

**Refuel Bar, Soho Hotel**  Exemplary hotel bar for hip media dahlings, with a fine wine list, fresh cocktails and a buzzy (read: noisy) atmosphere; also a quieter drawing room (4 Richmond Mews, Soho, W1; 020 7559 3000; see SLEEP).

**Le Bar at Joel Robuchon**  Glamorous lounge bar of the Michelin-starred restaurant: red velvet curtains, black floors and petal-garnished cocktails (13 West Street, Covent Garden, WC2; 0871 971 4546; see EAT).

**Skylon Bar and Grill**  New bar at the Royal Festival Hall: a serious wine list, panoramic views of London and modern-retro glamour (South Bank Centre, Belvedere Road, SE1; 020 7654 7800).

**Zuma Bar & Grill**  Japanese restaurant with lounge bar, sake and shochu cocktails for goodtime girls and boys (5 Raphael Street, Knightsbridge, SW7; 020 7584 1010).

# drink... (pubs)

It's often said that alcohol oils the wheels of society, and in Britain it's in pubs where this oiling happens. But the British pub is more than a mere purveyor of potation – it's the very heartbeat of the community. Pubs are such social institutions that all Britain's soap operas have one written into the plotlines (usually as the setting for scandals, showdowns and scurrilous gossiping). Every neighbourhood has a love-worn local – aka the old man's pub, after the demographic of its most loyal regulars.

Pub culture even has its own vernacular – so if invited for a cheeky half (half a pint, a euphemism for very many pints) down the old rub-a-dub-dub (pub), where after a few pig's ears (beers) the guv (landlord) might take to the old Joanna (piano) for a right old knees-up (fun), never turn it down. Beer is to Britain as wine is to France – where they have Bordeaux, Chablis, Chardonnay etc, we have bitter, stout, lager and ale. Some connoisseurs go to great lengths to seek out 'real ale' pubs (such as The White Horse and The Salisbury): these serve traditionally brewed, non-carbonated, unpasteurized 'live' beer, which, unlike the mass-produced stuff, continues to ferment and improve right up until you drink it.

Currently, beer-pairing is the thing, as some gastropubs are now matching beer with food, as sommeliers would for wine. Note that if you find a palate-pleasing beverage, you'll only find it in establishments owned by the same brewery – such as Youngs, Fullers, etc. Freehouses (independently owned pubs) can sell any beer they like, though more and more are controlled by the breweries or replaced by chains such as All Bar One, Pitcher & Piano and The Slug & Lettuce – fine if you want homogeneity, not if you want soul.

While getting drunk is a favourite British pastime (and ever more so on cider, by the by; with ice to be totally cool), pub culture is also about relaxing – many boozers have pool tables, fruities (fruit machines), pinball machines, dartboards and a tatty selection of games – chess, backgammon, cards etc. Pub quizzes are often taken scary-seriously in London (some travel the capital daily to satisfy their competitive streak) but there is always room for new faces. Meanwhile the recent indie rock wave is filling more and more pub backrooms with cheap gigs from young bands keen to take their music beyond their parents' garages.

Pub grub is no longer the pork scratchings/stale crisps/chicken-in-a-basket of days gone by, and London's gastropubs (The Eagle, The Anchor & Hope, The Greyhound, below) are now attracting punters on the merits of their restaurant-quality cuisine alone – a trend only accelerated by London's smoking ban in 2007. And as the superchef goes global, gastropubs are starting to pop up in their portfolios, for instance, Gordon Ramsay at The Narrow.

With the newly relaxed licensing laws, many pubs are calling 'Time, please!' an hour or two later these days; others prefer the traditional lock-in – where pints carry on being pulled till the (usually fabulously eccentric) landlord/lady decides the party's over. Certainly some are becoming more like clubs than pubs (The Lock Tavern, The Old Queen's Head, New Cross Inn, The George & Dragon).

Thankfully, the classic pub is remarkably resilient to change – 'Website? What's that?' – and like great oaks, many stand for centuries and centuries (see The Salisbury and Ye Olde Mitre). In summer, people brave the Great British Weather to drink in beer gardens, and in winter, tables around open fires are highly prized. And of course, there's always the great tradition of the pub-crawl – where you drink a pint in each pub until very well oiled indeed.

## The Anchor & Hope, 36 The Cut, Waterloo, SE1

Tel: 020 7928 9898

Open: 6–11pm Mon; 11am–11pm Tues–Sat; 12.30–5pm Sun

After a recent makeover (think pleasingly simple scrubbed wood), The Anchor & Hope no longer looks like the kind of joint where meat might be raffled and men might meet their ends. Now, the only aspect of this gastro pub (serving robust British dishes, many say it is London's finest) to grumble

about is its no-booking policy, which can mean a long, long wait in the admittedly agreeable tavern-style bar. However, it definitely is worth the wait, so start with a sherry – there's a proper selection, not the rubbish you serve to mad, deaf Auntie Joan at Christmas (don't worry, there's also plenty of gastropub-worthy wines and beers) – and sample some of the tapas-style nibbles at the bar if you're too hungry to wait. It's best to come here with company, as many of the dishes on the twice-daily changing menu are made to share (including the legendary stuffed duck) – if that is, you can be trusted only to eat your fair share, after one too many sherries on an empty stomach.

## The Boogaloo, 312 Archway Road, Highgate, N6

Tel: 020 8340 2928   www.theboogaloo.co.uk

Open: 6pm–midnight (1am Thurs, 2am Fri) Mon–Fri; 2pm–2am Sat; 2–10.30pm Sun

Everyone who's anyone has played an acoustic gig here. The jukebox has every song you'd ever want to listen to and none that you wouldn't. It's Shane McGowan's 'office'. It's still in single figures, but it's already close to achieving the founders' ambition of becoming one of the greatest rock'n'roll bars of all time. Located unprepossessingly on a main road within sight of Archway's 'Suicide Bridge', this pub, since throwing open its cheery red doors in 2002, has become a mecca for music lovers, musicians, groupies and wannabes – and is where the volatile (now ex) lovers Pete Doherty and Kate Moss famously duetted. If you're feeling knowledgeable enough, the Tuesday evening music quiz is fiendishly hard and pits the geekiest musos against

the music-makers, plus literary readings, poetry slams and club nights. Hungry? Shut up and have another Guinness: the Irish landlord – Gerry O'Boyle of Filthy McNasty's infamy – knows how to pull a proper pint.

## The Cow, 89 Westbourne Park Road, Notting Hill, W2
Tel: 020 7221 0021   www.thecowlondon.co.uk
Open:  daily, noon–11pm (10.30pm Sun)

You might expect The Cow to be named after a particularly meat-heavy menu – and it's true that The Cow's draw first and foremost is its excellent gastropub fare. However, the name comes not from an animal, but a human – it's how the locals used to refer to the pub's original landlady. Now the landlord is one Tom Conran, son of uber-restaurateur Sir Terence Conran (see Bibendum, SNACK) and is unlikely to be attracting such abuse: this small pub, authentically styled on old Irish pubs – scruffy cream walls, wooden pub furniture and ironic lino floors, is still attracting Notting Hill's finest, with a smattering of celeb regulars for that extra head-turning factor. With Tom's foodie pedigree (he has his own deli/café nearby: Tom's Deli), there's due praise for a menu that's subtly Celtic in theme – think modern Irish without the 'Oirishness'; Guinness and oysters are a favourite (it's seafood

and not steaks that is the focus here). If you can't bear the scrum at the bar, head upstairs, although peace doesn't come cheap. Though not a reason to hurl farmyard insults.

### The Dove, 24–28 Broadway Market, Hackney, E8
Tel: 020 7275 7617  www.dovepubs.com
Open: daily, noon–11pm (midnight Fri/Sat, 11pm Sun)

Broadway Market, nestled in between London Fields and Hackney's canals, is the current address of choice for East End hipsters, and The Dove, a pub serving yum Belgian beers, is their New Best Friend. Here, the liquid equivalent of the latest haircut is The Dove's wonderful cherry beer, but for those with beer fear there's also a decent wine list. The menu features hearty Flemish dishes while its Sunday roasts have acquired legendary status – book ahead or expect a wait for a table. There's a bohemian mittel-

European feel to the décor (candle-strewn checkered tablecloths and a jumble of dark wooden chairs and benches), but in layout, The Dove is classic English – all higgledy-piggledy with various alcoves for lounging in comfort. There's a roaring fire in winter and coveted spots in the garden when the sun is out. Its sister pub, The Dovetail in Clerkenwell (9–10 Jerusalem Passage; 020 7490 7321) is equally charming, though maybe after working through its selection of over 101 Belgian beers, anything would be.

## The Eagle, 159 Farringdon Road, Clerkenwell, EC1
Tel: 020 7837 1353
Open: noon–11pm Mon–Sat; noon–5pm Sun

The Eagle was London's first gastropub, kick-starting the welcome trend of honest, high-quality dishes served up in pubs that had been given a bit of polish. Since it was founded in 1991 by Michael Belben and chef David Eyre, The Eagle's tiny kitchen has been so successful that it even cooked up its own recipe book, *Big Flavours and Rough Edges: Recipes from The Eagle* (now

out of print and collectible). 'Food that asserts itself successfully in such an environment', it declares, 'must be robust in flavour and not too finicking in presentation' – think bold Mediterranean flavours, with an all-wood rustic interior decorated to match, fittingly festooned with chillies and spices. Service can be slapdash and the menu is straightforward, with no side dishes or starters per se, just a daily selection on an ever-changing blackboard of whatever's good; so widespread is its reputation that it's sometimes standing-room only, and always noisy. It's the local watering-hole-cum-dining-room for the nearby *Guardian* and *Observer* newspapers, so keep your antennae alert for tomorrow's news.

## The Fat Badger, 310 Portobello Road, W10

Tel: 020 8969 4500  www.thefatbadger.com

Open: noon–11pm Mon–Fri; 11am–midnight Sat; noon–10.30pm Sun

Just down from the Trellick Tower council estate, way north of Portobello Road's twee antiques shops, is a pub where hoodies swig from bottles, victims are held at gunpoint and vagrants are slumped on benches... on the wallpaper. Deeply cool Timorous Beasties wallpaper, no less. Opened late 2006, The Fat Badger knows (a little too self-consciously, perhaps) just

where cool lies. Soften that tough edge with some seat-pleasing Chesterfields, fine glass chandeliers, and slow-cooked, trad-Brit gastro-grub and West London's show ponies are sure to trot up. Indeed they did, beelining for the upstairs restaurant where head chef Will Leigh, previously of The Cow, is delivering an enthusiastic yet mercifully uncomplicated menu of roasts, game and fish – that is, when he's done with his big beef of rigorously examining the provenance of his ingredients. Those who couldn't extricate themselves from their Chesterfield for the sake of dining (surprisingly easy) could invest in a 'Badger in the Bag' – a DIY dinner kit, complete with those locally sourced, artisan-produced ingredients and a recipe card. Minus the ability, of course.

## The George & Dragon, 2 Hackney Road, Shoreditch, E2

Tel: 020 7012 1100

Open: daily, 6pm–midnight

This grubby-looking old boozer has become the coolest watering hole in

Shoreditch since its kitsch gay makeover by part-time queen Richard Battye, who, as an employee, liked the place so much he bought it. In fact, The George is now such an institution that the Institute of Contemporary Arts (see CULTURE) recreated it as a live arts installation – right down to his

late great-grandmother's antiques, heart-shaped lights and vintage cowboy ephemera that adorn its original fag-stained walls. Tranny DJs spin unashamedly trashy pop to a crowd that is gay, straight and somewhere in between; all sport the local dress code of thrift chic and studied cool. Raid your dressing-up box or just admire the exhibitionism as the scene hags overflow onto the pavement (be sure to hide your pashmina or face their withering looks). The George doesn't bother with the practicalities of food (the peckish should forage in Kingsland Road's Vietnamese noodle bars) – The George is just one small room, unless you count the White Cubicle art gallery: yes, located in the ladies' toilet.

## The Greyhound, 136 Battersea High Street, SW11

Tel: 020 7978 7021   www.thegreyhoundatbattersea.co.uk
Open: 11.30am–midnight Mon–Sat; noon–5pm Sun

Perhaps this pub-cum-restaurant is a sign of things to come: with the arrival of the smoking ban – and the departure of that oppressive fug of stale smoke – food is taking over London's drinking floors. And we're not talking cooked-from-frozen chicken Kiev: The Greyhound's highly original, adventurous menu, courtesy of Italian chef Diego Sales, trips your tongue along *amuses gueules*, then delicately garnished fish or succulent meats, other-worldly desserts (beer compote, for example) and finishes on a fine cheese selection – the emphasis is very much more on 'gastro' than 'pub'. This is

not to say you can't get a decent drink. Owned by sommelier Mark Van der Goot, it's no wonder there's a 32-page wine list and wine-food recommendations. There's also Leffe on tap, authentically misty draft cider and a prestigious selection of whiskies, rums, gins and vodkas, and for after dinner, lip-smacking liqueurs. And if you're missing a kick from a pub full of nicotine, there's always their absinthe.

### The Golden Heart, 110 Commercial Street, Spitalfields, E1
Tel: 020 7247 2158
Open: daily, 11am–11.30pm

The Golden Heart is an exemplary East End boozer – rough and ready (ie, bare and bruised), classic pub drinks (ie, no highfaluting quadruple distilling), hugely popular (ie, loved by the avant-garde arts crowd that includes Tracey

Emin and Sarah Lucas) and, crucially, run by an eccentric landlady (ie, local celebrity Sandra Esquilant, recently voted one of the most influential people on the international arts scene). Sandra rules the roost here, and keeps the City slickers as well as the paint-spattered art brigade in line – if she doesn't like the cut of your jib, you'll be asked to vacate the premises (there's even a paparazzi ban); if she does like you, she'll give you her heart (cue framed photos of Ms Emin all around). The Golden Heart is located right opposite Old Spitalfields Market, the history of which is recorded in the old photos on The Golden Heart's panelled walls. Look out for the occasional piece of Brit Art – and those Young British Artists – too.

## The Holly Bush, 22 Holly Mount, Hampstead, NW3
Tel: 020 7435 2892  www.hollybushpub.com
Open: daily, noon–11pm (10.30pm Sun)

On a cold winter's evening, there are few better places to nurse a pint of real ale than fireside at The Holly Bush. This cosy pub nestles in the heart of

a most pictur-esque (and expensive) part of London, but when it opened in 1643, Hampstead was home to the working class. In Victorian times, having evidently taken to the pub, the middle classes instigated some kind of social and gender apartheid, dispatching the working class to the tavern bar, and ladies (to 'protect their dignity') to the Coffee Room – as much is writ in the antique window etching. Nowadays its warren of dark, woody rooms is less about social segregation, more about conjuring a vintage atmosphere (it's defiantly sport-free). It also boasts quite the creative heritage, once owned by painter George Romney and patronized by writers Dr Johnson and James Boswell. In fact, happily, about the only modernization is in its organic menu. Then again, 17th-century scoff was probably also certifiably organic.

## The Jerusalem Tavern, 55 Britton Street, Clerkenwell, EC1
Tel: 020 7490 4281   www.stpetersbrewery.co.uk/london
Open: 11am–11pm Mon–Fri

With its old-fashioned murky green bottles of beer and topsy-turvy layout, this is the kind of olde worlde pub you might find down Daigon Alley. The building was once a merchant's house and an artisan's workshop, and, prior to this 1720 incarnation, had occupied various other sites since the 14th century (it was named after The Priory of St John of Jerusalem, and it is said

that from here, the Knights of St John left to fight the Crusades). Perch in one of its many nooks and crannies to sample its unusual brews, all from St Peter's Brewery in Suffolk – if curious about what a pint tasted like a thousand years ago, try the King Cnut ale, a surprisingly delicious blend of barley, nettles and juniper; for more modern pleasures, try the lemon and ginger ale, the spiced ale and the organic bitter; there's also solid lunchtime sustenance (and dinner Tue–Thur). In summer, bag one of the outdoor tables, but don't leave it till the weekend when the old man puts its feet up and shuts up shop.

## The Lock Tavern, 35 Chalk Farm Road, Camden, NW1
Tel: 020 7482 7163   www.lock-tavern.co.uk
Open: daily, noon–midnight (1am Fri/Sat, 11pm Sun)

You don't have to be a wannabe rock star to drink here – but it helps. The Lock is co-owned by electro DJ Jon Carter, who's friends with all the right people, so the Thursday to Sunday night DJ line-up (eg, Rob da Bank, Erol Alkan, Filthy Dukes) and Next Big Thing live bands – not unknown to play

from the tabletops – keep the hip haircut crowd's hands up in the air. Drinks include Brothers pear cider from Glastonbury and Frulli strawberry beer, while the I'm-only-doing-this-till-I-get-a-record-deal bar staff are able to knock up respectable cocktails too. The Sunday roast is a major draw, while the regular menu features good pub nosh, sarnies and unfeasibly fashionable Square Pies. In fact, this self-described 'tarted-up boozer', channelling Camden's tatty glamour (bare brick walls, big slouchy sofas, and a 'smokers rule' roof terrace and garden), is so hip to the beat that there's now a regulars' card system operating at the weekend – if you don't have one, get a head start on the rest of the Lock crowd and aim for Barfly (see PARTY) to see the Next NBT bands.

## The Narrow, 44 Narrow Street, Limehouse, E14

Tel: 020 7592 7950   www.gordonramsay.com/thenarrow
Open: 11.30am–3pm, 6–11pm, Mon–Fri; noon–4pm, 5–11pm Sat/Sun (10.30pm Sun)

So this is what you get when you mix a pub with a triple Michelin-starred chef (see Gordon Ramsay at Claridge's, EAT): food so fresh it tastes like it was cooked in the field, and beer so sophisticated (for example, double chocolate stout, wheat grand cru) that it needs a sommelier. Gordon Ramsay's dockside delights are exquisitely turned out in a Grade II listed, 100-year-old dock-master's house resting peacefully among the scenic surroundings of historic canals and the Limehouse marina. Food is fashionably British renaissance (even with British wine on the list) – devilled this, braised that, and all elegantly so. And being located by the Waterways, there's a bit of an 'aye, aye cap'n' theme, with crustacea in pints, and posh

fish and chips. Décor is restrained (teals, plums, matt woods), and just beg-
ging for someone to scruff it up so it can really feel like a pub. Not that anyone would dare face the effing wrath of the captain himself. His Ramsayness
has also recently gastropub-ed The Warrington (93 Warrington Crescent,
W9; 020 7592 7960).

## New Cross Inn, 323 New Cross Road, SE14
Tel: 020 8692 1866  www.myspace.com/newcrossinn
Open: daily, noon–2am (midnight Sun)

This isn't just a pub, this is A Happening, whipped up by the art students of
nearby Goldsmiths and the melody-makers behind Angular Recording
Corporation (namely the Klaxons, The Long Blondes and These New

Puritans). This shabby,
shambolic 'music' pub is a
playground 'for the dream-
ing, the drowning and the
drunk', as is aptly scrawled
on its wall, and the goal is
clearly to leave in all three
states. With live art-punk
bands (see above), poets,
DJs, pool and pinball, plus
late, late lock-ins (for
'friends and family' – get
making friends), it's easy

enough to be creative with the bender here (try crowdsurfing for starters) and can be more like a wild house party than a pub. So infectious is its vibe that The Lock Tavern folk recently opened up the seriously sceney (if less authentic) Amersham Arms nearby (388 New Cross Road; 020 8469 1499), while the New Cross Inn has spawned a little sister in Deptford: Deptford Arms (52 Deptford High Street SE8; 020 8692 1180) – it's another new Happening.

## The Old Queen's Head, 44 Essex Road, Islington, N1
Tel: 020 7354 9993  www.theoldqueenshead.com
Open: daily, noon–midnight (1am Thurs, 2am Fri/Sat)

And so it came to pass that when late drinking licences were issued, pubs became clubs. With ex-Fabric founding partner Steve Blonde taking over the helm in 2006, The Old Queen's Head was evidently in well-connected hands: its almost nightly musical line-up far exceeds pub status (recently, Pete Doherty, New Young Pony Club and Andrew Weatherall; expect a weekend cover charge). That's not to say it's too big for the unsigned and the

unplugged – or the uninhibited, as a cool crowd equipped with concept haircuts, enviable jeans and all the right moves piles into its top room. No space? A warm welcome awaits downstairs: slouchy leather sofas, reindeer chandeliers and a real log fire. Its menu rightly puts drinking first, food first equal – home-made burgers, tempura fish and chips and Pie Minister pies, plus all-day Sunday roasts. But more important are its all-day benders – this is a party in a pub. Still no space? Check out its new kid sister in Clerkenwell: Queen Boadicea (292 St John Street, WC1; 020 7354 9993).

## The Prince Arthur, 95 Forest Road, London Fields, E8

Tel: 020 7249 9996   www.theprincearthurlondonfields.com
Open: 4–11pm Mon–Fri; 10.30am–11pm Sat/Sun

For years, this once-derelict corner spot was home to squatters and dusk-to-dawn ravers. Then Tom and Ed Martin, the duo behind gastropubs The Gun, The Well, Empress of India and The White Swan, arrived. The building's hedonist heritage lives on, but, with its original Victorian public house status reclaimed and décor thoughtfully restored, it's a much more refined take on

how to enjoy an East End evening. Push through the heavy wooden doors for a time warp into dark oak, rickety tables, lead-framed windows, Chesterfield banquettes, taxidermy, plenty of Prince Arthur portraits (Queen Victoria's favourite son) and that old East End favourite – a genuine, welcoming smile from behind the bar. Liquid offerings include award-winning ales (such as London Pride), continental lagers and interesting ciders. Food is British: traditional with a twist (roasts, pies, stews, deep-fried jam sandwiches – precisely) with a fish focus (all from Billingsgate Market), and novel bar snacks (feta-stuffed jalapenos, Bloody Mary crisps). In fact, rather like its previous incarnation, all too easy to overdo.

## The Prince of Wales, 38 Clapham Old Town, SW4

Tel: 020 7622 3530
Open: daily, 5pm (1pm Sat/Sun)–11pm (12.30am Fri/Sat)

Eschew Clapham's bland high street populated with suits and Sloanes, and make for the quaint Old Town and its local pub, The Prince of Wales – a true original (clue: it's the corner pub with blue neon POW POW POW on the walls). A favourite with local fashion doyenne Vivienne Westwood, this

pub is jam-packed full of 1960s ephemera and car-boot junk – artificial limbs even – much of which is strung from the ceiling. Unlike other self-conscious-ly 'eccentric' pubs, where jumble seems to have been stage-managed for maximum quaintness, the POW is more an authentic monument to the work of a life-long hoarder with a taste for taxidermy, toys and oddities of all descriptions. The music veers towards the indie end of the spectrum and is not so loud that you can't chat with Dame Westwood about design. No credit cards, no food – just drinks (and real ale), kitsch and chat, and a great big soul.

## The Salisbury, 90 St Martin's Lane, Covent Garden, WC2
Tel: 020 7836 5863
Open: daily, noon–11.30pm

If pubs had sexes, The Salisbury would most certainly be a lady. This ornate institution proudly announces on the saloon doors that it's been officially sports-free since 1892 – you wouldn't be tempted to throw a ball around after appreciating the 50 or so hand-etched windows and delicate mirrors adorning every sparkling nook and cranny. Amber and rose lighting stokes up a warm, convivial atmosphere – romantic even, once settled into the gilt-framed velour booths with a pint of exquisitely silky cask ale in your hands. The Salisbury is one of only two London pubs to receive the Beautiful Beer Campaign's Platinum Award (congratulations, too, to The White Horse): ie, excellent beer served with passion, knowledge and food recommendations – pub classics include pies, Ploughmans and roasts. It's one of London's best-

139

preserved Victorian pubs, except, needless to say, this lady doesn't care for darts.

### The White Horse, I Parson's Green, SW6
Tel: 020 7736 2115  www.whitehorsesw6.com
Open: daily, 11am–11pm (10.30pm Sun)

The White Horse is as much about the beer as it is the ridiculously stereotyped Sloane crowd. Brays of 'Oh, look Annabelle, there's Annabelle' resound from the rugby-shirted crowd as they discuss the day's shooting or upcoming skiing holiday to Val d'Isère. However, if you can look past all of this to

the welcoming interior, with deep Chesterfield sofas, a roaring fire in winter, a ludicrously popular outside terrace, summer barbeques and the ability to pick up your pint and meander onto Parson's Green to mull in the sunshine, then The White Horse has undeniable charms. What's more, The White Horse is a 'beer pub' — what pub isn't, you might ask? Perhaps one without beer festivals, beer-food pairing in its large dining room, up to 14 different beers on tap and some 55 varieties of bottled beers, and, deservedly, a platinum Beautiful Beer award. For that, there's a rival tribe in town: the bearded beer tourist, who in their specs and cagoules, present an amusing foil to the yah majority at The Sloaney Pony.

## Ye Olde Mitre, Ely Place, Farringdon, EC1
Tel: 020 7405 4751
Open: 11.30am–11pm Mon–Fri

There are few secrets left in London. Keeping one might be easier with the protection of a private road. Ely Place is one such gated lane (under the watchful eye of a top-hatted sentry guard, no less), built in 1772 to keep Londoners out of the pretty pocket of land around Ely Palace, the London residence of the Bishops of Ely. Now it simply serves to keep the roar of London to a distant hum when visiting Ye Olde Mitre (and it really is old; its

first incarnation opened here in 1546, to quench the servants of the palace). Enveloped in ivy, with antique beer barrels for outside seating, this quaint wooden warren is a step back in time: no music, no TV, just dominos and cribbage, real ales and real cider; food is vintage tavern tucker — pork pies, scotch eggs, sausage rolls and toasties. Look out for the diamond dealers from nearby Hatton Gardens who come for a quiet pint post-diamond-peddling and who are known for carrying their sparklers around in attention-deflecting plastic bags — no wonder they like Ye Olde Mitre.

# snack...

London's café culture, like the city itself, comes in many flavours. So while the big-bucks coffee chain pandemic may seem impossible to ignore, this guide will do just that, championing the capital's more historic, esoteric and characterful caffeine scene.

Time for tea: tea is Britain's national drink, and has been since the Industrial Revolution in the 18th century when it was recognized as a cheap, warming tonic for the work forces. So silly are the Brits about tea that it is often pre-scribed in hot weather as a refreshing beverage; how we drink it has always divided the classes. So Milk in First (MIF) or 'not our cup of tea' has become snobspeak to describe common folk whose tea-making methods are deemed distasteful. Meanwhile, that other great British institution, afternoon tea, is the ritual of high society, a tradition attributed to Anna, 7th Duchess of Bedford, who, in 1840, caved in to her afternoon hunger pangs and demanded a tray of tea, bread and butter in her room at 4pm. It was soon served in the grandest hotels, such as Claridge's and The Ritz, where the bourgeoisie (and arrivistes) still to this day take tea with scones and finger sandwiches. New tea salons such as Teasmith, The Tea Palace and the Parisian tearoom Ladurée are proof that tea is very much back in vogue.

'The other half' traditionally feasts at the Great British 'greasy spoon' – greasy for its full-fat full English breakfasts of bacon, eggs, bangers and fried bread (washed down with a nice cuppa, of course). Much of their charm is in their resolutely old-fashioned furnishings and community spirit – a sadly vanishing virtue in London. The most authentic is Bethnal Green's cockney caff E Pellicci, still with its original 1940s décor; the S&M (Sausage & Mash, of course) Cafés offer a smarter take on the theme with modern gloss and middle-class diners.

Café connoisseurs should check out the 13 Grade II listed Victorian cabmen's shelters. These wooden green sheds (no larger than a horse and cart, in accor-dance with a 1875 bylaw) are dotted around the capital – for example, in

Kensington Park Road, Northumberland Avenue, Temple and Hanover Square. Today they provide food (sometimes even à la carte), drink and a resting spot for London's black cab drivers. Many offer a takeaway service to the public, served through a hatch. Little do they know they're onto a trend – because the takeaway just got tasty as Londoners got more lazy (and bored of having to smoke on pavements): at The Diner, The Real Greek and Canteen and more. Also having a moment is tapas snacking, enabling the have-it-all generation to, well, have it all on their plate and share food with friends – it's Mexican at Wahaca, Japanese at Bincho Yakitori, Indian at The Urban Turban and even British at Bumpkin (below).

Tables are also being shared – at Daylesford Organic, Le Pain Quotidien, Baker & Spice, Ottolenghi etc – as London self-consciously tries to correct its unfriendly reputation by parking all at one big, communal table. The Brits' new-found love of brunch over the papers and gossip seems to be thawing the situation.

But lurking solitarily in corners is London's 'kinetic elite' – a new tribe of nomadic entrepreneurs who hotdesk at WiFi-enabled cafés, paying their office rent in the currency of coffee. Meanwhile, the green revolution powers on, as more and more menus get with the low carbon diet, the organic bandwagon and the was-once-happy meat movement (gold stars to Leon, Canteen and Daylesford Organic). Hopefully, though, that's not just a fashion.

### Aubaine, 260–262 Brompton Road, South Kensington, SW3

Tel: 020 7052 0100   www.aubaine.co.uk

Open: 8am–11pm Mon–Sat; 9am–10pm Sun

Le tout South Kensington gathers at this chichi bakers-cum-restaurant at weekends, drawn as much by the charming, French atmosphere as by the

food (to them there's truth in the meaning of Aubaine – 'godsend'). A light, airy space, the restaurant has a feminine feel thanks to the country-style white chairs, Venetian mirrors and a vintage ivory dresser adorned with fresh flowers. Aubaine prides itself on its breads, cakes and savoury food in equal measure so you can stop by at any time of day: a coffee and a croissant at breakfast, a soup or *tartine* (open sandwich) at lunch or a Gallic meat or fish dish in the evening. In summer it serves up a slice of pavement life when the glass frontage folds back. Don't be taken aback if your waiter addresses you in French – so many of the locals are from across La Manche that they often innocently assume customers speak the language.

### Balans, 60 Old Compton Street, Soho, W1

Tel: 020 7439 2183   www.balans.co.uk

Open: daily, 8am–5am (6am Fri/Sat, 2am Sun)

If Old Compton Street is Soho's gay parade, Balans – buzzy, clubby, queeny – is its Gossip Central. Dishing up bear-sized portions of trusty British, French, Italian and Asian staples through much of the night (steaks, roasts, grilled fish, Thai curries and all-night breakfasts – the perfect post-clubbing treat), Balans has served succour to many a spurned lover, and with its

lethal cocktails and happy hour, has seen a scandal or two over the years. Not that you need to be part of the queen scene: Balans offers some of the finest people-watching opportunities in London. If it's late, get a booth at the back – you never know who you'll end up swapping tales of debauchery with (may we recommend swallowing the shock with one of their exemplary Cosmopolitans). If however, yours is a daytime visit, then secure a table in the window and watch the world and his pretty boy go by.

## Bibendum Oyster Bar, 81 Fulham Road, South Kensington, SW3

Tel: 020 7581 5817  www.bibendum.co.uk
Open: daily, noon–10.30pm (10pm) Sun

The Bibendum Oyster Bar sits in Michelin House, of one of London's most

glorious Art Deco buildings – the former HQ of the Michelin Tyre Company. All around are reminders of its motoring heritage, with stained-glass windows of the iconic Michelin Man (think mummy with tyres for bandages) and original floor and wall tiles depicting historic motor races. Lifestyle supremo Sir Terence Conran added this building to his empire of restaurants and design shops in 1987, naming it after the Latin toast 'Nunc est bibendum', or 'Now is the time for drink'. On-site there is also a coffee bar, a seafood deli, a formal restaurant upstairs and the Conran Shop, Conran's high-end modern furniture and design store. The Oyster Bar is ideal for casual yet sophisticated lunches and quiet dinner trysts, and with the exception of the fresh soups all food is served cold. The seafood platters are the signature dish, and are usually accessorized with champagne and extra caviar on the side, and, of course, plenty of toasts.

### Bincho Yakitori, 2nd Floor, Oxo Tower Wharf, Barge House Street, South Bank, SE1

Tel: 020 7803 0858  www.bincho.co.uk.
Open: noon–3.30pm, 5.30–11pm Mon–Fri; noon–11.30pm Sat; noon–11pm Sun

Bincho Yakitori is Japanese for 'charcoal chicken skewers' – and does exactly what it says on the tin. In fact an entire section of the menu is dedicated to different chicken body parts (breast, wing, gizzard, skin), all served on skew-

ers. The restaurant is based on the *izakaya* drinking concept, where food is served to accompany beverages – or more specifically, an extensive selection of sake, shochus, Japanese beer and wine – although getting sozzled certainly isn't a pre-requisite; the food more than stands up on its own. Also skewered for your delectation are cuts of red meat, fish and vegetables, and there are also Japanese salads, soups, appetizers and rice dishes (and take-aways if you liked it so much, you want more). What's not to like? – this is sexy, slick snacking inside the handsome Oxo Tower with epic views over the river (NB: forsake Japanese etiquette for a window table). Oh yes. Getting drunk on sake.

## Bumpkin, 209 Westbourne Park Road, Notting Hill, W11

Tel: 020 7243 9818  www.bumpkinuk.com
Open: noon (11am Sat)–3pm (3.30pm Sat/Sun), 6–11pm. Closed Mon lunch.

Dogged cosmopolites regard trips to the countryside akin to being buried alive. Far better to get the only decent thing worth dislocating oneself for – farm produce – to come to London. And so there is Bumpkin, Notting Hill's

romanticized ideal of a country pub, serving up simple, trad food – think Toad in the Hole, Sunday roasts and fruit crumbles slathered in thick custards – with season-al fruit and veg from Secretts Farm near Guildford (sans chemicals) and free-range meat from family butcher Frank Godfrey. Its three dining rooms, each with their own open kitchen, lie in ascending snob factor – the pubbish brasserie on the ground floor (populated by young, blond thoroughbreds), the restaurant on the first floor (same menu, a generation older) and the private dining room on the second floor (for those reluctant to mix with the mere middle classes). On the fourth floor are the Whisky Rooms – two private dens for letting the Mulberry belt out a hole or two, playing chess, poker and backgammon and drinking whisky presented by a whisky Sommelier. An absence of village idiots cannot be guaranteed, however.

## Claridge's, Brook Street, Mayfair, W1

Tel: 020 7629 8860   www.claridges.co.uk
Open: daily, 7am (8am Sun)–10.30pm

Since the end of the 19th century, when taking afternoon tea became the done thing in British high society, the opulent surrounds of Claridge's Foyer and the more secluded Reading Room have done a roaring trade in the ritu-

al (served between 3 and 5.30pm). And it is obvious why – just sitting among the high-ceilinged chandelier-festooned Art Deco grandiosity makes you feel as starry as one of the many silver screen stars who've done the same over the years. There is a choice of over 30 teas including the Royal White Needles (a champagne among teas since the needles can only be picked at dawn on two days in the year), all served in Bernardaud china and accompanied by dainty finger sandwiches, scones with clotted cream and (tea-flavoured) Marco Polo jelly, and nostalgic tunes from the pianist at the grand pianoforte. Today journalists and businessmen congregate here for civilized end-of-day meetings for what is a less obvious and tourist-ridden indulgence than tea at The Ritz (booking essential). The smart casual dress code is loosely adhered to and little fingers are kept erect at all times.

## Daylesford Organic, 44B Pimlico Road, SW1

Tel: 020 7881 8060   www.daylesfordorganic.com
Open: 8am–7pm Mon–Sat (8pm April–Oct); 10am–4pm Sun

Lifestyle envy is a highly profitable syndrome, as the folk behind Daylesford Organic (namely Lord and Lady Bamford of JCB riches) have realized. Their new 4,500 square-foot lifestyle emporium is a temple to all you need to buy for a life just like theirs — ie, super-chic, super-pricey eco-luxury. Straight from the organic fields of Daylesford's Staffordshire farm are three floors of seasonal groceries, dairy goods and heritage breed meats (including Gloucester old spots and venison), plus artisan homewares, organic and biody-namic wines from the Bamford Estate in Provence, and, crucially, the chance to taste the Bamford 'brand experience' at the café. It's evidently too much for the

bourgeoisie to resist, as furs, cosmetic surgery and new teeth settle round the communal table for verdant salads, wild-caught fish, posh sandwiches, and louder-than-necessary posturing. To compare and contrast the moneyed construct of Daylesford with the reality of British farming, visit on a Saturday morning when the Pimlico farmers' market is in full swing.

## Dehesa, 25 Ganton Street, Soho, W1

Tel: 020 7494 4170 (no reservations)  www.saltyard.co.uk
Open: noon–11pm Mon–Wed; 9am–11pm Thur/Fri; 10am–11pm Sat;
11am–5pm Sun

Sod the slow food movement — sometimes life is just too short. This is the *raison d'etre* of the Italian/Spanish charcuterie and tapas bar Dehesa, named after the Spanish woodlands where the black-footed Iberico pigs live (before becoming very fine ham). In one corner you'll find a stand-up charcuterie bar where Atkins-friendly plates of freshly shaved *jamón* and Spanish cheese can be enjoyed on the hoof with a fortifying glass of Prosecco — perfect for a mid-shopping pitstop. Said savouries can also be enjoyed off the hoof, perched atop high wooden stools; also on the menu are very reasonably priced meat, fish and vegetable tapas and Spanish and Italian desserts. No

wonder queues form as soon as the local media offices close of an evening — oops, not always such fast food then. If oversubscribed, try your luck at its older sister restaurant Salt Yard (54 Goodge Street, W1, 020 7637 0657), winner of a Michelin Bib Gourmand for 'good food at moderate prices', or book ahead for Dehesa's 12-seater private dining room. Quickly.

### The Diner Shoreditch, 128–130 Curtain Road, EC2

Tel: 020 7729 4452  www.thedinershoreditch.com.
Open: daily, 8am (9am Sat/Sun)–11.30pm (10.30pm Sun/Mon)

Americana in London isn't as easy to find these days (can't imagine why), so for fans of all things starry and stripy, this authentic US-style diner and its sister branch in Soho (18 Ganton Street, W1, 020 7287 8962) has made a timely appearance on the snacking scene. Decked out with comfy booths and serving up classic diner fare — from burgers in baskets to blueberry

pancakes, all washed down with cocktails and bottomless cups of cwarfee – both venues manage to be refreshingly non-gimmicky, despite the painstakingly adhered-to diner theme; even the staff are mostly genuine rockabilly types. Seventeen – count 'em! – 'burger and dog' options should cater to all tastes, but be warned – while they look very reasonably priced, all the sides and sauces cost extra so the price of a plateful can soon mount up. The maltshakes, 'hardshakes' (with 'liquor') and all-day breakfasts are also a big draw; corned-beef hash perhaps intended for diner historians only. Themephobes should try the takeaway menu.

## Electric Brasserie, 191 Portobello Road, Notting Hill, W11
Tel: 020 7908 9696   www.electricbrasserie.com
Open: daily, 8am–12.15am (1am Thurs–Sat, midnight Sun)

For some years now The Electric Brasserie has been the hub of the Notting Hill scene, and was established by one of London's major players, Nick Jones, the man behind Soho House in London and New York. At weekends it is rammed with fashionable locals and TV personalities whose swanky cocktails and sharp elbows jostle for space at the crowded bar, though the inner circle of this scene takes to The Electric's private members' club, Electric House, upstairs. However, face-time anywhere in The Electric's sleek urban interior – complete with steel tables and lobster tanks – is good for status.

The back restaurant is a little more secluded, and an upmarket US dineresque menu of generously portioned breakfasts, lunches and à la carte dinners (that serve up those lobsters, plus prime steaks, caviar and oysters) is available all day. Next door, The Electric's playground continues with the historic cinema from which the Brasserie takes its name (see CULTURE).

---

## The Garden Café, Queen Mary's Rose Garden, The Inner Circle, Regent's Park, NW1

Tel: 020 7935 5729   www.thegardencafe.co.uk
Open: daily, 9am–4pm

---

Located on the site of the original 1960s Little Chef restaurant, the Garden Café specializes in 1960s-inspired British classics made using fresh, seasonal ingredients. The 1960s-furnished hexagonal structure and wooden-clad  interior are flooded with natural light thanks to the large glass panels that provide views onto the rose gardens of Regent's Park. A central service counter acts as a divide between the self-service café, which offers drinks, pastries and snacks and the restaurant, where warming roasts, casseroles and traditional Ploughman's lunches are the order of the day. In keeping with its natural setting, the experience varies according to the season – in summer, live jazz bands play in the outside area, and theatre-goers gather for pre-performance meals (Regent's Park's Open Air Theatre is right next door), while on winter weekends, musicians from the Royal College of Music perform. Glorious Englishness.

## Inn The Park, St James's Park, SW1

Tel: 020 7451 9999  www.innthepark.com
Open: daily, 8am (9pm Sat/Sun)–11pm (6pm Sun/Mon)

Inn The Park's wooden eco-chic structure (complete with turf roof) is perfectly in tune with the natural surroundings of St James's Park. A modern design dream, the organic sauna-style architecture is by the acclaimed

Michael Hopkins with interiors by Habitat's Tom Dixon, and is perfectly lined up for views of the London Eye – all from the sanctuary of this 19th-century park landscaped by Buckingham Palace's architect John Nash. With a strict policy for locally sourced ingredients, restaurateur Oliver Peyton (the man behind Mash and the National Gallery's eponymous restaurant; see page 155) has catered for all: there is waiter service and à la carte dining (set menu only at the weekend) at indoor tables in chunky white marble booths, a canteen serving hot dishes for speed-diners and those preferring to dine alfresco on the wooden-decked lakeside terrace, and sandwiches and hampers for picnickers in the park, where most agree the atmosphere of birdsong and rustling trees is far superior.

## Ladurée, Door 1A, Harrods, 87–135 Brompton Road, Knightsbridge, SW1

Tel: 020 3155 0111  www.laduree.com
Open: 8am–9pm Mon–Sat; noon–6pm Sun

Blinkering one's eyes from the tourist trap that is Harrods, make straight for the trademark mint green doors of the celebrated Parisian tearoom

Ladurée for its first home out-side the French capital (a bijou second home has recently opened at 71 Burlington Arcade; 020 7491 9155). The experience is rather like diving into an exquisite jewellery box – there's the airy White Room downstairs, the cosy Red Room with its rich, rust-coloured fab-rics and balcony overlooking a takeaway counter piled high with individual cakes (each a miniature work of art), and the very Versace-esque Black Room, all in black and gold with extravagant gold Roman-style statues – a popular setting for evening dining. The all-day menu is impressive (smoked salmon, caviar, club sandwiches etc); the afternoon tea an extravaganza, but what Ladurée is best known for is its delicate macaroons. These *gerbets* span the rainbow and an incredible variety of flavours – from white amber to dark chocolate – and have already become a fashionable gift, not least because of their chichi packaging. Admiring your takeout is an excellent blinkering device.

## Maison Bertaux, 28 Greek Street, Soho, W1
Tel: 020 7437 6007
Open: 8.30am–11pm Mon–Sat; 9.30am–9pm Sun

Maison Bertaux, a Soho sanctuary since 1871, doesn't care much for cool. And because of that, it has it in buckets. An intimate space set over two floors, this is classic Soho bohemia: a haphazard collection of wobbling, mis-matched furniture, charmingly chipped crockery (in which some of London's finest loose-leaf brews are served), and is full of character and characters. Not least the theatrical staff headed up by the eccentric Michelle – ask for a cappuccino and you'll be summarily dismissed to Bar Italia: this is a French café, and café au lait is what you're getting; ask for a (non-existent) menu

and expect a glacial glare. It's also known for its unapologetically full-fat patisseries, all freshly baked on the premises. This may be a timeless Soho throwback, but there's something very fashionable about Maison Bertaux – its unpretentious, effortless shabby chic draws in hip Japanese girls, scenesters hoping to refuel after some hard partying, and fashionistas – make sure you don't take Alexander McQueen's table (first floor by the window, last on the left).

## The National Café, The National Gallery, Trafalgar Square, WC2

Tel: 020 7747 5942  www.thenationalcafe.co.uk
Open: daily, 8am (10am Sat/Sun)–11pm (6pm Sun)

Suggest meeting a Londoner in Trafalgar Square and expect great ugly scowls of disapproval. Preface that with 'Oliver Peyton's eateries' and command rather more kudos: Peyton is the restaurateur resuscitating London's art gallery restaurants: The Admiralty at Somerset House, The Wallace Restaurant at the Wallace Collection, and, here, The National Café and National Dining Rooms. For slap-up lunches and afternoon tea 'as it should be', head for the Sainsbury Wing and The National Dining Rooms designed by David Collins – all neutral tones and understated neatness (020 7747 2525). The National Café is considerably more casual. Designed like a grand Viennese salon (praise be to Collins), its high ceilings, red-leather Thonet chairs and tall Georgian windows lend a sweeping elegance. But it's something of a local secret: there's always somewhere to sit, and no one to stare, making it ideal for an office affair. Ambrosial food (exotic salads, handmade

burgers, charcuterie and cheese boards etc) is served up by ex-Automat chef Sean Gilmore but there are also 'Grab & Go' delights by the bakery Peyton & Byrne should lovers prefer a takeaway.

## The Parlour at Sketch, 9 Conduit Street, Mayfair, W1

Tel: 0870 777 4488  www.sketch.uk.com
Open: 8am–6pm Mon–Fri; 10am–6pm Sat

When the entrepreneur and food-lover Mourad Mazouz (best known for his Moroccan restaurant Momo) set up the multi-tasking, multi-million-pound Sketch in 2003, the ground-floor Parlour tearoom was an instant hit with the fashion set, who came in droves to nibble its fanciful cakes and sip tea in its bijou environs – antique chairs, opulent fabrics and ornate mirrored doors artfully mixed up with a futuristic light fitting that's more like a

planetary constellation. The expansive tea list (all the right single estate loose leaves from China, Japan and India) was conceived by Pierre Gagnaire, the French chef of Sketch's haute cuisine restaurant (see EAT), and the cream teas (served from 3pm) are a visual treat perfect for pushing around one's plate. Breakfast and all-day savouries of the club sandwich/gourmet burger/salad variety are also available but the main draw is an invitation to one of the many fashion parties hosted there. Generating enough gossip to dine out on for weeks, it's no wonder the fash pack is off their food.

## E Pellicci, 332 Bethnal Green Road, Bethnal Green, E2
Tel: 020 7739 4873
Open: 6.15am–4.45pm Mon–Sat

The Ivy, Gordon Ramsay, Pellicci… three of London's most oversubscribed restaurants. The similarity ends there – Pellicci sits firmly, and proudly, at the silly-cheap end. It also trumps them both on history, having been run by the

Italian/cockney Pellicci family since 1900. Team Pellicci now comprises the octogenarian Nevio (born upstairs, no less), his wife Maria and their adult children Nevio Junior and Anna; every day Nevio leaves after the lunch rush to a round of hearty applause. 'Mama' cooks – English breakfasts, meat and two veg, steamed sponge puddings, and a fair bit of Italian pasta – while the others serve and exchange wise-cracks and football scores (Spurs supporters get special attention). With your meal comes instant community, which previously has included the Kray brothers, Eastenders actors and footballers – just ask to see Nevio Junior's autograph book. It's just as well there's no alcohol licence – Pellicci can't take much more buzz: zone out from the chatter and clatter by admiring its 1940s Grade II listed Art Deco marquetry and stained-glass windows. No wonder all eyes are on Nevio Junior and Anna to further the family line.

### The Real Greek & Mezedopolio, 14–15 Hoxton Market, N1
Tel: 020 7739 8212  www.therealgreek.co.uk
Open: noon–11pm Mon–Sat

Opened in 1999 by chef Theodore Kyriakou, The Real Greek has put Greek dining back on the culinary map. Here, in the space of an ex-pub, you can share *mezedes* (appetizers) before tucking in to your own individual *fagakia* (small dish) or *kirios piata* (main course). Next door at the more relaxed Mezedopolio (meaning *meze* bar), you can prop yourself up on one of the high stools circling the welcoming lantern-adorned bar or sit at a table to snack on individual *meze* or *souvlaki* – lamb, pork or chicken skewers served in flat bread – or drink from the 100% Greek wine list. The historical wall-

mounted plaques and religious mural at the rear date back to Victorian times when this building was a Christian mission hall set up to feed the poor children of Hoxton. Reservations for the restaurant are essential and takeaways are available; also branches at 140 St John Street, Clerkenwell, EC1 (020 7253 7234); 56 Paddington Street, Marylebone, W1 (020 7486 0466); and Unit 1, Riverside House, 2a Southwark Bridge Road, Bankside, SE1 (020 7620 0162). It's no wonder it's doing so well.

### S&M Café, 4–6 Essex Road, Islington, N1

Tel: 020 7359 5361   www.sandmcafe.co.uk
Open: daily, 7.30am (8.30am Sat/Sun)–10.30pm

The S&M Cafés (short for sausage and mash, what else?) pride themselves on offering the sort of traditional British comfort food once widely in greasy spoon cafés, albeit with the greasy bit discreetly tidied away. S&M specializes in all manner of bangers (from traditional pork to vegetarian, via

ones laced with apple, Guinness and chilli), full English breakfasts, hearty classics such as steak and kidney pie, and vintage British drinks like Dandelion and Burdock. The interior is a glossier, more uniform version of the classic caff, with chrome finishes, Formica tables, gingham tablecloths and 1950s furniture. Although the slick (some may say poncey, what with its dairy-free mash, wine list and fancy salads) image may go against the princi-ples of a working-class eaterie, this is all readily welcomed by its young, hip following. Besides, it also rescued Alfredo's, a 1920s Grade II listed greasy spoon from near-death (268 Portobello Road, W10; 020 8968 8898). Also at 48 Brushfield Street, Spitalfields, E1 (020 7247 2252). 'Eat yourself happy,' as the S&M folk say.

### Tea Palace, 175 Westbourne Grove, Notting Hill, W11

Tel: 020 7727 2600   www.teapalace.co.uk
Open: daily, 10am–7pm

Notting Hill's glossy Tea Palace has successfully glammed up the chintzy image of the classic tea room. Tables are decked in starched white linens

while intricate cream chandeliers loom over the regal purple chairs and carpet. In fact, the only nod to more traditional tea-taking environs is the delicate patterned pale grey and white wallpaper inspired by paper doilies. The 150-strong tea menu, with sections on oolong, black, green and white teas, reads like a fancy wine list and there is even a tea master (or tea sommelier) to help you decide. Settle in for an afternoon tea of cucumber sandwiches and cakes with Notting Hill's yummy mummies and fashionistas (Kate Moss and Stella McCartney have been known to have the odd cuppa here) or stock up on your favourite blend from the purple canisters that line the shelves; brunch and dinner are also available. No MIF please in front of the tea snobs, now.

### The Troubadour Café, 265 Old Brompton Road, South Kensington, SW5

Tel: 020 7370 1434  www.troubadour.co.uk
Open: daily, 9am–11pm

Founded in 1954, the bohemian Troubadour Café has retained the lively ambience of a 1950s coffee house, despite spilling over upstairs with an art gallery in 2001 (necessary because the downstairs walls had become overcrowded with the work of the many artists who frequent the café). And it is a lot more besides, with its long-standing tradition for troubadours playing live music in the moody basement club, from Joni Mitchell, Jimi Hendrix and Bob Dylan back in the day, to today's sounds of indie, R&B, blues and funk. Eclectically and busily decorated with coffee pots, original enamel advertising signs and wooden church pews, the warren of dark rooms harbours a

history of intellectual mindmelds – this is where the satirical magazine *Private Eye* was first produced and where Ban the Bomb meetings were held. The Troub is quietly proud of its café fare – acclaimed breakies, free-range omelettes, steaks and burgers. And now The Troub's service to wandering minstrels is complete, with The Garret, a one-bedroom hotel on the top floor. With, of course, room service and a fully stocked bar.

## The Urban Turban, 98 Westbourne Grove, Notting Hill, W2
Tel: 020 7243 4200   www.urbanturban.com
Open: 5–11pm Mon–Fri; noon–3pm, 6pm–10.30pm Sat/Sun

Diffusion dining has made its way to Indian cuisine. You'll find no Michelin prices at the Michelin-starred chef Vineet Bhatia's new 'street food eaterie' in Notting Hill. Taking from his Mumbai roots rather than his fancy restau-

rant, Rasoi (10 Lincoln Street, SW3; 020 7225 1881), Bhatia has made his plates smaller, his prices cheaper and has outsourced some of the cooking to the customer. Exactly – order a Volcanic Rock Grill Platter and you get to cook at your own table on sizzling slabs of, yes, volcanic rock. Fret not – if you're a bit wet (or wetted with alcohol), there are plenty of other 'street-eats' to feast on: sharing tapas of kebabs, samosas and tikkas, and mains such as biryani and rogan josh. The late-night-lounge décor is a major selling point (think mirrors, banquettes and sultry lighting), and attracts the young Notting Hill Billies happier for their Mumbai street food to come from a sanitized West London kitchen.

### Villandry, 170 Great Portland Street, Marylebone, W1

Tel: 020 7631 3131   www.villandry.co.uk
Open: Restaurant: noon–3pm, 6–10.30pm Mon–Sat; 11.30am–4pm Sun
Bar: 8am–10pm Mon–Fri; 9am–10pm Sat

Named after the French Chateau de Villandry, it's true Villandry is something of a castle to cuisine – all cream stone floors and tall, whitewashed walls, it's

an emporium of gourmet delicacies and speciality foods from around the world. With three kitchens catering variously for those who want to enjoy their food slowly, fast or off-site, there's a crisp, 100-seat restaurant with a daily-changing European-flavoured menu, frequented by discerning media types, a 40-seat bar area that whips up lighter, less formal meals and tapas with more wallet-friendly price tags to match, and a vast food hall, resembling an old-fashioned food market, with its counters of meats, cheeses, sweets, fresh bread baked on-site and three-course meals from its takeaway kitchen. Bespoke picnic hampers are also available – Regent's Park would be the nicest and nearest location to tuck into Villandry's takeaway treats, and there's even an outside catering service, should you have a castle-sized budget.

## Wahaca, 66 Chandos Place, Covent Garden, WC2

Tel: 020 7240 1883  www.wahaca.co.uk.
Open: noon–11pm Mon–Sat; noon–10.30pm Sun

Leaving no gaps along the spectrum of 'Mexican market eating' – from tortilla chips (of course) to tapas-style sharing dishes, a selection of hearty soups and salads, and big dishes for big appetites – one senses the presence

of a chef with some ambition at Wahaca (named phonetically for fick people, after the fertile Mexican region Oaxaca). Step forward the winner of MasterChef, Thomasina Miers, who in 2007 opened her first restaurant after working at Villandry and Petersham Nurseries. She's also pretty keen to ensure that her food is up there environmentally – all meat is from the UK, chicken and pork is free-range, and produce is seasonal and locally sourced (chillies from Devonshire, no less). To describe Wahaca as 'the Mexican Wagamama' might be accurate in (sprawling) spatial terms, but is a disservice to the colour and buzz that seems to lure large groups with its Latino soundtrack and sociable staff, and pushes waiting time for a table up to an hour in the evenings – tortilla chips time.

# THE BEST OF THE REST

It's a slippery slope between independent success and global domination. Some of the more commercial café chains have grown and grown, probably because they're not half bad.

## Baker & Spice  www.bakerandspice.com

A buzzing neighbourhood deli and café that's mouth-wateringly tasty and eye-wateringly expensive – European salads and roasts made from seasonal, organic ingredients. SW3: 47 Denyer St; 020 7589 4734. NW6: 75 Salisbury Rd; 020 7604 3636. SW1: 54 Elizabeth St; 020 7730 3033. W9: 20 Clifton Rd; 020 7266 1122.

## Canteen  www.canteen.co.uk

Quiet on décor, loud on philosophy: nationally sourced ingredients, using only meat from farms practising good animal husbandry, and fish from the south coast, for a modern take on traditional British recipes: pies, roasts, crumbles. E1: 2 Crispin Pl, Spitalfields. SE1: Royal Festival Hall, Belvedere Rd; 0845 686 1122

## Leon  www.leonrestaurants.co.uk

Leon's opening in 2005 heralded a new era in fast food: healthy, locally and ethically sourced food – wholesome salads, hearty soups and cheeky cakes, in friendly, retro settings. W1: 35 Great Marlborough St; 020 7437 5280. E1: 3 Crispin Pl; 020 7247 4369. SW3: 136 Brompton Rd; 020 7589 7330. WC2: 73 The Strand; 020 7240 3070.

## Maison Blanc  www.maisonblanc.co.uk

Michelin-starred French chef Raymond Blanc's *salons de thé* selling *sandwiches gastronomiques* made from *pain au levain* (a yeast-free loaf) and a glutton's paradise of tarts, gateaux and patisseries. W11: 102 Holland Park Ave; 020 7221 2494. W8: 7A Kensington High St; 020 7937 4767. NW8: 37 St Johns Wood High Rd; 020 7586 1982.

## Ottolenghi  www.ottolenghi.co.uk

This café/deli specializes in Mediterranean food with a Middle Eastern slant, which pays tribute to both Tuscany (from where the Ottolenghi family originates) and Israel (where they emigrated to). W11: 63 Ledbury Rd; 020 7727 1121. N1: 287 Upper St; 020 7288 1454. W8: 1 Holland St; 020 7937 0003.

**Le Pain Quotidien**  www.painquotidien.com
The Belgian organic bread specialist also does a mean salad, eggs any way you like 'em and wickedly tasty chocolate spreads. W1: 72 Marylebone High St; 020 7486 6154. SW7: 15 Exhibition Rd; 020 7486 6154. SE1: Royal Festival Hall, Southbank Centre, Belvedere Rd; 020 7486 6154.

**Patisserie Valerie**  www.patisserie-valerie.co.uk
Established in 1926 by the Belgian Madame Valerie in Soho, its reputation has hinged largely on its outrageous chocolate cakes covered with thick leaves of solid chocolate. Also serves scrummy savouries, pastries and gelaterie.  E1: 37 Brushfield St; 020 7247 4906. SW3: Duke of York's Sq; 020 7730 7978. W1: 105 Marylebone High St; 020 7935 6240 and 44 Old Compton St; 020 7437 3466.

# party...

Naughty, naughty London! Don't believe what they say about British reserve. After dark, decorum is safely tucked up and the wildcats come out to play: fetish is now fashionable, pool parties are making a splash (at Shoreditch House, Haymarket Hotel and Aquarium), and illegal drinking dens (knock thrice on that blue door next to the sex shop) is where the too-cool-for-school crowd like to hang.

But we don't have to take our clothes off to have a good time. Oh no. London is a boogie wonderland for 24-hour party people: whatever your bag is — be it prog rock or the nostalgic sound of 78s — it will provide. While dance music continues to shake the capital to its foundations (reverberating from clubs like Fabric, The End and Ministry of Sound), a fresh wave of promoters is laying on new thrills, including poetry slams, open-mic/-deck nights, and ever more outrageous cabaret. Although the Weimar-era burlesque revival (tassel-twirling and saucy stripping) high-kicks onwards, the next frontier is twisted: surreal, grotesque, pervy — it's all about the shock of the new (see CABARET).

And yet nostalgia for The Way Things Were continues to see fair ladies pour themselves into the tightest corsetry, and gentlemen cultivate twirled moustaches, at the moveable feasts of Ladyluck ('hot gangster sounds from the 1920s to the 1940s') and Viva Cakes (rockabilly dance workshops, live bands and cake), and at the vintage establishments of Black Gardenia and Volupté Lounge. If it's all starting to sound awfully polite, worry not: another tribe, the post-nu-rave generation, is out to alarm as they out-dress each other in outrageous DIY drama and drag; you'll find them congregating around the East End.

'Up west', however, it's business as usual in the pose pavilions — over-designed, overpriced 'table clubs' (ie, where you buy status by reserving a table): for example, Amika, Chinawhite, Mo*vida, Mahiki. But be warned, the elitist door whores micro-manage their crowd, for some reason preferring celebs, WAGs, bankers, rich russkis and debutantes on exeat; there's rarely any walk-in trade at the weekend. 'It's a New York-style door policy' they say (like that makes it OK), ie, it's appearance-based – exploit it for all it's worth (questionable) and dress up. Alternatively, call ahead for the (payable) guest list or to reserve a table, or work it on the night with boasts of dropping £5,000 on a table. The West End on the weekend can get ugly – flesh-flashing girls in gutters, barfing boys in disco shirts (no coats), couples copping off and police sirens screaming. No wonder those guest lists, and no wonder the cool crew party during the week, when the townies are safely on the other side of those bridges and tunnels.

The scene is more specialist (and laidback) outside the centre – King's Cross and Smithfield are dance-music destinations, Brixton is thumping with urban music (ragga, dancehall, drum'n'bass) and the East End is more experimental, with kooky cabaret, word-of-mouth warehouse parties (clue: get with Bugged Out and Mulletover) and indie rock bands performing secret gigs; a fringe gay scene is usurping the stronghold of Soho's Old Compton Street. And across London the ironic power ballad seems to be staging a comeback, at nights like Punk's Smash and Grab (a reference to the recommended pulling technique), and Guilty Pleasures' spin-off, Erection Section. Very, very naughty.

## 12 Acklam Road, 12 Acklam Road, Notting Hill, W10

Tel: 020 8960 9331   www.12acklamroadclub.com

Open: 9pm–2am Weds; 6.30–2am Thurs (sometimes closed Weds/Thurs; see website for listings); 9pm–3am Fri/Sat

This address has always had a little parking spot reserved in the hearts of London clubbers. It was once Subterrania. Then it was Neighbourhood. Now it is the very perky 12 Acklam Road and it's still very much churning out the choons. Its enduring popularity is possibly because it's the only decent-sized club in West London: against the industrial setting beneath the Westway dual carriageway, its 'tough but friendly' interior (read: 1980s New

York warehouse – concrete walls, steel piping) accommodates 640 in what is just a darned successful layout: three bars, two floors, one of them a gallery over the other so friends are never lost, and a drink is never far away. '12 Acklam' is ably maintaining its hedonistic legacy with some wild new nights – for example, the monthly Rodigan's Reggae Lounge (Wednesdays), author Patrick Neate's monthly Book Slam (Thursdays) and Death to All Culture Snitches (disco, indie, house and techno; Fridays monthly) – that are even attracting the spoilt-for-choice East Enders, and of course, the ubiquitous Notting Hill fillies who if nothing else make for pretty wallpaper.

## 93 Feet East, 150 Brick Lane, Bethnal Green, E1

Tel: 020 7247 3293   www.93feeteast.co.uk

Open: 5–11pm Mon–Thurs; 5pm–1am Fri; noon–1am Sat; noon–10.30pm Sun

Set in the gorgeous Georgian brick buildings of Brick Lane's sprawling Truman Brewery (now a shopping/business complex), 93 Feet East lies precisely 93 feet and 57 inches east of the brewery's original foundation stone. Its main dance-floor was once the employees' social hall and – when empty

– still resembles a provincial village hall. The similarity ends right there – even among the no-flies Hoxton trendies, 93 Feet East's programming has a consistently good reputation for plucking out unknown bands and DJs (mostly indie, electronica and rock'n'roll) before they make it big. There are usually three live bands a night most weekdays, club nights on Fridays and Saturdays, and bands, films and DJs on Sundays, all set within three big rooms – that dance hall, a great big lounge with slouchy brown leather sofas, and an overspill gallery bar. There's also a rather lovely cobbled courtyard with garden furniture and gas heaters – particularly pleasing when the club lays on its all-day dance festivals and summer barbeques. With all this multi-tasking, there's little point in straying beyond that foundation stone.

## Bethnal Green Workingmen's Club, 42 Pollard Row, E2
Tel: 020 7739 7170   www.workersplaytime.net
Open: 8pm–2am Thurs–Sat; 7pm–midnight Sun (sometimes Mon–Weds)

The BGWC is a members' club with a difference – money, power and good looks won't get you anywhere here. Since 1953, it's been a social club for real East Enders and until 2002 was a closed shop. However, faced with financial ruin, the committee opened the doors to local events producer Warren Dent, who let in non-members (not of the working-men variety) whose beer money has kept the club a-go-go. The 1970s interior is unchanged (mock teak panelling, swirling red carpets, leatherette chairs and laminate tables), and an authentic scuzz lingers. Members have their own private floor downstairs while Dent's delights take place upstairs – the

BGWC has one of the most creative (and fun) programmes in London. There's all kinds of 'oke, cabaret (from amateur show-offs to out-there performance artists), dance classes and, of course (it's a club after all), live music, DJs and dancing. It's crawling with sharply dressed scenesters ('So ironic!' they squeal), though the charm (and cheap prices) of a workingmen's club lives on. And now with infamous guerrilla artist Banksy's Yellow Lines Flower Painter painted on its outside wall, the BGWC has been granted immortality.

## Black Gardenia, 93 Dean St, Soho, W1
www.myspace.com/blackgardenia93
Open: 6pm–1am Tues–Sat

So-called after Chicago gangsters spray-painting their buttonholes inky black, Black Gardenia echoes the seedy speakeasies of Prohibition Era. A new reincarnation of an old classic Soho basement dive bar (née Push), its shabby red paint, low ceilings and poky corners are atmospherically filled with shifty-looking characters and femmes fatales – ladies in vintage skirt suits, seamed stockings and shampoo-and-set hair, lads in baggy flannel suits, fedoras and dodgy 'taches (NB: 'no jeans' states the dress code, and, take note all obnoxious, cash-brandishing egomaniacs: 'no cunts' – old-fashioned manners rule at Black Gardenia). It's run by vintage aficionados Jake Vegas, Ronnie King (who both started Ladyluck Club) and Zimon Drake, so expect

on the music menu some post-war blues, black rock'n'roll and voodoo jive. It's a tiny slice (literally) of the twilight zone in central London – and not unlike a David Lynch movie. There's twisted cabaret, live music and expert dancers showing up the dilettantes on the dance-floor. And like any dive worth its salt, there's no aircon or ventilation. Quite the authentic time warp then.

## Boujis, 43 Thurloe Street, South Kensington, SW7
Tel: 020 7584 2000  www.boujis.com
Open: 9pm–3am Tues–Sun

Among certain circles (namely aristos, models, visiting A/B/C-list celebs and Eurotrash social climbers), Boujis is the best club in town. Others wouldn't stoop to sully their souls with it, but that's just as well – it's a bijou 'boutique' club in sloaney South Kensington that can afford to be selective about its clientele (and

171

it is, in no uncertain terms), thanks to the frequency of champagne orders (and champagne only comes as vintage here while vodka is quadruple distilled). The official door policy is members and their guests only, but contamination is possible for the exceedingly beautiful (the aesthetically challenged should befriend a member in the queue, or pester A Small World associates). Inside this intimate basement club – all low ceilings, dark lighting and secluded banquettes – impeccably groomed lovelies in towering heels and designer slips-of-dresses dirty-dance to nice and accessible cheese old and new and poppy R&B for their male counterparts – preppy, Chino-ed and drooling. We couldn't possibly say that Paris Hilton has done as much for Prince William, but both are certainly regulars, drawn perhaps to its ban on photography and secret back exits.

## Cargo, Kingsland Viaduct, 83 Rivington Street, Hoxton, EC2

Tel: 020 7749 7840  www.Cargo-London.com
Open: 12.30pm–1am Mon–Thurs; 12.30pm–3am Fri; 6pm–3am Sat;
1pm–midnight Sun

Housed under three cavernous arches of a disused Victorian viaduct, Cargo is a lair for the Hoxton homie – he/she of concept haircut and Rough Trade East loyalty card. As a one-stop shop, Cargo provides all they require – in arch one, the Street Food Café serves up global flavours in clubbers' portions (read: small), arch two is for lounging on leather benches, levering foreign bottled beer down necks and nodding just-so to bass-heavy beats, and

arch three is for pogoing on one's limited-edition Japanese-import trainers. All around is reassuringly hard-edged exposed brickwork and street art from, among others, Banksy. Like the food and beer, the music menu is an international mash-up – DJs and live bands play anything from dancehall and grime to Kiwi or Eskimo sounds (often with themed food to match) – anything, in fact, as long as it is cutting-edge, played on an impeccable, all-enveloping sound system. In summer, there's even an 'urban' barbecue in its fag garden. 'Is it is it wick-ed', as the homies say.

## The End, 18 West Central Street, Holborn, WC1
Tel: 020 7419 9199  www.endclub.com
Open: 10pm (10.30pm Sun)–3am (5am Tues, 4am Thurs, 6am Fri, 7am Sat)

Set up in 1995 by The Shamen's Mr C and Layo of DJ duo Layo & Bushwacka, The End's electronic music pedigree and hardcore sound system (with speaker walls and everything) is still attracting the pro clubbers. Its two dance-floors pay host to superstar DJs such as Laurent Garnier, LTJ Bukem and Goldie, as well as the founders themselves – DJs are elevated in altar-like booths for maximum hero-worship – err, sorry, 'for a greater connection between DJ and clubbers' (devout fans can buy the End's compilation CDs or even enrol at its music academy). With a 1,000-strong capacity

and a futuristic, industrial design, The End has a superclub vibe (especially when its conjoined twin, the DJ bar AKA is interconnected). But it's not just a music industry hangout – it's also about the only club outside the East End that the Hackney hipsters deign to dress up in blue lipstick and Grayson Perry frocks (tourists of the night, take note, or be dismissed) for DJ Erol Alkan's Durrr on Mondays. And with its Sunday/Monday benders, the biggest problem is being able to actually find the end.

## Fabric, 77a Charterhouse Street, Farringdon, EC1
Tel: 020 7336 8898  www.fabriclondon.com
Open: 9.30pm–5am Fri; 10pm–7am Sat

It's all about the beat in Fabric. It used to be all about meat, as the building was originally a meat cellar to service Smithfield's meat market. With three dance-floors – including a full-on warehouse rave den with a 'bodysonic' floor that pumps bass through the soles of your feet, and a constantly upgraded surround sound system – Fabric is for anyone into a racing bpm. It is renowned for supporting new, underground DJs playing the latest breaks, drum'n'bass, house, techno and electro, and, to stay with the game, has introduced live music (electronic orchestras, rock bands, MCs, etc). But as a destination club, it lacks that vibe that only locals bring – this disparate 1,500-capacity crowd includes stag parties, bridge-and-tunnellers and

tourists, happy to wait in Fabric's massive queues (it even sells queue-jumping rights with monthly membership). There's some convergence around the unisex loos, where surprised strangers often slip into conversation, and there's some warmth in the chill-out areas. But Fabric – modern, cool and loud – is considered London's best dance club and, for that, not intended as cosy and cute (nor indeed a meat market).

## The Ghetto, 5 Falconberg Court, Soho, W1
Tel: 020 7287 3726  www.popstarz.net
Open: daily, 10.30pm–3am (4am Thurs–Fri, 5am Sat)

The Ghetto was born of frustration in 2001 by the late gay club promoter

Simon Hobart after despairing of Soho's high prices and lack of originality (cf. the factory-farmed G.A.Y. and the industrial sexuality of Heaven). A spearhead of the alternative gay scene, he also started the much-copied indie night Popstarz (now at Sin, 144 Charing Cross Road on Fridays) and cult bar Trash Palace (11 Wardour Street, 020 7734 0522 – as hallowed as ever since its recent refit; think neon period furniture, skull wallpaper and cockroach cabinets). With its 'cheap and gorgeous' motto, the Ghetto keeps prices down and musical diversity up. Club kids and fashion folk flock to electro nights Nag Nag Nag (Wednesdays) and The Cock (Fridays), where

DJ Princess Julia rules the decks. In contrast, guilty pleasures are indulged on Saturdays with 'seriously unserious' tunes, and Thursday is 'technically' ladies' night (yes, a dykes' disco). And with determinedly friendly bar staff, the atmosphere is always upbeat and laidback in this small basement venue (all sweaty red walls, and cream pleather bonkettes). Unlike your typical homo hangout, cruising is much more covert, resulting in a truly pansexual crowd.

## Madame Jojos, 8–10 Brewer St, Soho, W1

Tel: 020 7734 3040   www.madamejojos.com
Open: 8pm–3am Tues, Thurs; 10pm–3am Fri; 7pm–3am Sat; 9.30pm–3am Sun

It's a dilemma. What night to go-go to the long-running Madame Jojos? Pick a day, any day: there's the legendary deep funk Friday night that pulls in the coolest break-dancers (NB: amateur roly-polies inside the breakers' magic circle doesn't usually go down so well), tranny cabaret on Saturdays, Whiteheat's indie live band night every Tuesday, and rockabilly and blues to

jitterbug along to midweek. As well as a variety of ska, soul and disco nights, Madame Jojos has been known to put on some rockin' one-off live gigs with bands such as the Scissor Sisters, Kings of Leon and The Fratellis taking to the stage. Whenever you decide to visit this former strip club, you will come away feeling a little bit decadent and a little bit dirty – possibly something to do with the venue's retro trashy-chic décor of plush velvet booths, gilded balustrades and mirrored walls that still channels seedy Soho boudoirs.

## Mahiki, 1 Dover St, Mayfair, W1
Tel: 020 7493 9529   www.mahiki.com
Open: 5.30pm–3.30am Mon–Fri; 7.30pm–3.30am Sat

You'd be forgiven for thinking the flashing lights emitting from Mahiki are from an electrified dance-floor – no: it's the paparazzi snapping away, hoping to catch one of the young princes or their escorts spilling out. Mahiki is their club of choice possibly because it takes the pocket money of a prince to afford its lavish sharing cocktails served up in treasure chests, frozen pineapples and other exotic wotnots, and pan-Asian tapas by that celebrity fruitcake chef Nancy Lam. It's a tiki theme bar, see, that just about gets away with all the crazy coconuts because its holiday spirit (and super-strength cocktails) just reminds its conservative posh-chav crowd of their rum-soaked holidays at the Sandy Lane Hotel in Barbados. Set over two floors, the upper bar is a wicker/bamboo-lined beach bar (think Hawaii Five-0, all palm fronds and exotic flowers); the lower bar is darker, glossier and home to the dance-floor. And often somewhere in there are those naughty

princes, girls that want to pull them, and hedgefunders happy to mop up the princes' leftovers (note that the clipboard bitches can afford to sieve out the unwashed masses). Why else would you need to order look-at-me cocktails? Aloha, sailor!

## Maya, 1a Dean Street, Soho, W1
Tel: 020 7287 9608  www.mayalondon.com
Open: 10pm–4am Weds–Sat

Given the British trend for drinking ourselves silly, a club that requires zero thought to get you through the party is surely a no-brainer. Maya's neat one-room layout puts partying on a plate. So you arrive. Bar. Right in front of you. Alcohol tickles your toes. Start feeling atomic. Dance. Dance a lot, infected by the evangelizing DJ in his elevated DJ island. Dance. Drift off-

course onto leather banquettes that hug the dance-floor. Disco nap. Wake up. Where are my friends? Ah, in front of me. The Goldilocks of clubs, its just-right size and design may be a simple luxury, but frankly necessary, once past midnight on the cocktail count. To jolly proceedings, there are rock-chick waitresses dressed in cheeky PPQ frocks; there are palm trees, burnished gold pillars and a super-glam, sleek black backdrop ('New York-style décor!' they boast). Less jolly are its extortionate cocktails, its Euro-heavy weekend crowd getting their freak on to St Tropez sounds, and its looks-based 'New York-inspired velvet rope culture' (try emailing rsvp@mayalondon.com in advance). And its obsession with the Rotten Apple.

## Notting Hill Arts Club, 21 Notting Hill Gate, W11

Tel: 020 7460 4459   www.nottinghillartsclub.com
Open: daily, 7pm (4pm Sat/Sun)–2am (1am Sun). Closed Mondays.

To say that the NHAC's line-up is eclectic is understatement akin to 'the Queen has savings'. All-encompassing might be more accurate, and by arts is meant anything from photography exhibitions to fanzine showcases to music to craft sessions. That's not to say that clubbers are required to come equipped with a crochet hook (that's provided) – music is its prime concern, and is yet more diverse – classical, country, flamenco, ska, rock, and all in the least obvious take. In fact the only things the NHAC doesn't do are open-mic nights ('we have standards', they say) or anything that is clichéd or boring. With the emphasis on its cultural programme, the NHAC is a small,

no-frills basement club that's mostly standing room only, and it can get hot and cramped (space by the industrial fans at the back of the dance-floor is particularly prized). Bar snacks, cocktails, absinthe and champagne afford welcome comfort to a loyal crowd, all enlightened in the NHAC's philosophy that 'a world created by artists is better than a world created by politicians'. Pseuds welcome.

## Plan B, 418 Brixton Road, SW9
Tel. 0870 116 5421   www.plan-brixton.co.uk
Open: 5pm–midnight Tues/Wed; 5pm–2am Thur; 5pm–4am Fri; 7pm–4am Sat

If B is for Brixton, Plan A – for many party-hardies – is often Anywhere East. Few head deep into South London, but Brixton – a destination for urban music – has its draw (wink, wink – you'll smell it as soon as you step out of Brixton tube). Nestling on the authentically unlovely Brixton Road is Plan B, luring in some of London's best DJs: Basement Jaxx, Norman Jay, Gilles Peterson and DJ Yoda have all played recently, no doubt seduced by its spasm-inducing, bass-heavy Funktion One sound system (the best, some

say). They and others variously deliver hiphop and breaks on Thursdays, funk, soul and old-school hiphop on Fridays, and house and electro on Saturdays; lovely fresh-fruit cocktails come all week long, but be warned: predatory males tend to come along towards the end of the night (it goes with the tough territory). Rather proud of its 'post-industrial chic' (bare brick, concrete and large open spaces 'post-ified' with padded leather seating and chunky wooden tables), urban reprobates should note that hoodies and general scruffiness are not on, innit.

## Proud Camden, The Horse Hospital, Stables Market, Chalk Farm Road, NW1

Tel: 020 7482 3867  www.atproud.net

Open: daily, 7pm–1am (3am Fri/Sat)

Once home to vintage vendors selling old oak tables and 1920s pyjama sets, Camden Market's Horse Hospital has been taken over by another Camden institution, Proud Camden. Founded by the gallerist Alex Proud, Proud started out as a photography gallery in the nearby Gin House, showing more than 150 exhibitions only to become better known for throwing riotous parties with live music from over 1,000 bands (including Arctic Monkeys, Amy Winehouse and Coldplay). It was soon anointed the spiritual home of

that naughty indie-rock tribe, the Camden Caners (featuring more Winehouse, the Geldof scionettes, Razorlight, etc). Opened in April 2008, it's now settled in at new premises that are five times as large as The Gin House's music space – this 200-year-old listed building has been refurbished by Russell Sage Studio and Proud's wife, the craft queen Danielle Proud: think large skylights, exposed brick walls and high-beamed ceilings, an outdoor terrace and booths which were once stables, still with the stable door intact. But who cares about the décor once the Caners come home?

## Punk, 14 Soho Street, Soho, W1

Tel: 020 7734 4004  www.myspace.com/punksoho

Open: 7pm–3am Mon–Fri; 9pm–3am Sat

Dispel all ideas of anarchy and tartan Mohicans – after all, wouldn't a true punk club name itself after genitalia or queen-bashing? But what better idea than to borrow from the safety-pinned iconoclasts to give edge to a shiny new club in town. Punk's music policy is considerably easier on the ears:

already its Thursday night Smash & Grab (orchestrated by the Queens of Noize) is seeing all the city's scenesters drop in for an ironic slow song'n' smooch, while FourPlay on Fridays encourages even more of the up-close-and-personal with notepads distributed on every table. But Punk isn't about romance – instead it's channelling the unholy trinity of sex, drugs and rock-'n'roll (apart from the drugs bit, they say) to contrive a sense of anti-estab-lishment, though perhaps 'sex slaves' slogans on the bar staff's T-shirts is tak-ing it a bit far... As for rock'n'roll, live indie bands play in the week while DJs buoy the weekend 'aving-it crowd into (they hope) a writhing mass with back-to-back floor-fillers. Décor is less punk, more polite, with chinoiserie chests, faux Louis XIV chaises longues and fringed lampshades, but, thanks to its popularity, is rapidly getting the punk treatment.

## Shunt Lounge, London Bridge Station, 20 Stainer Street, SE1
Tel: 020 7378 7776   www.shunt.co.uk
Open: 6pm–late Weds–Fri; 8pm–late Sat. Last entry 11pm.

Digging ever deeper underground in the quest to escape London's samey pose palaces, it was only a matter of time before finding oneself in a vast, derelict, dank brick vault far beneath the city's foundations. This is Shunt. Named after the resident avant-garde theatre collective, this is its play-ground and incubator for forthcoming productions. Strictly speaking a

members' club (because stray commuters do come a-knocking), day membership is available for a fiver (Wed/Thur) or tenner (Fri/Sat).

Each week, the space is 'curated' by a different Shunt member – there may be film, live music, 'installations' of sorts, or nothing at all (they also lend a creative licence to opening hours, so 'late' could be any time between midnight and 3am). Whichever, there's always a thrilling, chilling walk of fear down into the space: yes, those are bats flying above (all very London Dungeons – appropriate, since it's next door). It also includes curios that you just don't find in your average overground lounge bar – a garden shed for trysts, a shoes-off snuggery and random HG Wells-style machinery. The entrance is predictably elusive – heading south from Tooley Street, walk through the station down Joiner Street until almost out the other side and look for a small door set back on the left – very Platform 9 3/4.

## St Moritz, 161 Wardour Street, Soho, W1

Tel: 020 7734 3324
Open: 10pm–3am Thurs–Sat

Spending the evening in St Moritz couldn't sound more misleading – it's not exclusive and it's nowhere near a mountain. There are some Swiss connections – it is run by two charming Swiss patriarchs, who have been known to entertain diners in the adjoining fondue restaurant with alpine horns, bells and an accordion (no yodelling, unfortunately). No such sounds down in the basement – St Moritz is a 'rawk' club, respected equally by rockerati (from Motörhead to the Kings of Leon) and the rockletariat – bikers, mods, skins and indie kids. Gaz's Rockin' Blues on Thursdays is still going strong after

more than 25 years with blues, rockabilly and ska plus live bands; its road-blockingly popular Friday nights (indie rock) and Saturday nights (1980s glam rock) are almost as long-running. This vintage club resembles the cellar of a Swiss chalet and its quaint alpine décor and intimate size makes for an atomic atmosphere. What's not to like? Well, with all that air-guitar action and rock-hopping, it gets pretty hot, and its primitive acoustics often induce tinnitus. But with resolutely cheap prices, at least you won't be needing a Swiss bank account here.

## T–Bar, 56 Shoreditch High Street, Shoreditch, E1
Tel: 020 7729 2973   www.tbarlondon.com
Open: 8pm–2am Thurs–Sat; 5pm–midnight Sun

Housed in a former tea warehouse (hence 'T'), the T-Bar means industrial-

sized and -styled clubbing. As a much-loved East End dance-music institution, coupled with its no-fee door policy, there's always a bit of a freeze-frame to your night, spent waiting in line, comparing outfits with your neighbours (or sniggering snobbishly at stray Leicester Square types that are inevitably drawn here) and anxiously watching the T-bar's large clock that counts down the seconds till last orders. Once in, past the laughably cantankerous door staff, there's space to run and run (or dance and dance) within its open-plan, stark concrete interior punctuated with design-classic seating. Acclaimed electro residents Damian Lazarus and Andrew Weatherall play monthly, and in between them is an annoyingly popular programme of all the things you might like to party to, including lots of gonnabe DJs and the much loved dirty house night Dig Your Own Rave for filthy-dirty Sundays.

### Victory, 55 New Oxford Street, Holborn, WC1
Tel: 020 7240 0700  www.clubvictory.com
Open: daily, 9pm–4am

Entering the newly opened Victory, you'd be forgiven for thinking that you'd followed the White Rabbit down the hole. You're inside but out – in a mini street complete with double yellow lines, street lamps and terraced houses. Shop fronts lead into private rooms (one even contains a bath), and there's a Parisian-style wine bar. It's like a movie set, a fact which becomes less sur-real knowing that the man behind the façade is Youcef Aden, a former Hollywood set designer and founder of the gothic-set members' club Hedges & Butler (and, apparently, costume designer for Dynasty – as well as a big bank balance, the man is clearly possessed of a sense of humour). At the back, sprawled louchely on armchairs among dusty old books, you'll find black-clad Clerkenwell architect types and graphic designers studiously grooving to live bands midweek. Weekends pull in a younger party crowd made up of art stars, actors and models all getting down. Eyes on that bath for the competitive exhibitionism.

## BEST OF THE REST

**Annabel's**  Exclusive members club, with a strict dress code. A London insitiution among the society set has been going for years, find a friend to get you in to party with the young and old, beautiful and rich. (44 Berkeley Square, W1; 020 7629 1096)

**Chinawhite**  Notorious haunt of celebs in the late nineties, this sumptuous, cushion-scattered club remains undeniably popular, even if the A-list clientele have moved on. (6 Air Street, W1; 020 7343 0040)

**Embassy**  Ever wanted to meet a real-life footballer, soap star or Big Brother contestant, if for some strange reason the answer is yes then Embassy is your mecca. Real-time Heat magazine for the socially unaware. (29 Old Burlington St, W1; 020 7851 0956)

**Fire**  If you ever have the need to head out at 5am on a Monday morning then Fire's the place. A gay dance club underneath the arches in Vauxhall has a very sweaty, very pumped up crowd who party their way through the weekend (38-42 Parry St, SW8; 020 7582 9890)

**Jamm**  No pretensions, no dress code, just a cool Brixton warehouse vibe in an appealingly scruffy ex-Victorian pub, which hosts live music most nights, as well as film screenings, after parties and organic roast lunches during the day (261 Brixton Road, SW9; 020 7274 5537)

**Raffles**  A recent revamp has seen Raffles catapulted back into the social pages of London newspapers as the glamorous party crowd indulge in behind-closed-doors debauchery (287 Kings Road, SW3; 0871 971 3794)

**Tramps**  Old School club full of glitz, glamour and just a touch of cheese, tabs run off the scale as the international clientele try and impress the ridiculously pretty girls (40 Jermyn Street, SW1Y; 020 7734 0565)

# LIVE MUSIC

Since every teenager in the country saw starting a band as their fast track into adulthood, venues large and small have seen to it that their creative angst gets an audience. Our favourites, below, are of the more intimate, soulful variety where performers are within ogling distance; also recommended are the 12 Bar Club on London's guitar mile, Denmark Street, WC2 (020 7240 2622), the long-serving 100 Club (100 Oxford Street, W1; 020 7636 0933), the acclaimed Vortex Jazz Club in Dalston (11 Gillett Square, N16; 020 7993 3643), the jazz players' jazz club, 606 (90 Lots Road, Chelsea, SW10; 020 7352 5953), and the love-worn but right-on-it Windmill right on the edge of a Brixton council estate (22 Blenheim Gardens, SW2; 020 8671 0700). Then there are the fun factories: KOKO (standing for 'keep on keeping on'), which hosts club nights and one-off, sell-out gigs (14 Camden High Street, NW1; 0870 432 5527), The Roundhouse, a Victorian steam-engine turning shed where Hendrix, Pink Floyd and The Doors have all played (Chalk Farm Road, NW1; 0870 389 1846), The Mean Fiddler, a 1,000-capacity rock box (165 Charing Cross Road, WC2; 020 7434 9592), and The O2 Centre (née The Millennium Dome and finally fit for purpose) in Greenwich (0871 984 0002).

---

**Bardens Boudoir, 38–44 Stoke Newington Road, N16**
Tel: 020 7249 9557   www.bardensbar.co.uk
Open: 8pm–midnight Mon–Thurs; 8pm–2am Fri/Sat (only open for events; check website for listings)

---

Named after the furniture shop that it once was before opening in 2005, Bardens Boudoir has succeeded in creating a loyal following (no mean feat) among the hippest Hoxtonites and savvy musoheads, who know that whoever plays in this 350-capacity basement will be musts for the iPod. Don't be put off by its remote Stokey address – certainly The Gossip, Bloc Party, Simian Mobile Disco, Lady Sovereign and Kate Nash, just a few of the biggest new names in music that have played here, haven't been. Its pioneering programme focuses on up-and-coming indie bands, sleazy electro, dirty punk and haunting folk, spliced with cutting-edge comedy and book readings; it climaxes at its sweaty, volatile dance party, Club Motherfucker (every second Saturday of the month). The décor is comfy and lived-in with battered old red Chesterfields, green leather stools and high-backed dining chairs – the kind of place you wish the smoking ban had never reached; cosy booths have been decorated by local artists giving it even more of a boho feel. Leave your sensible head at home.

## Barfly, 49 Chalk Farm Road, Camden, NW1
Tel: 020 7424 0800  www.barflyclub.com
Open: 7pm–midnight Sun–Weds, 7pm–3am Thurs–Sat

Not one known for throwing around the niceties, Noel Gallagher said of Barfly, 'Ten years ahead of anybody's time.' Maybe it's just a thinly veiled self-compliment – seeing as Barfly plucked Oasis from obscurity – but nurturing new talent has been their speciality since 1996, and puts over 1,000 bands on their stage each year, not without some kind of Midas touch: pedigree rock bands (such as Blur, Stereophonics, The Strokes) all cut their teeth on its small, dingy stage. That they've since opened two others in London (at the University of London Union, Malet Street, WC1; 020 7664 2000) and The Fly (36 New Oxford St, WC1; 0844 8472424), plus several nationwide, is proof that polish and pretensions are not requisites for rocking live music. Expect talent scouts to be lurking in the standing-room-only space (arrive early for a good view), alongside other musicians and musos, all in artful scruffiness and prog-rock hair, exuding couldn't-care-less cool. Sticking around in the downstairs pub after the gig to buy the band a beer is as good a start as any to a night of rock'n'roll mayhem.

## Jazz Café, 5 Parkway, Camden, NW1
Tel: 020 7485 6834 (box office 0870 150 0044)  www.jazzcafe.co.uk
Open: daily, 7pm–2am

It doesn't just play jazz, and it's not really a café – the Jazz Café is so much more, and for that it's a live-music institution. Black music is a speciality but not a necessity – a huge, brave range is guaranteed, from gospel choirs and drum'n'bass collectives, to beat box and Mexican rock, and beyond. Big and breaking stars alike take to its stage (though if it's the likes of De La Soul, Courtney Pine and Desmond Dekker – exemplary Jazz Café guests – be sure to book in advance). The sedentary can dine in the gallery restaurant overlooking the stage, but committed music lovers know that there's most space for bouncing around to the right of the stage (they also know that the food can underwhelm). With its industrial, Blue Note-esque steel/blue neon décor and a laidback dress code, the vibe here is modern, upbeat and unpretentious. There's no need to hear a pin drop during performances, and in fact some artists are so relaxed, they have been known to invite their famous musician friends from the audience to jam with them.

## The Luminaire, 311 High Road, Kilburn, NW6
020 7372 7123   www.theluminaire.co.uk
Open: daily, 7.30pm–midnight (1am Thurs, 2am Fri/Sat)

'Welcome to your new favourite venue,' says The Luminaire, with uncharacteristic self-regard. That it was Music Week's UK Venue of the Year 2007 arguably gives it the right. With friendliness written into its mission statement, The Luminaire's commitment to putting on first-class gigs with a happy attitude towards bands, sound engineers and punters has reaped its rewards. Since opening in 2005, the venue's forward-thinking music policy has seen it become a music-lover's lair, presenting a line-up that ranges from futuristic-electro Japanese carnivals to blues heroes, as well as bands such as Au Revoir Simone, Babyshambles and Bat for Lashes – and that's just the As and Bs; OK, so it is in Kilburn – but lower rents mean reasonably priced drinks. Plush red curtains lining the back of the stage, flickering candles and cared-for toilets give this venue a slightly more dignified feel than most – that is, until the mad moshing starts.

## Ronnie Scott's, 47 Frith Street, Soho, W1
Tel: 020 7439 0747   www.ronniescotts.co.uk
Open: daily, 6pm–3am

Such a national treasure is Ronnie Scott's that two entire books have endeavoured to tell its story. The potted version is thus: it was opened in 1959 by one Ronnie Scott (plus fellow musicians Pete King and Leo Green) – Scott is largely credited with importing modern jazz to Britain and was awarded the OBE in 1981 for services to jazz. He died in 1996 and in 2005, King sold it to theatre impresariette Sally Greene, who brought in Hotel Costes' designer Jacques Garcia for a £2 million facelift, but thankfully, when the lights are down it looks exactly the same (1950s Soho – warm, dark, rich, red, and lined with black-and-white photos of all the musicians who have played here: Dizzy, Miles, Ella, etc). She's also brought in a decent menu, and opened a members' club upstairs (here, think Hotel Costes – all luxe lounge bar). But when the old jazz cats are smoking up the smoothest tunes, there's nowhere else to be but in the magic and romance of the main room; ideal for conversationally challenged dates. Booking advised.

---

**Soho Revue Bar, 11–12 Walkers Court, Soho, W1**
Tel: 020 7437 4400   www.sohorevuebar.com
Open: 5pm–4am Tues–Sat

---

Purposefully OTT, this high-camp cabaret-cum-nightclub opened – appropriately enough – in the shell of historic strip joint Raymond Revue Bar in the dark heart of seedy Soho. Sleaze was firmly shown the door in 2004, but outrageousness is still high on the agenda, with a high-quality (if at times high-risk) schedule that includes (drag) cabaret, (nude) magicians and comedy (porn stars). Evenings start out quite civilized, with dinner, cocktails and cabaret served at tiered leather banquettes in the auditorium; by 11pm the space segues into a (usually house-heavy) nightclub. Extravagant décor – all rich reds and pinks, kitsch chandeliers, a Swarovski-studded bar and the original (planet-sized) disco ball from Raymond's days – sets the tone, as does a mixed clientele that includes trannies and screaming queens (Elton John held his hen night here). That said, anyone's welcome, provided they're up for fun, and are prepared to observe the celebrity-penned house rules – including gay TV darling Graham Norton's: 'Best behaviour will not be tolerated.' And with the nudity licence still active, the management encourages punters to dress daringly.

## CABARET

It's showtime! London is having a 21st-century variety moment. What began as a fringe phenomenon in abandoned East End warehouses and festivals in fields is now taking root in the mainstream as new cabaret lounges and supper clubs crop up across the capital. King of Clubs Vince Power (he who founded Mean Fiddler) knows on which side his bread is buttered – he's ditched the dance music to invest in **The Pigalle Club**. Dressed up like a 1940s Chicago gangster joint (all warm red tones, aged wood panelling, twinkling mirrors and authentically uniformed staff), The Pigalle is a dinner/dance club with its own 26-piece swing band and guest performances from Power's seriously good connections (215–217 Piccadilly, W1; 020 7287 3834, www.lepigalleclub.com). In Holborn is the rather less commercial and pleasingly alternative **Volupté Lounge** (9 Norwich Street, EC4; 020 7831 1677, www.volupte-lounge.com), where cabaret of a more vaudeville (and risqué) nature is performed in an intimate 20th-century-styled salon. Other clubs are increasingly including cabaret into their line-ups (see Soho Revue Bar, Black Gardenia). But for the freshest, most original take, it's best to head back to the wilderness. At Hackney's **Bistrotheque** (see DRINK) there are bearded trannies up to all sorts of mischief; the **Bethnal Green Workingmen's Club** (see page 169) frequently offers something suitably sideways, and then there are guerrilla cabarets that require ear-to-the-ground tracking to see where they'll land next. **Medium Rare** (020 8749 7781, www.mediumrare.tv) is a roving supper club whose regular perform-ers include Tina C (country goes drag) and Gunther the German porn star; the vintage club night Ladyluck (www.ladyluckclub.co.uk) usually incorpo-rates 'burlesque and grind'. Life, as they say, is a cabaret.

For some assistance on that ear-to-the-ground business, there are a number of excellent weekly web listings. Tune in to www.flavorpill.com/london, www.urbanjunkies.com, www.kultureflash.net and www.run-riot.com and all bases should be amply covered.


## ADULT ENTERTAINMENT

London's adult entertainment scene is as eclectic and cosmopolitan as the city, and ranges from the louchely retro to the downright seedy. Starting at the higher end of the spectrum are the likes of Stringfellows and The Windmill Club (OK, there are no great heights to the scene); **The Windmill Club** (17–19 Great Windmill St; 020 7439 3558), in the heart of London's red light district of Soho, is a strangely alluring combination of a Weimar cabaret bar and a 1980s soft porn Playboy video. As London's first nude dancing bar it was the subject of the film *Mrs Henderson Presents* (star-ring Dame Judi Dench), which now means the club is also packed with tourists and couples. **Stringfellows** (16 Upper St Martin's Lane; 020 7240 5534) and **Peter Stringfellow's Angels** (201 Wardour Street; 020 7758 0670) are both owned and run by the legendary leathery lothario Peter Stringfellow. With half-decent restaurants and some of the more beautiful girls in town it is a classier night out alongside London's suited and booted voyeurs. Slightly less exclusive and slightly more seedy is the **Secrets** chain – five in all with the Holborn branch arguably being the best (3 Grays Inn Road; 020 7242 6266). **Spearmint Rhino**, the American chain, has a large club in the West End (161 Tottenham Court Road; 020 7209 4488), which is often rumoured to be close to closure for all sorts of shenanigans. Slipping a little further down the greasy pole is the likes of **Metropolis** (234 Cambridge Heath Road; 020 8980 2917), located on the edge of Hackney Road's 'Titty Mile'. Finally, at the bottom of the pile, at the end of the mile, are the pubs that offer lunchtime strips, where punters put a pound in the pint pot for the privilege of watching – for example **Browns** (1 Hackney Road; 020 7739 4653).

## CASINOS

London's gaming laws changed in October 2004 to allow immediate access to casinos. In order to play, bring along an approved form of ID – a pass-port, driving licence, or if a UK resident simply a credit card. Most of London's casinos are found in the West End and offer a similar variety of games – Blackjack, Roulette and Poker, all ringed by a glittering and noisy array of slot machines. Some have begun to jump on the Texas hold'em poker bandwagon and hold regular tournaments where players can 'buy-in' for around £100. **Hard Rock** have just opened their first casino in London (3–4 Coventry Street, 020 7287 7887) in the neon tourist hell of Leicester Square and, accordingly, attracts the lowest common denominator of clien-tele; similarly there is the new **Casino at the Empire**, offering 'a touch of Vegas' (5–6 Leicester Square; 0870 870 7731). More upmarket, which also means higher minimum bets and a smarter dress code (no trainers or frayed jeans), are **Palm Beach Casino** (30 Berkeley Street; 020 7493 6585) and **The Sportsman** (Old Quebec Street; 020 7414 0061). The Sportsman offers regular poker nights on Mondays, Fridays and Sundays, with the Sunday afternoon session offering tuition for beginners. Those wanting to don a tux and play with the high-rollers should try **Fifty** (50 St James's Street; 08704 155050) or **Aspinalls** (27–28 Curzon Street; 020 7499 4599), but be warned – there's no such democracy here, but a large annual mem-bership fee and a tight screening process that requires new members to be proposed by two existing ones. Time to start making friends in high places.

## MEMBERS' CLUBS

One capitalist commodity that apparently proves you've made it is club membership, as it requires many hundreds of pounds lying around *and* powerful friends – it seems Londoners are ever more eager to wear that badge of honour. The ultimate collection of membership cards would include **Bungalow 8**, Amy Sacco's New York outpost at St Martin's Lane Hotel with affections for Studio 54 and all manner of celebrities, socialites and opinion-formers; **Shoreditch House**, the new satellite of corporate media haunt **Soho House**, which has upped the ante with its rooftop swimming pool, private bowling lanes, East End location, and high fashion and high camp regulars; **The Groucho** in Dean Street, Soho, the playground of more mature media luvvies, and especially useful for its bedrooms; **The Hospital** in Endell Street, Covent Garden, Dave Stewart's incubator of creativity and harbour for the hungrily ambitious; and **Dex** in Brixton with its 24-hour bar, outdoor hot tub and eight bedrooms. As everyone wants to look popular, there's sure to be some members keen for the services of rent-a-friend.

## CAN'T SLEEP?

Beat sleep with **Bar Italia**'s espressos and *paninis* (22 Frith Street, W1; 020 7437 4520), join the off-duty chefs at **Vingt Quatre**, a posh greasy spoon (325 Fulham Road; SW10, 020 7376 7224), try not to be put off your halal food by gurning Fabric clubbers at the American diner **Tinseltown** (44 St John Street, EC1; 020 7689 2424), buy salt beef bagels just to laugh at the cool kids all drunk and not cool anymore at **Brick Lane Beigel Bake** (159 Brick Lane, E1; 020 7729 0616), and indulge in home-cooked Turkish food, at **Somine** (131 Kingsland High Street, E8; 020 7254 7384).

# culture...

Warning: this chapter may cause serious harm to a hedonist's partying pro-gramme. London is a veritable heritage theme park. It's taken a few knocks, such as with the Great Fire in 1666, and the Blitz – though of course these only add to its rich history – and has been continually added to ever since the Roman invasion in AD43 (if you're visiting the Tower of London, check out the remnants of Londinium's city walls at Tower Hill). Rome's legacy doesn't stretch to town planning, however: blame the capital's haphazard layout on the merry-makers of medieval times – though its distinct lack of right angles and order makes for a quirky charm with surprises around ever corner.

Getting lost in London's 2,000-year history is another hazard. A visit to the tri-umvirate of the Tower of London, the Houses of Parliament and Westminster Abbey will provide a crash course in British history, while tombstones in the Abbey and St Paul's Cathedral present a near-full pack of flash-cards of the city's VIPs. Also look out for the blue circular plaques on buildings, denoting famous Londoners' residences. The most famous residence of all needs no such introduction – the seat of the British monarch, Buckingham Palace.

Architecture anoraks will find plenty to forage on in London's chaotic patch-work of fashions through the ages – Gothic, Romanesque, neoclassical, Art Deco, modernist, postmodernist and High Tech. But indulging in London's cul-ture needn't involve excessive brain engagement. There are plenty of handsome buildings to gaze at idly – such as those royal residences (also Clarence House, Prince Charles' present home, and Kensington Palace, home of the late Princess of Wales). An amble along the river's south bank offers a fine vantage point – not least if you take the London Eye, or there are all manner of tours that will do the hard work for you (see PLAY).

London's performing arts scene offers yet more passive entertainment of all genres that easily competes on a world stage – there really is something for everyone, be you a Druid or a droog. And while London's national institutions and historical monuments add gravitas to the city, much of its cultural character comes from its independent enterprises, from the house museums of Sir John Soane and Dennis Severs (an extraordinary candlelit Huguenot residence) to the hothouses of avant-garde arts such as the ICA, Whitechapel Art Gallery, White Cube, The Saatchi Gallery (due to re-open in 2008, though they said that about 2007) and The Wapping Project. Indeed, while London has a rich heritage of monarchy and aristocracy, empire and industry, it maintains a progressive outlook – and a sharp edge. The new guard – including those naughty, controversy-courting YBAs (Young British Artists), an ever-rolling wave of rebel rock stars and all those steel-and-glass-loving visionary architects – is redefining London's cultural and physical landscape.

What follows are edited highlights of London old and new, with, inevitably, glaring omissions that could fill this section many times over – namely, Trafalgar Square and Nelson's Column, the National Gallery, the National Portrait Gallery, the art collections of Somerset House, the war museums, the Museum of London, the Royal Courts of Justice and the Old Bailey, Number 1 London (the residence of the Dukes of Wellington past and present), Temple Church (now a tourist destination thanks to *The Da Vinci Code*) and so on and on and on. Save these for a rainy day – though with London's inclement climate, that might obliterate any chance of hedonism whatsoever.

### The British Museum, Great Russell Street, Bloomsbury, WC1

Tel: 020 7323 8000  www.thebritishmuseum.ac.uk
Open: daily, 10am–5.30pm (8.30pm Thurs/Fri)

So important are the collections in the vast neoclassical British Museum that it seems that every schoolchild in the land is required by law to see them firsthand. Our advice is to hire an audio guide to block out their unrestrained delight when they see the Egyptian mummies, the Lindow Man (a peat-preserved 1st-century body) or 'Ginger' (a sand-preserved 3,400-year-old man with, you guessed it, ginger hair). Thankfully there are quieter wonders of antiquity, including the Rosetta Stone, a rock inscribed with Egyptian hieroglyphics from 196BC, and the Elgin Marbles, those friezes and statues

c. 440BC controversially taken by Lord Elgin from the Parthenon in Athens in 1816 – in fact the British Museum has so much, it's a wonder what can be left in the countries of origin. Less contentious is Norman Foster's masterful architecture in the Great Court, Europe's largest covered square with 3,300 triangular glass panels that shed a magical luminescence onto the pale limestone courtyard, and the domed Reading Room where Lenin, Marx, Dickens and Hardy once studied, and where you can almost hear the sound of silence.

## Buckingham Palace, The Mall, Green Park, SW1

Tel: 020 7766 7300  www.royal.gov.uk

State Rooms: daily, 9.45am–6pm (last admission 3.45pm) end July–end Sept;
Royal Mews: 11am–4pm Sat–Thurs end March–end July; daily, 10am–5pm
end July–end Sept
Queen's Gallery: daily, 10am–5.30pm

Britain's most famous house boasts something of a trophy case of superlatives – the world's largest working palace, London's largest private gardens and Britain's most obvious tourist destination. Some say it's one of the worst places to visit because it's expensive and most of it is out of bounds.

Freeloaders can witness Changing the Guard, a daily traffic-stopping tradition of pomp and circumstance where 20-odd bearskinned guards parade up the Mall (11.30am in summer; otherwise on alternate days in clement weather). Access beyond that famous neoclassical façade (actually the back of the building) is limited – only the State Rooms can be visited and only when the Queen trots off to Balmoral Castle in Scotland in the summer. The Royal Mews – home to the palace's horses and State carriages (and the ludicrously look-at-me 24ct gold-plated Coronation Coach) – are open for half the year; only the Queen's Gallery, which displays the Royal Collection – dour oil paintings by Dutch masters, gilt parade furniture and precious jewels – is open year round. Otherwise, try appropriating an invitation to one of her garden parties, or a knighthood.

## The Design Museum, Shad Thames, SE1

Tel: 0870 909 9009  www.designmuseum.org
Open: daily, 10am–5.45pm

With a museum that champions the equal merits of style and substance, form and function, there are high expectations for its own architecture. Needless to say, the Design Museum is the apotheosis of good taste – an angular, whitewashed building in the style of the Bauhaus Dessau, built in

1989 under the direction and financial support of Sir Terence Conran (the man behind Habitat, the Conran Shop and a portfolio of fine restaurants in London; see Bibendum, SNACK). A temple to design, it pays tribute to the best of all areas – product design, graphics, fashion, architecture and engineering – and hosts the annual Designer of the Year award (previously won by Apple's Jonathan Ive). For recharging one's batteries, there's the Blueprint Café (a Conran restaurant, no less) with binoculars set out on the tables for spying on design in the distance – being riverside, there are panoramic views of the Thames and Tower Bridge.

## Institute of Comtemporary Arts (ICA), The Mall, Trafalgar Square, SW1

Tel: 020 7930 3647  www.ica.org.uk
Open: daily, noon–1 am (11pm Mon, 10.30pm Sun)

Somewhat out of place plonked literally on the Queen's front drive is the Institute of Contemporary Arts, a homage to experimental and cutting-edge art, music, film and people, founded in 1947 and still very much at the forefront of modern culture. Step inside away from the grandeur of The Mall

pinhole cameras. Also recommended: Magnum Print Room (Magnum Studios, 63 Gee Street, EC1) – the exhibition space of Henri Cartier-Bresson's photographic co-operative; and the Proud Galleries – a pair of commercial galleries offering cool photography exhibitions and plenty of Kodak moments at their rock'n'roll parties (Proud Camden: Horse Hospital, Stables Market, Chalk Farm Road, NW1; 020 7482 3867; Proud Central, 5 Buckingham St, WC2; 020 7839 4942).

## The Royal Academy, Burlington House, Piccadilly, W1
Tel: 020 7300 8000   www.royalacademy.org.uk
Open: daily, 10am–6pm (10pm Fri)

The Royal Academy of Arts is rather like an order of knights for the art

world. Founded in 1768 by King George III, there's room around the proverbial table for 80 elected Academicians – sculptors, architects, printmakers and painters –

who must be professionally active in Britain. Past Academicians include Sir Joshua Reynolds (its first president), Constable, Gainsborough and Turner; current members include Peter Blake, Norman Foster, David Hockney, Elizabeth Blackadder and, since 2007, Tracey Emin. Academicians' privileges include choosing its major loan exhibitions, curating the famous Summer Exhibition, and of course hanging their own masterpieces ('Whoops: that's a whole wall taken out; no room for non-members. Oh well – our club'). And with the RA's architectural pedigree, the building itself is a work of art (and a welcome sanctuary, set back from Piccadilly) – built in 1668 for the Earl of Burlington, it's since been embellished by numerous Academicians including Sidney Smirke (who with his brother designed The British Museum) and Lord Foster, Knight of modern London.

### Royal Albert Hall, Kensington Gore, South Kensington, SW7
Tel: 020 7838 3105  www.royalalberthall.com
Open: daily, 9am–9pm. Tours 10am–3.30pm Fri–Tues.

London has much to thank Queen Victoria and Prince Albert for, a lot of which can be found in 'Albertopolis' – a veritable village of epic national institutions designed to bring arts and sciences to the people. Its symbolic heart is the Albert Hall, a love story in red brick built in Albert's memory after he died of typhoid in 1861. Victoria mourned his death till her own and apparently always drew the curtains of her carriage when driving past

as she couldn't bear to look; at the opening ceremony in 1871 she was too emotional to speak, and the Prince of Wales had to do the honours. For more heartache –

and eyestrain – cross the road into Kensington Gardens to see the dazzling-ly gaudy Albert Memorial, some 176ft of gilded Gothic revival. The Albert Hall – a 6,000 capacity rotunda – is vastly more tasteful and is affectionately known as the nation's village hall, thanks to a diverse programme including boxing, tennis and concerts; it's also famously home to the BBC Proms. It's even available for hire, so any secret ambitions of performing in the Albert Hall could be just a cheque away.

## St Paul's Cathedral, Ludgate Hill, City, EC4
Tel: 020 7236 4128   www.stpauls.co.uk
Open: 8.30am–4pm Mon–Sat. Sunday services at 10.15am, 11.30am, 3.15pm and 6pm

While Westminster Abbey is the 'House of Kings', St Paul's is the people's cathedral, and where, in 1981, Lady Diana Spencer married Prince Charles. It was built in 1710 by Sir Christopher Wren – as the first ever Protestant cathedral, Wren was instructed not to make it too 'Catholic'; the lavish gold artwork is the result of Queen Victoria's influence, after she complained that it was 'most dreary, dingy and undevotional'. During World War II, Churchill famously insisted on saving St Paul's 'at all costs'. It was relatively safe though – its Portland stone dome can be seen from all over London, and served as a German landmark. And from its vertigo-induc-ing external galleries (via

some 530 steps), one can see the whole of London (plus the odd architec-tural photographer taking advantage of its view). Visitors can also climb to the base of its massive freestanding dome, so-called the Whispering Gallery since a whisper can be heard on the opposite side. Those with OBEs or upwards can get married here – so really a cathedral for people who happen to be Very Important.

## Serpentine Gallery, West Carriage Drive, Kensington Gardens, W2
Tel: 020 7402 6075   www.serpentinegallery.org
Open: daily, 10am–6pm

Much of the Serpentine's appeal is in its snack size compared with some of London's cultural heavyweights. Indeed its setting – in a Grade II listed tea pavilion (built in 1934 in the heart of Hyde Park for the park's 'poorer visitors' because the authorities thought they might cause trouble if left without refreshments) – is also a pleasing antidote to the pandemonium of plan-

et London. Since becoming a contemporary art gallery in 1970, however, its provocative exhibitions – from the likes of Bridget Riley, Damien Hirst and Cindy Sherman – have stood as a pleasing counterpoint to the tranquillity of the park. Each year from July to September the gallery reclaims some parkland with its Pavilion – a temporary showcase for pioneering and internationally acclaimed architects (such as Zaha Hadid, Oscar Niemeyer and Rem Koolhaas) under which a café operates. Park Nights runs throughout August showing open-air films, talks and 'sound' events. Awfully refreshing.

## Shakespeare's Globe, 21 New Globe Walk, Bankside, SE1
Tel: 020 7902 1400   www.shakespeares-globe.org
Open: daily, 10am–5pm Oct–April; 9am–noon May–Sept

They say they don't make them like they used to, but here on the south bank, a group of thesps led by the late American actor Sam Wanamaker has done just that. Shakespeare's Globe Theatre, originally built at the end of the 16th century, was authentically reconstructed in 1997 right down to the 12 million wooden pegs used to hold the playhouse together, and has the only thatched roof in London since the Great Fire in 1666 – needless to say, the original burnt down (daily tours and an exhibition tell the full story). Even if you despise theatre, the polygonal amphitheatre is unarguably spectacular, with its elaborate jewel-box stage and repro Tudor exterior of oak beams and whitewash. The auditorium comprises the pit for 700 'groundlings' and tiered benches for 900 (though the bard would have packed in a riotous 3,000). The programme is Shakespearean, plus some plays by his contemporaries, as it would have been in Elizabethan times. In fact the most dramatic change to the experience is you, the audience – the throwing of rotten eggs has sadly been consigned to history.

## Sir John Soane's Museum, 13 Lincoln's Inn Fields, WC2
Tel: 020 7405 2107   www.soane.org
Open: 10am–5pm Tues–Sat

Sir John Soane was a very popular British architect of the 19th century, not least for bequeathing his house as a free museum to the nation when he died in 1837. His greatest work was his design of the Bank of England – sadly this was later replaced, but since he used his home as a test-bed for his grand designs produced in miniature and crammed into every inch, it has become a pilgrimage for architects and historians alike. Indeed as a prolific

collector with considerable taste – and a fabulous eccentric streak – he also attracts art lovers with his Hogarth series (including The Rake's Progress) and his Turners (he was great friends with the artist), and archeologists with his sarcophagus of Pharaoh Seti I (c.1,370 BC) that at the time was too pricey for the British Museum. But the appeal for all is in the townhouse's original – and mostly untouched – function as a home, so also on view are his breakfast parlour, drawing rooms, kitchen and study – all of course designed by Soane's gifted hand. Booking essential.

## South Bank Centre, Belvedere Road, South Bank, SE1
Tel: 0870 380 4300  www.southbankcentre.org.uk
Open: daily, 10am–10.30pm

It's arguable that the South Bank Centre's concrete 'carpark-itecture' (aka Brutalism) is a strategy to repel the hordes of zombie tourists that invade

the scenic south bank. For this is a no-frills, highbrow culture bunker largely populated by the elite intelligentsia and built in 1951 to celebrate the Festival of Britain (an enterprise to kick-start British post-war culture). On site is the Royal Festival Hall (now a Grade I listed building – ie, exceptional and therefore protected), which hosts ballet, dance and gigs, the Queen Elizabeth Hall and the Purcell Room, both smaller venues for dance, concerts, 'live' art and talks, and the Hayward Gallery, a fine arts and photography exhibition space; nearby are the independently managed National Theatre and National Film Theatre. All around are cultural phenomena, official and otherwise – there are free exhibitions and concerts in the SBC's open foyers, a skate park in the complex's graffiti-ed underbelly, secondhand book stalls huddling under Waterloo Bridge, and a kinetic light sculpture atop the Hayward Gallery that changes colour in the wind. And unwitting tourists – aka 'live' art.

## Tate Galleries

Tel: 020 7887 8000   www.tate.org.uk
**Tate Britain**, Millbank, SW1. Open: daily, 10am–5.50pm.
**Tate Modern**, Bankside, SE1. Open: daily, 10am–6pm (10pm Fri/Sat).

The Tate name has had various associations over time. Today it paints a picture of contemporary art, as in Tate

Modern: a vast, riverside ex-power station, opened in 2000 as the national gallery for international modern art. Within some 4.2 million bricks it holds works by Picasso, Matisse, Dalí, Magritte, Miró, Rothko, Lichtenstein and Warhol. The star attraction is usually whatever installation is being exhibited in the colossal Turbine Hall. But before Swiss architects Herzog & de Meuron converted this building into Tate Modern, if you said 'Tate', you would mean what is now known as Tate Britain on Millbank, which since 1897 has been the national gallery

207

of British art from 1500 to the present day, with works by Turner, Blake, Constable, Gainsborough, Hogarth, Reynolds and Bacon, plus all those YBAs, and is host to the annual Turner prize exhibition for contemporary art. And preceding the original Tate gallery, the name was simply associated with its benefactor, Sir Henry Tate, as in Tate & Lyle sugar – we surely have him to thank for many pleasures.

## Tower of London, Tower Hill, EC3
Tel: 0870 756 6060  www.tower-of-london.org.uk
Open: daily, 9am (10am Sun/Mon)–6pm (5pm Nov–Feb)

Only Britain's most esteemed villains – among them, naughty royals, high-society traitors and notorious cockney gangsters the Kray Brothers – have been behind bars at the Tower of London. The Krays were among the few to leave alive. Most (including two of Henry VIII's wives) were subjected to gruesome torture and bloody execution. The last prisoner is long gone, leaving a well-preserved medieval fortress built over 900 years ago for William

the Conqueror. Actually it's an entire town of towers, with charming cobbled lanes, cottages and a chapel. Add to that the jolly Beefeaters carrying out bizarre traditions, the royal ravens and the Crown Jewels (yes, they are the real deal apparently), and the result is rather like a Disney film set. Except for the bloodstains. If stamina allows, visit Tower Bridge – that iconic landmark so often (and occasionally expensively) confused with London Bridge. Opened in 1894, the upper walkway (45m/148ft up; intended for crossing the bridge while its drawbridges were raised) is still accessible, as is the Engine Room's original steam-powered machinery. Now, however, electric motors lift the two 1,200-ton arms in 90 seconds, and since it's one of the Thames' lowest crossings, do so over 500 times a year ( 020 7403 3761, www.towerbridge.org.uk).

## The Victoria and Albert Museum, Science Museum and Natural History Museum, South Kensington, SW7

**V&A**, Cromwell Road. Tel: 020 7942 2000  www.vam.ac.uk
open: daily, 10am–5.45pm (10pm Weds)
**Science Museum**, Exhibition Road. Tel: 0870 870 4868
www.sciencemuseum.org.uk; open: daily, 10am–6pm
**Natural History Museum**, Cromwell Road. Tel: 020 7942 5000
www.nhm.ac.uk; open: daily, 10am (11am Sun)–5.50pm

Tackling 'Museum Central' does not require Tefal-headed learnedness – this cluster of world-class national museums caters for dilettantes and PhD types alike. All were built in Queen Victoria's reign as an initiative to make information available to all. The Victoria and Albert Museum specializes in decorative art and design, fashion and textiles. Its seven miles of galleries, halls and corridors hold over 4 million items. The Science Museum is rather more left-brain and among its treasures are patent models of Stephenson's Rocket and Arkwright's textile machinery, plus medical artefacts (some nec-

essarily pickled) from Ancient Greece to the present-day, flight simulators and, for those in need of a brain break, an IMAX cinema. The Natural History Museum, with its grand Romanesque architecture, is hailed as a temple of nature, and as 'the animal's Westminster Abbey'. Its most famous inhabitant is the diplodocus cast but it boasts over 70 million other exhibits, from microscopic cells to mammoth skeletons and Martian meteorites.

## Whitechapel Gallery 80–82 Whitechapel High St, E1

Tel: 020 7522 7888  www.whitechapel.org

Open: 11am–6pm (9pm Thurs, 11pm Fri). Closed Mondays and Tuesdays.

That the East End is now a major centre for fine art, the Whitechapel has come to be its unofficial flagship gallery, despite arriving long before the bandwagon. Founded in 1901, it introduced artists into the UK such as Picasso, Rothko, Pollock and Kahlo, and was the first to showcase Hockney, Gilbert & George and Freud – eat that, establishment! It's now having such a moment that it's due to double in size by 2009, and its programme also stretches to talks, film and Friday night fun with live music and the obligatory trendoids. Close behind the flagship is the commercial gallery White

Cube (48 Hoxton Square; 020 7930 5373, www.whitecube.com) run by art dealer Jay Jopling who has a near-monopoly on YBAs (who aren't really that Y any more): Hirst, Turk, Quinn, Gilbert & George, Emin, the Chapman brothers, and of course Jopling's wife, Sam Taylor-Wood. Such is the eminence of White Cube that there is even a rip-off/tribute 'gallery space' in epicentre-of-cool The George & Dragon pub (see PUBS), called White Cubicle (yes, housed in the ladies' toilet, measuring precisely 1.4m by 1.4m).

## GALLERIES

### Mayfair Galleries

Once rife with stuffy galleries run by old Etonians, Mayfair has seen a steady invasion of international commercial galleries only too happy to feed It-art to hedgefunders with bonuses to blow and uber-rich 'non-doms'. From

Zurich came **Hauser & Wirth** to 196a Piccadilly (020 7287 2300), opening in 2003 in an old Lutyens-designed bank, representing Louis Bourgeois, Martin Creed and co. They then went into business with the old master dealer Colnaghi creating – you guessed it – **Hauser & Wirth Colnaghi** (15 Old Bond Street; 020 7399 9770). **Sadie Coles HQ** (35 Heddon Street; 020 7434 2227) has expanded her eponymous mini-empire (that looks after the likes of Sarah Lucas and Matthew Barney) by opening another gallery at 69 South Audley Street. Also with the requisite two galleries is the British dealer **Timothy Taylor** who sells, among others, Alex Katz and Craigie Aitchison: Mark I at 21 Dering Street, Mark II at 15 Carlos Place (020 7409 3344). Then from the Big Apple with big ideas and big names (like Jeff Koons and Carsten Höller) is **Gagosian**, at 17 Davies Street (020 7493 3020). In their spatially challenged ex-bag/glove shop is the German duo **Monika Sprüth and Philomene Magers** (7A Grafton Street; 020 7408 1613) who represent artists such as Andreas Gursky, Cindy Sherman and Karen Kilimnik. Previously they were in business with **Simon Lee** who still sells Larry Clark et al at 12 Berkeley Street (020 7491 0100). Tucked away in **Haunch of Venison** mews is a gallery of the same name (020 7495 5050) – once the residence of Nelson and now of art, by the likes of Bill Viola and M/M. Meanwhile at 25 Mason's Yard is Jay Jopling's **White Cube** (020 7930 5373), a satellite gallery to Hoxton Square's mothership that is equally white and cube-shaped, and at 99 New Bond Street is **Max Wigram**'s gallery (aka Mr Phoebe Philo; 020 7495 4960). Interestingly, both Jopling and Wigram happen to be old Etonians. Over at 34 Bruton Street, run by Rolling Stones scions Jamie and Tyrone Wood, is **Scream** (020 7493 7388). Which is what you might feel like doing after all that.

### Vyner Street Galleries

Ever since **Maureen Paley** (21 Herald St, E2; 020 7729 4112) and **Victoria Miro** (16 Wharf Road, N1; 020 7336 8109) paved the way to the Hackney art scene, dealers, collectors, artists and budding art students have descended on East London in their droves, largely settling in Vyner Street and Herald Street. A particular little stretch has become the place du jour. Visit Vyner Street in the evening and you will no doubt be met by many a private view-goer spilling onto the street from the plethora of galleries that have moved in of late. The multitude of bright young things in the evening creates a vibrant buzz that is in contrast to Vyner Street's somewhat low-key grey daytime vibe. Dominating the end of the street is **Wilkinson's** (50–58

Vyner Street; 020 8980 2662) new two-storey gallery. Having moved from just around the corner, the first purpose-built gallery in E2 covers 6,000 sq ft of museum-inspired space. Over the way, set back off the road, No.45 is home to three galleries. Hidden downstairs, **One in the Other** (45 Vyner St; 020 8983 6240) although small shouldn't be missed if for nothing else but the emerging talents of James Wright. Then there is **Fred [London]** (45 Vyner St; 020 8981 2987) who moved here after parting ways with his former partner of Rhodes + Mann; also setting his sights on music, he's now set up a record label and a space in Leipzig. Also in the same building is the co-founder of Zoo Art Fair, **David Risley**'s gallery (45 Vyner St; 020 8980 2202), which is always brimming with talent both on the walls and in attendance. Still going strong is **Stuart Shave/Modern Art** (10 Vyner St; 020 8980 7742). Undeterred by being next door to a car repair garage, the exhibitions programme is always diverse. Keeping it young and giving the more established a run for their money is **Ibid Projects** (21 Vyner St; 020 8983 4355), which recently moved from Cambridge Heath Road, and **Netti Horn** (25b Vyner St; 020 8980 1568), a recent addition, which is committed to showing emerging artists.

## OPERA, BALLET AND DANCE

In the heart of theatreland is the seat of both the Royal Ballet Company and the Royal Opera. The **Royal Opera House** (Bow Street, Covent Garden, WC2; 020 7304 4000, www.royaloperahouse.org.uk; open: 10am–3.30pm (telesales till 8pm) Mon–Sat) is actually in its third incarnation after the first (built 1732) and second (built 1809) both burnt down. Backstage tours (often filled with obnoxious stage school kids; booking recommended) cover much of the 2.5-acre site and 10 floors, including the Grade I listed auditorium in splendid 24ct gilt and red velvet, the Fame-style dance studios that are maintained at 80°C so that dancers' muscles stay warm, and the bewitching prop-making room. If your take on opera and ballet is more sedentary, be sure to snap up one of the 67 tickets made available each day for that evening's performance, or take tea in the gorgeous Floral Hall, a Victorian crystal arcade where monthly tea dances and weekly jazz sessions are held. **The London Coliseum** (St Martin's Lane, Covent Garden, WC2; 020 7632 8300, www.eno.org; open: 10am–8pm Mon–Sat) has been home to the English National Opera since 1968 in a splendidly plush structure that since 1904 has been a music hall, cinema and a greyhound track. The ENO company is rival only to the Royal Opera but is the more populist since all performances are sung in English and surtitles are provided. For dance, with its 300-year heritage, **Sadler's Wells** (Rosebery Avenue, Islington, EC1; 0870 737 7737, www.sadlerswells.com) is considered London's premier contemporary dance venue. Its portfolio comprises three theatres – two on-site (the main auditorium and the more experimental Lilian Baylis Theatre) and the Peacock Theatre in W1. All show international and UK dance of all varieties, from the Shaolin Monks to disabled troupes. There's good reason to get on the inside of the **Barbican** (Silk Street, Barbican, EC2; 0845 120 7553, www.barbican.org.uk; open: 9am–11pm Mon–Sat; noon–11pm Sun and public holidays). Despite being the titleholder of 'London's Ugliest Building' shame, it is also Europe's largest performing arts centre (set over seven acres). Take refuge from its Grade II listed Brutalist architecture within its 2,000-seat concert hall, two theatres, two art galleries and three cinemas for some of London's most progressive arts programming.

## THEATRES

London's Broadway lives in the West End, and is where all the big-budget productions, long-running musicals and cheesy pantos sell out by the coachload (check *Time Out*, London's listings magazine, for what's on; for tickets, www.ticketmaster.co.uk; tel: 0870 534 4444). But honouring its rich heritage of playwrights – including Shakespeare (see The Globe), Alan Bennett, David Hare, David Mamet and Nobel Prize-winner Harold Pinter – are plenty more challenging theatres, as follows. Widely regarded as London's leading theatre, the **Royal National Theatre** (South Bank, SE1; 020 7452 3000, www.nationaltheatre.org.uk), or the National as it is known, is also considered its ugliest – built in 1976, Prince Charles once described it as 'a clever way of building a nuclear power station in the middle of London without anyone objecting'. Still, the show must go on, and a diverse programme of new and classical plays is overseen by artistic director Nicholas Hytner over three auditoriums. Slightly lower key is **The Almeida** (Almeida Street, Islington, N1; 020 7359 4404; www.almeida.co.uk) under the artistic directorship of Michael Attenborough – son of veteran actor Lord Richard Attenborough – which fills its 321 rather fashionable seats with creatively produced classical and contemporary plays. Then there's the **Donmar Warehouse** (41 Earlham St, Covent Garden, WC2; 0870 060

6624, www.donmarwarehouse.com). Named after theatre impresario Donald Albery and his friend, the ballerina Margot Fonteyn (Don and Mar, see?), who in 1961 together set up this space in an old warehouse, the Donmar is an internationally acclaimed yet intimate studio theatre with just 250 seats, renowned for its edgy, new productions. With Kevin Spacey as artistic director, the historic **Old Vic** (The Cut, Waterloo, SE1; 0870 060 6628, www.oldvictheatre.com) first opened in 1818 and later renamed after Queen Victoria, has seen its fair share of drama – and Spacey – on its stage. The programme is an eclectic mix of old classics and brave new theatre. For some, **Battersea Arts Centre** (Lavender Hill, SW11; 020 7223 2223, www.bac.org.uk) is the only reason to go to Battersea, or even South London for that matter: always a lovely line-up of alternative theatre, cabaret and comedy in this Grade II listed ex-town hall. The world's longest running play – Agatha Christie's *The Mousetrap* – has been shown at **St Martin's Theatre** (West Street, Covent Garden, WC2; 020 7836 1443, www.stmartinstheatre.co.uk) for over 50 years (more than 23,000 times). It's become a national treasure from one of Britain's greatest crime writers, and most Londoners know whodunit. If you're after something that's much more than just a theatre, the **Soho Theatre** (1 Dean Street, W1; 0870 429 6883 www.sohotheatre.com) hosts plays, comedy, writers' workshops and talks on current events. And even if you abhor all of that nonsense, its late-licence bar is an excellent undiscovered refuge in amongst the chaos of Soho. And for those at one with nature, the **Open Air Theatre** (The Ironworks, Inner Circle, Regent's Park, NW1; 08700 601811, www.ope-nairtheatre.org) offers theatre in the fresh air, a magical (if risky) combination in the inner circle of Regent's Park, weather permitting – sensibly, it's only open during summer months. Genres range from Shakespeare to family plays.

## CINEMAS

Leicester Square is Cinema Central, showing the latest popcorn movies at the highest prices. **Odeon** (www.odeon.co.uk; 0871 224 4007) and **Vue** (www.myvue.com; 0871 224 0240) cover most releases. London has plenty of independent cinemas and lovingly restored picture palaces that show art house and world films (see also the ICA and the Barbican). For the ultimate big screen experience, try the **BFI London IMAX Cinema** (1 Charlie Chaplin Walk, Waterloo, SE1; 0870 787 2525, www.bfi.org.uk). Inside a dramatic cylindrical glass building situated on a busy roundabout is the UK's largest cinema screen. The BFI's IMAX typically screens films set in extraordinary landscapes – such as the North Pole, the moon, the summit of Everest – in 2- or 3-D, and with such steeply raked rows, even getting to your seat is a thrill. Also under the administration of the British Film Institute and as part of the South Bank Centre is the **National Film Theatre** (Belvedere Road, South Bank, SE1; 020 7928 3232 www.bfi.org.uk/nft), London's leading art house cinema with three screens, directors' talks, the London Film Festival in November and an awful lot of film buffs cerebrating in its quite lovely riverside bar. The family-run Curzon cinema chain specializes in European and art house films. Curzon Soho, built in the 1950s, has three screens, while Curzon Mayfair, built in 1934, is a Grade II listed building with two screens. It has recently acquired the Chelsea and Renoir cinemas – a sign of the times for independent picture houses **Curzon Cinemas** (www.curzoncinemas.com) **Chelsea Cinema** (206 Kings Rd, SW3; 0871 7033 990); **Curzon Mayfair** (38 Curzon St, W1; 0871 7033 989) **Curzon Soho** (99 Shaftesbury Ave, W1; 0871 7033 988) **Renoir Cinema** (The Brunswick, WC1; 0871 7033 991). **The Picturehouses** (www.picturehouses.co.uk) chain is slowly gobbling up independent cinemas, which might sound like the plot of, say, Nightmare at the Cinema but this group has trodden carefully. Expect a programme of cult, foreign language and independent films, a select few commercial films that 'they like' and themed festivals: **Clapham Picturehouse** (76 Venn St, SW4; 0871 704 2055); **The Gate** (87 Notting Hill Gate, W11; 0871 704 2058); **The Ritzy** (Brixton Oval, Coldharbour Lane, SW2; 0871 704 2065). For a more chi-chi experience, the see-and-be-seen screen **The Electric** (191 Portobello Road, Notting Hill, W11; 020 7908 9696, www.electriccinema.co.uk) is decked out like a modern gentleman's club with the baroque backdrop of one of London's oldest cinemas (built 1905) – all chunky leather armchairs, foot stools and kissing couches. The bar serves cocktails, champagne and swanky snacks; the programme leans towards the critically acclaimed mainstream. Finally, for something a little bit hipper, try **Rich Mix** (35-47 Bethnal Green Road, E1; 020 7613 7490 www.richmix.org.uk). It's the epitome of East End gentrification: a six-storey cultural centre moves into an ex-garment factory. Three cinema screens (showing documentaries and respected Hollywood films), an exhibition space and a 200-seat auditorium comprise a 'cross-cultural arts and media centre'.

# shop...

'I shop therefore I am' is the mantra of London's majority tribe of capitalists (read: compulsive materialists). 'Buy, buy, buy!' hums the ambient noise on the frenzied drags of Oxford Street, Regent Street and Knightsbridge. 'I predict a riot!' is the spiritual soundtrack at the latest over-hyped launch of a designer diffusion range on the high street. Fact: police marshalling smash-and-grab fashion victims at such launches frequently makes the evening news.

Recession? What recession? London is a veritable circus of consumerism and its attractions range from superluxe designer flagships and dazzling department stores to offbeat independent boutiques and scruffy street markets. London is one of the four fashion capitals, and where New York fashion is commercial, Milan's is high-glamour and Paris's sophisticated, London is considered the experimenter. Fuelled by the capital's renowned design schools and a much-vaunted stable of agents provocateurs (Vivienne Westwood, Alexander McQueen, John Galliano), London is a hothouse of young, out-there designers (flavours of the month are Gareth Pugh and House of Holland). Supply and demand for such creativity is amply catered for by the capital's avant-garde boutiques such as Dover Street Market, Pineal Eye and b Store.

All this experimentation is a symptom of something much more core to Britishness: eccentricity, and it's for this reason that London's vintage scene is so well established. John Galliano pops back from Paris to draw inspiration from Virginia in Notting Hill, and Paul Smith from Portobello Market; but it's the East End, with its glut of empty warehouses and (relatively) cheap rents, that has become the main destination for vintage vultures.

Meanwhile, Bond Street and Sloane Street offer everything any label slave could ask for, while the fiercely competitive British high street – Top Shop, Warehouse, Oasis and Primark (which, in irony, we call Primarché because it is so low-grade) – is known and loved for replicating the catwalks in a matter of weeks, plus there are all the key high street imports including H&M, Mango,

Uniqlo and Zara. For fast, affordable fashion, sharpen your elbows, pack your patience and head for Oxford Street, Regent Street, Kensington High Street and the King's Road; for a high concentration of edgy and urban boutiques and the media darlings who depend on them, beat a path to Soho and Covent Garden. But for calmer consumption, there are numerous lovely villagey streets (Marylebone High Street, Walton Street, Chelsea Green, Exmouth Market, Broadway Market), where you'll find one-off boutiques, bijou jewellers and local delis and cafés that, with admittedly some knowingness, hark back to a more

old-fashioned era of shopping: a world apart from the mayhem and mass production of the homogenous high street.

Then there are London's specialist streets – rummage for literature in Charing Cross Road, guitars and rock music in Denmark Street, diamonds in Hatton Garden, and antiques in Pimlico Road and Portobello Road. There are also the fabulously elegant Victorian and Edwardian arcades of Piccadilly and Mayfair (The Royal Arcade, Princes Arcade, Royal Opera Arcade, Burlington Arcade) where dainty shops sell fine jewellery, art and suchlike.

The best example of anachronism (and, sadly, fighting the biggest battle against the developers) is London's hallowed heritage of classic craftsmanship and fine tailoring, located in the bespoke shops of Savile Row and Jermyn Street (even the very word bespoke originated in Savile Row, meaning that a suit is spoken for). Many of these historic stores have been trading for generations and offer a wonderfully personalized and genteel service – now you don't get that in Primarché.

## COVENT GARDEN

The enormous flower, fruit and vegetable market of *My Fair Lady* days is long gone but Covent Garden still has a quirky character and buzzing atmosphere. Serious shoppers ignore the rejuvenated picturesque piazza, a tourist magnet, and head to the area's more subdued cobblestone pedestrian side streets where fashion boutiques are interspersed with vintage shops and London's best streetwear and surf shops.

### EARLHAM STREET

**Carhartt** American streetwear shop selling sweatshirts, jackets, jeans and their trademark carpenter jeans
**Fopp** Records (both rock and mainstream), CDs, and art house films
**Magma** Specialist store selling deeply cool arty mags and design books
**Urban Outfitters** Industrial-style emporium for retro/modern culture, music, clothing and homeware

### FLORAL STREET

**Betsey Johnson** Loud pinks, flirty dresses and playful jewels for coquettes
**Paul Smith** The historic first shop from Britain's reigning knight of fashion Sir Paul Smith, who lends a quirky spin and lots of colour to classic English tailoring

### MONMOUTH STREET

**Coco de Mer** Classy yet kinky lingerie and erotica from Sam Roddick, daughter of Body Shop founder Anita Roddick
**Kiehl's** Flagship store for slick American cosmetics line
**Koh Samui** The hottest, high-end womenswear and vintage collectibles
**Pop** Retro relics (clothes and kitsch curios) from the disco era, beloved by scores of stars whose photos pepper the walls
**Poste Mistress** Eccentric designer shoes in a kitsch 1950s boudoir

### SHORTS GARDENS

**Boxfresh** Young, hip and affordable streetwear
**Duffer of St George** Cult menswear line plus more obscure labels
**Fred Perry** Classic British sportswear brand with of-the-moment guest

designers
**G-Star Raw**  Blokey streetwear and trainers for boys and tomboys
**Jelly Pong Pong**  Quirky, playful cosmetics for grown-up girls

## EAST END

Despite a steady corporate invasion and now even a shiny new mall at Spitalfields, the East End is less commercially adulterated than most of London. Still thankfully outnumbering the multinationals are thrift and vintage shops, kooky independent boutiques and street markets where enterprising young designers sell their kitchen-table-produced wares. For that, its treasures are not neatly town-planned along one convenient street, but scattered around in among the knock-off designer shops of the old East End. On your wander, keep your radar tuned for the many sample sale outlets in the area.

**Blondie**  (114 Commercial St) Absolute Vintage's older sister where quality trumps quality. Head to AV on Hanbury St for the reverse
**Bordello**  (55 Great Eastern St) Boudoir boutique stocking Myla, Damaris and Pistol Panties
**CA4LA**  (23 Pitfield St) Japanese-run hip hat boutique (pronounced kashira)
**Columbia Road**  A dear old East End street lined with tiny cafés and cottage-industry shops variously selling ceramics, cupcakes and jewellery, with a long-running Sunday flower market
**Hoxton Boutique**  (2 Hoxton St) Current and vintage wardrobe staples for any self-respecting Hoxtonite
**No-One**  (1 Kingsland Rd) Mens- and womenswear with Shoreditch sensibility
**Relax Garden**  (4 Kingsland Rd) Shoebox fashion store full of choice and charm
**SCP**  (135 Curtain Rd) Modern, upscale interiors emporium
**Sh!**  (57 Hoxton Sq) Pink and perky erotica for women; an East End institution
**Start**  (42 Rivington St) Probably Hoxton's glossiest boutique – key men's and women's fashion, plus jeans solutions for all
**The Three Threads**  (47 Charlotte Rd) Under-hyped and rare streetwear brands for boys and girls

## BRICK LANE

**Bernstock Speirs**  Modern millinery for sharp boys and girls
**Rokit**  A well-edited selection of vintage, all according to the trends of the season
**Tatty Devine**  Playful plastic accessories, plus art, fashion and zines from all their clever and creative friends
**The Laden Showroom**  A platform for young designers who have outgrown their market stalls, plus vintage treats

## CHESHIRE STREET (off Brick Lane)

**Beyond Retro**  Over 10,000 pieces of second-hand American clothes and accessories in a good old East End warehouse
**Labour & Wait**  Resembling an old-fashioned general store, L&W sells wondrously traditional things for the home and garden
**Mar Mar Co**  Scandinavian design: lamps, ceramics, prints and stationery
**Shelf**  Charming and quirky shopette selling English retrorama – wooden, tin, ceramic and paper knick-knacks

## DRAY WALK (off Brick Lane)

**A Butcher of Distinction**  Boys' boutique selling cool, casual menswear from underground, overground and traditional labels
**Gloria's**  A sneaker freak's fantasy – all sorts of rare, collectible trainers
**Rough Trade East**  Indie heaven: records, live stage, coffee

## KNIGHTSBRIDGE AND CHELSEA

These pretty, posh neighbours are where many well-heeled shoppers start, where reassuringly large price tags hang from comfortingly conservative objects of desire. Ladies who lunch worship in the holy houses of Harrods and Harvey Nichols, and the numerous other shrines to designer fashion on Sloane Street (a less busy – more staid – version of Bond Street), and take their communion in San Lorenzo on Beauchamp Place; if they're feeling crazy, they explore around Brompton Cross and Chelsea Green. The King's Road has lost its mojo of the Swinging Sixties, but the further west you walk the more originality you'll find.

## BROMPTON CROSS

**Joseph** Stylish womens- and menswear designer and own-brand clothes spread over three boutiques

**The Conran Shop** British designer Sir Terence Conran's flagship store, selling furniture, kitchenware, books and gadgets, all housed within the magnificent Art Deco Michelin Building

**The Library** Menswear boutique selling cool, casual labels including Dries Van Noten, Alexander McQueen and Martin Margiela

## KING'S ROAD

**Antiquarius** Antiques arcade full of stalls offering everything from Georgian glasses to vintage Louis Vuitton luggage

**Austique** Girly heaven selling fashion by Karen Walker, Olivia Morris and Alice McCall

**Bamford & Sons** Lifestyle solutions – cashmere, casuals, gadgetry and an organic café – for the cash-rich, time-poor modern gentleman

**Daisy & Tom** Fantasy toyshop complete with merry-go-round, children's hair salon and a huge array of children's games, books and clothing

**Ekyog** Chic French organic cottons for women and kids

**R. Soles** Cowboy boots in every conceivable style (note the naughty pun)

**Rococo** Chocolate heaven, from traditional violet creams to vegetable-shaped pralines, all beautifully packaged

**The Shop at Bluebird** Inside the original 1920s Bluebird garage is impeccably edited fashion from the fashion capitals, Antwerp, LA and well-preserved attics; next door in the Bluebird Epicerie is impeccably made food

**Vivienne Westwood** The queen of punk's original store with its anti-clockwise clock

## SLOANE STREET

**Chloé** Glamorous French fashion: wishlist frocks and trophy handbags

**Gina** Hazardously high shoes coveted by London's moneyed party girls

**Jo Malone** Beautifully packaged and deliciously scented bathroom goodies

**Paule Ka** Stylish fashion from a French designer with an aunt named Paule

**Pickett** Eclectic treasure trove of gloves, jewellery and handmade leather luggage

**Shanghai Tang** Elegant Chinese-inspired clothing, from silk pyjamas to velvet Mao jackets

221

## WALTON STREET

**Bentleys** Antique gallery/shop selling vintage luggage, bowler hats and 1920s aeroplane propellers

**Blossom** Gorgeous maternity shop, with exclusive pieces by top designers. Surplus to requirements? Get a head start next door in the luxury lingerie store Myla

**Catherine Prevost** Beautiful and original jewellery – many four-figure modern classics

**Louise Bradley** London-based interior designer showcases her favourite stylish furniture and knick-knacks for the home

**Monogrammed Linen Shop** Lovely sheet sets, table linen and nightwear

## DEPARTMENT STORES

### Harrods, 87 Brompton Road, SW1

The grande dame of London's department stores comes with a caveat – as the UK's biggest shop (at 1 million sq ft), it's one massive maze crawling with tourists and arrivistes. There are 23 restaurants and countless (OK, 330 to be precise) different departments including fashion, furniture, food, sports, antiques and toys, not to mention two Dodi and Diana memorials. Just opposite is the new Harrods 102, selling 'gourmet food on the go'. Undoubtedly, Harrods' best (and cheapest) angle is from the outside after dark, when its splendid terracotta façade sparkles with 11,500 light bulbs.

### Harvey Nichols, 109–125 Knightsbridge, SW1

With a champagne nail bar, botox, fake tanning and blow drying, Harvey Nicks has become something of an Ab Fab parody: a one-stop shop to satisfy all of a narcissist's needs. Of course the daily trawl around the shop floor really is awfully hard work, what with four floors of all the best names in women's fashion, plus an accessories and beauty hall, interiors floor and two men's floors, so thankfully there are outposts from Daylesford Organic, Yo! Sushi, Wagamama and Fushi organic juice bar.

## THE WEST END

The West End is scored with exclusive shopping streets – none more so than New and Old Bond Street, which are lined with designer boutiques (and big spenders' attendant limos), and is said to have more royal 'By Appointment' warrants than any other thoroughfare. Savile Row is the golden mile of tailoring, while Jermyn Street is for shirts what Savile Row is for suits. Bruton Street and Conduit Street add a younger, more hip edge, while Brewer Street and Broadwick Street take shoppers into the seedier realms of Soho. Meanwhile, South Molton Street and Marylebone High Street provide a low-key antidote, with charming independent stores and eateries.

## Marylebone

### MARYLEBONE HIGH STREET

**Brora**  Gorgeous cosy cashmere, in a range of mouth-watering colours

**Calmia**  All you need for a holistic lifestyle: chic yoga clothing, aromatherapy products, an Eastern tea bar and a day spa

**Cath Kidston**  All you need for a chintzy retro existence: from petal-patterned tea towels to vintage china tea sets

**Daunt Books**  Everything you ever wanted to know about travel and more

**Divertimenti**  Luxury kitchen emporium selling the domestic goddess lifestyle

**Kabiri**  Jewellery 'gallery' selling Me&Ro, Alexis Bittar, Scott Wilson et al

**KJ's Laundry**  Unusual international fashion including Mike&Chris

**Sixty 6**  Tiny boutique with a variety of fashion-forward labels for women

**Space NK**  Cult beauty shop selling the coolest names in cosmetics

## Mayfair

### BOND STREET

**Alexander McQueen**  Sharp, dramatic tailoring from British fashion's reigning bad boy

**Jimmy Choo**  Exquisitely jewelled strappy sandals, foxy boots and chic bags

**Mulberry**  British bastion whose trad-with-a-twist fashion ranges from interesting tweeds to the latest It-bag

**Pringle**  Scottish sweater brand long associated with golfers but now competing on the catwalks with archive-inspired designs

**Smythson**  The Queen's favourite purveyor of luxury leather stationery

## BRUTON STREET

**Holland & Holland** Historic gun company established 1835, with chic outerwear for yomping in the country (or parading in the city)
**Matthew Williamson** Whimsical, colourful clothing – sexy, flowing frocks a speciality
**Stella McCartney** Delicious daywear, understated eveningwear and vegetarian shoes from the daughter of a Beatle

## CONDUIT STREET

**Connolly** Luxurious leather accessories from shoes to cigar boxes, from the brand responsible for Aston Martin's leather interiors
**Rigby & Peller** Made-to-measure lingerie with a royal warrant to the Queen. Guaranteed to find your perfect fit
**Vivienne Westwood** High drama meets outrageous tailoring from the punk queen

## DOVER STREET MARKET, 17–18 Dover Street, W1

When the highbrow Japanese label Comme des Garçons decided to open a London store, it shunned the obvious (ie ego and logo), instead opting for 'concept' and collaboration. On six floors of stark, spiky architecture (with sheds for cash desks and birdcages and Portaloos for changing rooms), DSM is the exemplar of curated consumption, with a thoughtful (if at times boggling) selection of fashion's darkest, edgiest offerings from Alaïa, Lanvin, Boudicca and of course Comme des Garcons and its protégé, Junya Watanabe. Sufferers of fashion fatigue may reward themselves at the instore Rose Bakery café.

## JERMYN STREET

**Dunhill** British stalwart selling made-to-measure shirts and suits, iconic lighters and all sorts of other accoutrements to make ladies swoon
**Emma Willis** One of the few female shirt-makers, renowned for her craftsmanship and fabrics
**Turnbull & Asser** Sharp shirts cut from a choice of 400 fabrics apparently good enough for Prince Charles, Al Pacino and James Bond

## SAVILE ROW

**b Store**  Shock news! Leftfield fashion on Savile Row. Stocks young, cutting-edge designers such as Peter Jensen, Bless and Bernhard Willhelm

**Gieves & Hawkes**  Has occupied the prized No.1 Savile Row address for over 90 years. Exemplary bespoke tailoring with design-led collections

**Kilgour**  (pronounced 'Kilgar') Cary Grant's erstwhile tailor, straddling tradition and modernity

**Huntsman**  One of the most expensive, famous for its tweeds

**Richard James**  An elegant, modern take on classic designs

## SOUTH MOLTON STREET

**Browns**  Cult emporium of men's and women's fashion. Browns Focus, opposite, is younger and yet more fashionable, while Labels For Less is just that

**Butler & Wilson**  A twinkling treasure box of vintage and new costume jewellery plus unusual, amusing fashion and frills

**Poste**  Eccentric designer shoe shop for men, styled like a gentlemen's club

**Tartine et Chocolate**  Luxurious French baby clothing

## Soho

## BREWER STREET

**Souvenir**  High fashion from dramatic labels like Hussein Chalayan, Westwood and Viktor & Rolf

**The World According To**  Basement boutique full of fashion's more affordable lines: Westwood's Red Label, Margiela's MM6 and Sonia Rykiel's Sonia

**Vintage Magazine Shop**  A unique source of entertainment memorabilia

## BROADWICK STREET

**Agent Provocateur**  Classy crotchless panties? Only at AP: lingerie from Vivienne Westwood's son, sold by staff wearing saucy nurses' outfits

**Pineal Eye**  Bleeding-edge fashion meets outré art at this ouch-cool Japanese-run boutique, with its beady eye closely trained on new talent

225

## TOPSHOP, Oxford Circus, W1

For virtually all female Londoners (and visitors), Top Shop's flagship is the ultimate fashion honey pot – there are 1,000 staff working at any one time, 200 changing rooms and around 200,000 visitors a week. With 90,000 sq ft of cheap (yeah, best not to ask why), fast fashion, 'ToSho' is always ahead of the game with more, bigger, better concessions, vintage collections and designer ranges by fashion's most current names. Resistance is futile.

## DEPARTMENT STORES

### Fortnum & Mason, 181 Piccadilly, W1

Established in 1707, Fortnum's is the grandmama of London's department stores. Beyond its *eau-de-nil* frontage is a taste of genteel, olde worlde England (and now with a sympathetic David Collins facelift). With a clutch of royal warrants, the Queen's grocer sells tasty comestibles – handmade chocolates, British cheeses and fine teas and coffees – at royalty prices. Escape the tourist stampede by buying a speciality hamper or by retreating to the sleepy upper floors selling women's accessories, lingerie, perfume and homeware: your gran would approve.

### Hamleys, 188–196 Regent Street, London W1

London's gigantic, seven-storey toy store is loud and frantic, with swarms of over-excited kids and model planes circling about your head. The enormous selection ranges from tin soldiers and a sweet factory to the latest in Jedi fighting equipment and remote-control choppers. There are dressing-up departments, a Lego World, and a café for birthday parties. Everything, in fact, except peace.

### Liberty, 214–220 Regent Street, W1

This iconic Tudor revival store started life in 1875 as a repository for Arthur Liberty's goods shipped in from the Orient. It still exudes an off-the-beaten-track charm with its gorgeous panelled interior and eclectic and original buying throughout. Fashion labels span the Brits, Belgians, French and Japanese, plus there are Arts and Crafts antiques, linen and homeware, and the store's famous Art Nouveau prints on any textile that will take it. Tea and scones and oysters and champagne await the weary.

## Selfridges, 400 Oxford Street, W1

With its grand neoclassical façade, Selfridges is something of a temple to consumerism. Many place their faith in its problem-solving powers: 'Argh: want cool outfit, need clever present, run out of aftershave and I'm starving… Selfridges!' As Britain's second biggest shop (after Harrods), there's room to please everyone: fashion from McTopshop to McQueen, books, toys, electrics, homeware, and food to satifsy the pickiest of eaters. It's arguably the most progressive department store, and hosts in-store festivals, previously themed on Bollywood, Vegas and Surrealism. If that requires a human window display, so be it.

## NOTTING HILL

For a more bohemian vibe head to Notting Hill, an area which exudes a laidback village atmosphere and offers a mix of vintage, urban and high-end shops. It is also home to Portobello Market, one of London's most famous street markets, which stretches down the area's geographic backbone, Portobello Road – a cute, colourful road beloved for its rugged character, and dotted with charming antiques shops, pubs, and fruit and veg stalls.

## LEDBURY ROAD

**Aimé**  Young boutique showcasing the brightest French labels
**Anne Fontaine**  Crisp white shirts in every conceivable style
**JW Beeton**  Less obvious, more original European womenswear labels
**Matches**  A perennial favourite selling key pieces from Chloé to Marni
**Melissa Odabash**  Glamorous swimwear for yummy mummies
**Paul & Joe**  Romantic, feminine fashion from French designer Sophie Albou

## PORTLAND ROAD

**Summerill & Bishop**  Stylish, unusual kitchen shop with a vintage French look
**The Cross**  Bohemian fashion boutique loved for its girly atmosphere and unusual trinkets
**Virginia**  Veteran vintage boutique specializing in antique lace in an outrageous pink boudoir setting

## PORTOBELLO ROAD

**Honeyjam**  Retro/eco toyshop co-owned by model Jasmine Guinness
**Hummingbird Bakery**  Cutesy cupcake cottage industry: so Notting Hill
**Olivia Morris**  Rising star's ladylike heels with quirky detailing
**One of a Kind**  Cult vintage store that sells rare designer treasures
**Portobello Green**  Arcade for 20-odd up-and-coming designers: womenswear, menswear and kidswear, including Preen's darkly romantic British fashion

## WESTBOURNE GROVE

**Bill Amberg**  Gorgeous leather accessories, luggage and those famous sheepskin papooses
**Feathers**  Womenswear boutique bursting with a global selection of labels
**Heidi Klein**  A one-stop holiday shop, with flattering bikinis, cool kaftans and wafty resort-chic clothing
**Nicole Farhi**  Interiors, menswear, womenswear and a great café (called 202) from which to watch Notting Hill's socialites waft by
**Question Air**  The answer to your denim dilemmas: whichever jeans brand people want this week, they have it
**Solange Azagury-Partridge**  Precious jewels in modern designs from one of Britain's boldest jewellery designers
**Twenty8Twelve**  Admittedly likeable fashion from Sienna and Savannah Miller

## SOUTH

## THE OXO Tower, Barge House Street, South Bank, SE1

One of the South Bank's most famous landmarks, the Oxo Tower (an ex-power station and later the HQ of Oxo beef stock cubes) is an essential address for fans of original works from little known design labels – and crowd-phobes. Many designers work on-site, making and selling fashion, jewellery, ceramics, art and photography. On the eighth floor is the Oxo Tower Restaurant and on the second, Bincho Yakitori (see SNACK), both with panoramic river views, while the (original) redbrick barge house opposite hosts interesting exhibitions. If you like this, you'll also like Gabriel's Wharf, nearby (Upper Ground, SE1).

## MARKETS

### Borough Market, Southwark Street, SE1

Endorsed by many celebrity chefs, a gigantic and excellent covered food market (known as the 'Larder of London') is held noon–6pm on Fridays, and 9am–4pm on Saturdays

### Brick Lane Market, E1

What was once just a flea market now also encompasses fashion, art, homeware and vintage (8am–3pm on Sundays). When hunger strikes, head for a curry house. Don't miss Sunday (Up) Market at the Old Truman Brewery

### Camden Market, NW1

Anthropologically historic market that spans various subcultures (Goth, punk, hippy, biker), selling fashion, music and tat (open daily, 10am–6pm)

### Gray's Antique Market, Davies Street, W1

Over 150 dealers selling antique textiles, sporting memorabilia and jewellery (open 10am–6pm Monday–Friday)

### Old Spitalfields Market, Commercial Street, E1

A hip, buzzy market all under an original Victorian structure selling everything from crafts and flowers to quirky creations by budding designers (open daily, 9.30am–4.30pm; records on Wednesdays and a fashion focus on Fridays)

### Portobello Road Market, W11

Pick your way through all the tourists and hundreds of antique dealers for clothes, collectibles and curios (Friday/Saturday 5.30am–4.30pm). Monday to Thursday sees the street lined with fruit and veg stalls

# play...

'When a man is tired of London, he is tired of life' – so goes the now clichéd quote of 18th-century writer Samuel Johnson. And of course, the cliché is entirely true – unless you've lost the will to live it's impossible to be bored in the capital. Distractions range from the conventional to the quirky to the extreme – from soporific spas to a swim in frozen waters, from a pedestrian walking tour to a chopper ride a thousand feet up, from circus training to 'Meet the Monkeys' at London Zoo.

Nature still holds ground in the metropolis, which has over 5,000 acres of royal parks. Hyde Park is London's answer to New York's Central Park and caters for the hyperactive (with 'black run' roller-blading, horse-riding, swimming and space to run and run) and the heavy-footed alike (also open-air concerts, picnics and a spot of boating on the lake). Further afield at Hampstead Heath, Kew Gardens and Richmond Park are the rewards of larger horizons and fewer people.

While the Thames struggles to support aquatic life, it remains the city's backbone – rushing with energy and studded with landmarks. Take a river cruise, a stroll down the Thames Path, or a flight on the London Eye, or be the sight itself by rowing the course of the Oxford and Cambridge Boat Race. This boat race, held in late March, essentially starts London's social calendar. Follow the aristocrats and *arrivistes* through this social whirl – the Grand National in April, Royal Ascot and Wimbledon in June, July's Henley Royal Regatta, polo at Windsor and Glorious Goodwood, and sailing at Cowes Week in August – and not only will you catch the season's main sporting events but also an insight into this top-hatted and tailed breed that travels the land to quaff champers from the back of their Range Rovers.

For inverse snobs, there is greyhound racing at E17's Walthamstow Dog Track – a much more proletarian pastime fuelled by lager, chicken-in-a-basket and a cheeky flutter. At Wimbledon Stadium, there's all this, plus stockcar racing, ie dodgems with clapped-out cars ready for the scrapheap. Of course, any good boozer (pub) will offer a game of arras (arrows – darts) and a few Britneys (Britney Spears – beers).

Rugby, cricket, tennis and football all have their origins in England, with London serving as the spiritual home to rugby at Twickenham, to cricket at Lord's and tennis at Wimbledon. Most (male) Londoners support a local football team, though few are truly local, for example, Chelsea and Arsenal, with players of every nationality attracting five-figure weekly wage packets, trophy girlfriends and international fame. And beyond the most common sports, there are more peculiar pursuits such as crown green bowling, croquet and fencing.

For those with a pathological aversion to sports, there are festivals throughout the year – Chinese New Year in January, the Great Spitalfields Pancake Race on Shrove Tuesday, St Patrick's Day on 17 March, Gay Pride in July, the Notting Hill Carnival over August's bank holiday, the Brick Lane Festival in September, the Pearly Kings & Queens Harvest Festival in October, and Bonfire Night on 5 November – the day, if any, for a London Eye night flight. Check out *Time Out*, London's fortnightly listings magazine, for current highlights – but if all that fails to leave you smiling, check out London's comedy scene for a 'giraffe' (laugh).

## BIKE HIRE

Plenty to choose from; see www.lcc.org.uk for cycle route maps. As with many other cities, London's cycling enthusiasts take to the streets on the last Friday of every month (starting at the National Film Theatre, South Bank) to form Critical Mass – 'we aren't blocking traffic; we are traffic', so goes the motto, and can be something of a traffic stopper with numbers in the thousands. There's a lively carnival spirit with fancy dress and noisy sound systems strapped onto bikes. It can get political and the police are threatening a crackdown – all the more motivation to attend (www.critical-masslondon.org.uk).

### The London Bicycle Tour Company
Tel: 020 7928 6838   www.londonbicycle.com

Claims to have the largest fleet in London with 150 bikes, and a good mix of mountain bikes, hybrids, tandems and kids' bikes.

### OYBike
Tel: 0845 226 5751   www.oybike.com

This ever-expanding initiative (standing for 'on yer bike') is an automated system activated by mobile phone – you'll be texted a map and combination code for one of OYBike's 130 distinctive yellow, chainless bikes (wonders for white-jean wearers) available at numerous collection points around London. It's a one-way system so no need to return to the start, and it claims to be the best value in town for 24-hour rental with the first half-hour free.

### Velorution
Tel: 020 7637 4004   www.velorution.biz

Has 16 Brompton folding bikes (excellent for train tours) and will deliver within central London for a charge.

## CANALS

Still waters run deep – alongside over 100 miles of canals is a London that most Londoners don't even know. The waterways are a vestige of the Industrial Revolution – shire horses have not trotted the towpaths since

1956 — but they now provide a behind-the-scenes window on the gracious Regency architecture around Regent's Park, Hackney's forgotten industrial landscapes and the enviable backyards of Primrose Hill. It's a tranquil hiding-place for anglers, 'yuvs', and houseboat-dwelling bohemia, with floating restaurants and canalside pubs aplenty, most scenically between Camden and Little Venice. The London Waterbus Company (020 7482 2550, www.londonwaterbus.com) offers trips on traditional narrow boats (week-ends Oct–Mar, daily April–Sept) — pack a picnic and Pimms.

## CIRCUS TRAINING

### Circus Space, Coronet Street, Hoxton, N1
Tel: 020 7613 4141   www.thecircusspace.co.uk

In an old Hoxton power station (so plenty of room to swing a cat), the Circus Space runs courses and evening classes in trapeze, juggling, tightrope walking, stilt walking, acrobatics and general clowning around. For those ready to remove the safety net, there's even a degree in circus arts on offer.

## COMEDY

London is the Hollywood of comedy (without the looks), and jokesmiths from around the world gravitate towards this rare platform for political incorrectness where heckling is actively encouraged. Apart from during August (when all migrate to Edinburgh's Fringe festival), comedians little and large can be seen rattling off their routines, from pub backrooms to pur-pose-built comedy club chains.

### Comedy Café, 66 Rivington Street, Hoxton, EC2
Tel: 020 7739 5706   www.comedycafe.co.uk
Open: 6pm–midnight Tues–Thurs; 6pm–1am Fri–Sat

A relative newcomer, the popular Comedy Café has followed the failsafe template — stand-up comedy served to seated punters plied with table serv-ice and snackage, followed by floor-filling disco music on the weekend.

**Comedy Store, Haymarket House, 1a Oxendon St, SW1**
Tel: 020 7930 2949   www.thecomedystore.co.uk
Open: daily, 6.30pm–3am; shows 8pm (midnight Fri/Sat)
Tickets from www.ticketmaster.co.uk,  0870 060 2340

This is London's premier comedy venue and arguably the most sanitized,
usually with a famous line-up (Mike Myers, Ruby Wax, Paul Merton and
Graham Norton have all trodden its boards) performing stand-up, improv
and topical satire; it has a capacity of 400 and a diner and bar.

**Jongleurs**
Tel: 08707 870707   www.jongleurs.com
Bow: Bow Wharf, 221 Grove Road, E3. Open: 7pm–2am Fri–Sat
Battersea: 49 Lavender Gardens, SW11. Open: 7pm–2am Thurs–Sat
Camden: Middle Yard, Camden Lock, Chalk Farm Road, NW1. Open:
7pm–2am Fri–Sat

Now with three venues in London and 16 nationwide, Jongleurs is the UK's
biggest comedy chain, playing host to both the emerging and the established.
Pitching itself as a party venue, its disco (from 11pm) is often swarming with
hen and stag partygoers.

## COOKERY

**Books for Cooks, 4 Blenheim Crescent, W11**
Tel: 020 7221 1992   www.booksforcooks.com
Closed: Sun/Mon, last three weeks in August, Christmas week

What started out as a bookshop now has two purpose-built kitchens for its
workshops taught by French, Italian, Japanese, British and vegetarian chefs
(often featuring names such as Mark Hix, Skye Gyngell and Sam and Sam
Clark). Most courses are demonstration only, plus a few hands-on classes.
For instant gratification, its café serves fresh international meals, and for
swots, books galore.

**Leith's School of Food and Wine, 16–20 Wendell Road, W12**
Tel: 020 8749 6400   www.leiths.com
Closed 2nd and 3rd weeks of August

Leith's is London's best-known cookery school so waiting lists are often on the menu. It's right up to date with its demonstration theatre and teaching kitchens, but still retains a rather charming school-ma'amish manner. Cuisine is contemporary and international, but there's a British focus with workshops in marmalade and curd-making, fish and game. There are also wine and champagne appreciation courses, and for those wanting to go the whole hog, professional courses.

## CRICKET

---

### The Brit Oval, Harleyford Road, Kennington, SE11
Tel: 020 7582 6660  www.surreycricket.com

---

The Oval is home to Surrey Cricket Club – Middlesex's biggest rival and the venue and birthplace of the Ashes (although they are always kept at Lords). As the story goes, England lost the Test Match to Australia on native soil in 1882, and *The Sporting Times* published a mock obituary to English cricket. When England won the Test in Australia, the English captain was presented with an urn of ashes. The ground is called The Oval after an oval road was laid round a cabbage patch in the 1790s, which was re-turfed as a cricket ground in 1845. Tours are available by arrangement, but if you fancy a go yourself book one of the bowling machines to see what it's really like facing the likes of Harmison, Warne or McGrath.

---

### Lord's Cricket Ground, St John's Wood, NW8
Tel: 020 7616 8500  www.lords.org
Open: tours at 10am, noon and 2pm daily except match and preparation days April–Sept; noon and 2pm Oct–Mar

---

The English cricket scene has recently found its mojo again thanks to its tabloid-friendly national team (and their WAGs), frequent streaking, and the new, more entertaining one-day Twenty20 games (essentially speed cricket). Lord's is 'the home of cricket' and also to both Marylebone and Middlesex cricket clubs, and remains the guardian of the Laws of Cricket. Matches are now sell-out events – the easiest tickets to get are for the last day of test matches, since these are not sold in advance. Book well ahead and then pack a picnic, champagne and a bat and ball – at the end of play, there's usually a pitch walk-on, where fans have a knock-up on the hallowed ground.

## FOOTBALL

Britain's Premiership League is known for its highly charged and fast-paced games; roughly half of London's 11 professional clubs are in this top division. Chelsea (or 'Chelski' since it's owned by Russian oligarch Roman Abramovitch) is probably the world's richest club – when the opposition is losing, the 'Blues' supporters wave wads of cash at them. Tickets are harder to get than scoring against Petr Cech, though tours of Chelsea's century-old ground are available. Chelsea's main rival in status is Arsenal (or 'the Gunners' – since the club was started by a group of employees of the Woolwich Arsenal Armament Factory in 1886). Some tickets are available from www.ticketmaster.co.uk or from the clubs direct (see www.thefa.com). If all else fails, try one of the touts, who loiter around the grounds on match days. Lesser leagues – the Coca-Cola Championship and Coca-Cola Leagues 1 and 2 – are far easier to access (www.football-league.co.uk).

---

**Arsenal Football Club, Emirates Stadium, Ashburton Grove, Highbury, N5**
Tel: 020 7704 4040  www.arsenal.com

---

**Chelsea Football Club, Stamford Bridge, Fulham Road, SW6**
Tel: 020 7915 2900  www.chelseafc.com

---

## GOLF

---

**Richmond Park Golf Courses, Roehampton Gate, Priory Lane, SW15**
Tel: 020 8876 1795  www.richmondparkgolfclub.org.uk

---

Set in the gorgeous surroundings of Richmond Park are two public 18-hole golf courses, a driving range, club hire, and a restaurant and bar. Daily tuition is available from PGA professionals.

## Urban Golf, 33 Great Pulteney Street, Soho, W1
Tel: 020 7434 4300  www.urbangolf.co.uk

What central London lacks in rolling golf courses, it makes up for with technology. Urban Golf is a virtual indoor course that digitally simulates over 50 of the world's most famous courses, providing full sets of Callaway clubs at each simulator. PGA professionals are on hand for guiding that swing, as are bar staff to bring the 19th hole right to your feet (also at 12 Smithfield Street, EC1; 020 7248 8600).

## HORSE-RIDING

## Hyde Park Riding School, 63 Bathurst Mews, W2
Tel: 020 7723 2813  www.hydeparkstables.com
Open: 7.15am–4pm Mon–Fri; 9am–4pm Sat, Sun (last hack at 3pm in winter)

There are five miles of bridleways and two arenas in Hyde Park. Its most famous bridle path, Rotten Row (from 'Route de Roi'), runs the length of the south side and was once a short cut between Buckingham and Kensington palaces. The Household Cavalry can still be seen on morning exercise here on their majestic, glossy mounts. Rather less glamorous nags can be rented from this British Horse Society-approved riding school, and note that it's safety first (read: 'quiet' horses, leading ropes across roads, and no cantering without prior tuition).

## Stag Lodge Stables, Robin Hood Gate, Kingston Vale, SW15
Tel: 020 8974 6066  www.ridinginlondon.com
Open: 8am–6pm Thurs–Sun; 8am–9pm Mon–Wed in winter; 8am–9pm daily in summer

For vast green horizons speckled with beautiful wild deer, the more accomplished rider should head out to Stag Lodge at Richmond Park, which offers group hacks up to two hours. Madonna has previously hired the entire stables.

## ICE-SKATING

Temporary ice-rinks are set up each winter in London's most lovely historic settings (from mid-November to end January) – in the neoclassical court-yard of Somerset House (home to three art galleries), in front of the Natural History Museum, and at Kew's Royal Botanic Gardens. Ali McGraw scarf-and-hat sets, mulled wine and much hand-holding all paint a romantic, festive scene – thus it's a popular venue for office parties and first dates; book ahead. Fanatics and amateur anthropologists should check out Queens Ice-skating & Bowling (17 Queensway, W2; 020 7229 0172) – its diner, ten-pin bowling alley and games arcade attract a rather different social scene. **Somerset House**, Strand, WC2; 020 7845 4670, www.somersethou-seicerink.org.uk; **Natural History Museum**, Cromwell Road, South Kensington, SW7; 020 7942 5000, www.nhm.ac.uk; **Kew Gardens**, Richmond, TW9; 020 8332 5000, www.kew.org (tickets for all also available from www.ticketmaster.co.uk, 0870 534 4444).

## KARAOKE

**Karaoke Box, 18 Frith Street, Soho, W1**
Tel: 0871 971 643  www.karaokebox.co.uk

The opposite of sleek, and none the worse for it: cocktails on demand; all the guilty pleasures you could ask for and a relatively modest bill at the end of it. Advance organisation advised.

**Lucky Voice, 52 Poland Street, Soho, W1**
Tel: 020 7439 3660  www.luckyvoice.co.uk
Open: 5.30pm–1am Mon–Thurs; 3pm–1am Fri/Sat; 3–10.30pm Sun

Nine private, sleekly designed 'pods', touch-screen technology, Japanese-influenced cocktails at the touch of a button, and over 4,500 songs including that hard-to-find Bros B-side. Ditto on the organization.

## LIDOS AND SWIMMING POOLS

A throwback to pre-jumbo jet days when holidaying in Britain was the only choice, lidos – large outdoor (unheated) pools, often still with Art Deco features, sunbathing decks and candy-coloured wooden changing cabins – bring a little bit of the seaside to the city. Fashionable in the 1920s and 1930s, they numbered around 30 in London; now just a third remain, and still represent the steely British spirit – lifelong regulars swim at the crack of dawn every day of the year. The weaker of will may prefer the new, sceney pools at Shoreditch House and Haymarket Hotel.

## Hampstead Ponds and Lido, East Heath Road, NW3
Open: 7am–6pm May–Sept; 7am–10am Sept–April

Among the lush, undulating hills of Hampstead Heath are three deep fresh-water ponds (two single-sex and one mixed) and a lido – the subject of a recent row between overzealous Health & Safety officials and locals over the dangers of unsupervised swimming in chilly waters. Now they recommend a medical check-up before taking to the waters – pah! Unaccompanied males should take note that the Heath is a cruising zone; its male pond is prone to 'shark infestation' and many swimmers prefer to be, ahem, at one with nature.

## Oasis Sports Centre, 32 Endell St, Covent Garden, WC2
Tel: 020 7831 1804
Open: 6.30am–9.15pm Mon–Fri; 9.30am–5.30pm Sat–Sun

A literal oasis in the centre of town, and no need to bring bravado since its 27-metre (88ft) outdoor pool is heated, and there's a back-up indoor pool. Also with squash courts, a gym, exercise classes and lovely sun terraces – make like the proverbial German and his beach towel on summer weekends though.

## Serpentine Lido, Hyde Park, W2
Tel: 020 7706 3422  www.serpentinelido.com
Open: daily, 10am–6pm mid-June to mid-Sept

A sectioned-off part of the Serpentine Lake, the lido has lured Londoners for over 100 years. At its maximum, there are 100 metres of straight swimming; there are also deck chairs, a paddling pool, a sandpit, a slide and swings, and the Lido Café in the old pavilion. The Serpentine Swimming Club swims there all year round; many of the 'serps' compete in the Peter Pan Christmas Day Race when water temperature averages 4°C.

**Tooting Bec Lido, Tooting Bec Road, SW16**
Tel: 020 8871 7198
Open: daily, 6am till dusk end May–end Aug

Built in 1906, Tooting is London's earliest purpose-built lido and is still Europe's largest, at 91 metres by 30 (300 by 30ft). It remains unheated and swimmers have been known to break the ice rather than break their habit. For winter madness, swimmers will need membership to the South London Swimming Club (020 8762 1416; open to all for an annual fee) to swim in the lido, and slatherings of goosefat.

## LONDON EYE

**London Eye, County Hall, Westminster Bridge Road, South Bank, SE1**
Tel: 0870 500 0600   www.ba-londoneye.com
Open: daily, 10am–8pm (9pm June–Sept)

This giant Ferris wheel serves both as a radical shake-up to London's skyline and as the city's tallest public viewing platform. At 135 metres (443ft) high, it was the world's largest observation wheel, built to celebrate the new millennium, but inevitably has since been trumped (by Singapore); on a clear day, it offers 20 miles' visibility. 32 glass pods each hold up to 25 people; the 'flight' takes 30 minutes, and whole pods can be booked out for champagne flights.

Other places to get high in London include Sir Christopher Wren's Monument, a single Doric column in EC2 (020 7626 2717). At 65 metres (213ft), it's the world's tallest isolated stone column. It was built in 1677 to commemorate the Great Fire, and its height is equal to its distance from Pudding Lane bakery where the fire started; inside are 311 dizzying steps to the top. Meanwhile, it's 530 steps up to the top of St Paul's Cathedral (85m/278ft up; see CULTURE) but those who'd prefer not to sweat for the view should take the lift direct to Vertigo 42, a champagne bar at the top of Tower 42 (née the Natwest Tower), situated 183 metres (600ft) up on the 42nd floor of London's fourth tallest (and dropping fast) building. By reservation only (020 7877 7842, www.vertigo42.co.uk).

# LONDON ZOO

**London Zoo, Outer Circle, Regent's Park, NW1**
Tel: 020 7722 3333  www.zsl.org
Open: daily, 10am–5.30pm (4pm Nov–Mar)

The conservation work of the Zoological Society of London has thrown animal rights activists off their high horses. Of London Zoo's 650 species, 112 are endangered and there are breeding programmes for over 130. It was founded in 1826 by Sir Stamford Raffles in Regent's Park as the world's first scientific zoo (Charles Darwin was a Fellow) and still retains some original Grade I and II listed structures, including the neoclassical Giraffe House (built in 1837), Lord Snowdon's aviary (built in 1964) and the 1930s modernist Penguin Pool (now for porcupines). Its most famous inhabitants are the Komodo dragons that grow up to 3.5m (10ft) long and can eat up to 80% of their bodyweight in one sitting.

# THE RIVER

The River Thames, at 215 miles long (rising in Gloucestershire), is no record breaker – although the city authorities claim it is the cleanest river in the world that runs through a city. Most Londoners wouldn't take a running jump, but it's certainly recognized as the city's most important feature, and harbours many historic landmarks – particularly striking after dark. The best and longest view is from Waterloo Bridge; some bridges are views in themselves (such as Tower Bridge), while others should be walked for posterity – for example, Norman Foster's Millennium Bridge (aka the Wobbly Bridge). Opened by the Queen in 2000, it was closed two days later, deemed unsafe due to the swaying motion pedestrians felt walking over it (all water under the bridge now). Take a river cruise from Westminster Pier to Greenwich (recommended is City Cruises, 020 7740 0400, www.citycruises.com). Most of the action is between Westminster and Tower Bridge, but in Greenwich is the line of longitude that marks GMT, plus maritime attractions including the Old Royal Naval College and the *Cutty Sark*, a 19th-century tea clipper. The river is also home to other floating museums, including:

## HMS Belfast, Morgan's Lane, SE1

Tel: 020 7940 6300  www.hmsbelfast.org.uk
Open: daily, 10am–6pm (5pm Nov–Feb)

Permanently moored just west of Tower Bridge, this 11,500-ton British war-cruiser served as a flagship in World War II. Set over nine decks are variously the engine room, the ops rooms, officers' cabins and (unintentionally) creepy waxwork sailors. There's a poignant chill on board as its recent history unfurls itself – it opened the bombardment of the Normandy coast on D-Day.

## The Golden Hinde, Cathedral Street, SE1

Tel: 0870 011 8700  www.goldenhinde.co.uk
Open: daily, 10am–5pm

Just to the west of HMS Belfast is an authentic reconstruction of Sir Francis Drake's 16th-century wooden galleon that circumnavigated the world in three years. Essentially, it's a Peter Pan stage set on five decks, with costumed pirates and sailors in authentic conditions (call ahead for availability).


## ROLLER-BLADING

Hyde Park sees most of the skate action – there's a hip black scene (complete with retro quad skates, legwarmers and ghetto blasters on shoulders (still!), snaking the Serpentine Road through DIY slalom courses), and sportos and skate punks who beat the life out of pucks and shins playing street hockey next to the Albert Memorial – join in if you care/dare. For the social skater, Citiskate organizes group skates – and, thankfully, tuition (020 7731 4999, www.citiskate.co.uk). The 'green run' Easy Peasy Skate (traffic-free and two miles long) is every Saturday morning in Battersea Park; the seven-mile-plus 'blue run' Rollerstroll is every Sunday afternoon in Hyde Park, and the 'black run' Friday Night Skate charges all over town at speeds of 32mph over 12-plus miles. There's also a roller-disco every Thursday, Friday and Saturday at The Renaissance Rooms, Vauxhall (020 7630 6625, www.rollerdisco.info; entry includes skate hire). Pogo-dancing not recommended.

**Slick Willies, 12 Gloucester Road, South Kensington, SW7**
Tel: 020 7225 0004
Open: 10am–6pm Mon–Sat; noon–5pm Sun

A skate shop just down the road from Hyde Park that rents skates and protective equipment.

## ROYAL PARKS

The 'lungs of London' were historically the playgrounds of kings and queens. Now they're open to all for picnics, play and oxygenating. The romantic St James's Park, designed by Buckingham Palace's architect John Nash, is the oldest Royal Park in London. Hire a stripy deckchair, sip on Prosecco at Inn the Park (see SNACK) or stroll along the lake to spot the scores of bird species there (the park's bird keeper even lives on site, at Duck House). Hyde Park is over 350 acres in size, with its own boating lake, lido and numerous cafés. Next to Marble Arch is Speakers' Corner where anyone is free to take to their soapbox (mostly it's just ranting religious fanatics). Centuries ago, Hyde Park was cleaved in two to make Kensington Gardens, Kensington Palace's 260-acre back garden (the palace has been home to Princess Diana, Queen Victoria and Princess Anne and is open to the public). Regent's Park covers 487 acres (including Primrose Hill), of which much is gloriously ornamental. Within its ring of palatial white Regency terraces are London Zoo, the Central London Mosque and the Open Air Theatre. For more information tel: 020 7298 2000, www.royalparks.gov.uk.

## RUGBY

**Twickenham Stadium, Rugby Road, Twickenham, Middlesex**
Tel: 020 8892 2000  www.rfu.com; tickets from www.ticketmaster.co.uk

On London's southwest outskirts is Twickenham, HQ of English Rugby Union and the venue for England's most important matches. Most – from premiership to World Cup matches – are played Saturday and Sunday afternoons. The main premiership teams in London are London Irish, London Wasps, NEC Harlequins and Saracens. Smaller games are played on their home grounds in and around London.

# SIGHT-SEEING

While lofty types may regard sightseeing tours with some hauteur, taking a tour is undeniably a fast way of getting your bearings, as well as delivering an ample portion of tapas tourism – London's most important nuggets presented with bite-sized information direct to your seat.

## The Big Bus Company
Tel: 020 7233 7797  www.bigbustours.com
Open: daily, 8.30am–4.30pm

Bus tours are not classy (the Queen has even banned them from passing in front of her house) but they are a pleasant, lazy way of nailing the key sights. The Big Bus Company has two hop-on, hop-off lines – the shorter red line has a live guide; the longer blue one has a recorded commentary in eight languages. Get the top deck for top views. Also recommended is the Original London Sightseeing Tour (020 8877 1722, www.theoriginaltour.com).

## Black Taxi Tours
Tel: 020 7935 9363  www.blacktaxitours.co.uk
Open: daily, 8am–midnight

A tourist attraction in their own right, cabbies train for at least three years to get the 'knowledge' – a comprehensive mental map of London. Black Taxi Tour cabbies are also trained guides and will conduct two-hour door-to-door tours for up to five people any time of day or year.

## Duck Tours
Tel: 020 7928 3132  www.londonducktours.co.uk
Open: daily, 10am–1hr before sunset, or 6pm in summer

So-called because the tour covers both land and water in a World War II amphibious DUKWS craft, the route starts and finishes by the London Eye, takes 75 minutes and covers just the very central sites, with a rather dramatic launch into the Thames itself. Since it's such an odd-looking vehicle (painted a conspicuous yellow), the Duck and its passengers become something of an attraction themselves.

## Heli-tours
Tel: 020 8953 4411  www.cabairhelicopters.com
Open: 9.45am–4pm Sat–Sun

With an average speed of 120mph and with zero congestion, helicopter tours are by far the most efficient way of joining up the dots – in 30 minutes the captain covers Kew Gardens, Westminster, the Tower of London and the Thames Barrier, while giving a full commentary. However, you will have to negotiate London's traffic to get to your chopper – they're based in Elstree, Hertfordshire (weekends only).

## The London Bicycle Tour Company, Gabriel's Wharf, SE1
Tel: 020 7928 6838  www.londonbicycle.com
Open: daily, 10.30am–1.30pm Oct–Mar; 2–5pm April–Sept

While London is no Amsterdam, two-wheelers certainly have the advantage in traffic and it's the fast track to engaging with the city. Tours run daily (bespoke rides available) and are mostly quite leisurely, though sloths might consider hiring one of their driven rickshaws.

## London RIB Voyages
Tel: 020 7928 8933  www.londonribvoyages.com
Open: daily, 10.30am–1hr before sunset (Sat/Sun only Oct–Mar)

RIB being, of course, Rigid Inflatable Boat, this one-hour tour gets you very close to Thames Water in a very fast 12-seater dinghy, travelling from the Houses of Parliament, out past Greenwich to the Thames Barrier. Available for private charter.

## Tour Guides Ltd
Tel: 020 7495 5504  www.tourguides.co.uk

Walking tours are the best way to discover London's nooks and crannies. Of course, trotting en masse in matching cagoules after an erect umbrella is route one to loss of street cred, but this company is far more discreet, with tailored tours from approved 'blue badge' guides to most of London's lures, including the 2012 Olympics, the *Da Vinci Code*, *Love Actually* and *Notting Hill* film locations, Royal London, Westminster and the cultural heritage sites. Driver guides are also available.

## Urban Gentry
Tel: 020 8149 6253   www.urbangentry.com

Creative and tailor made tours of London from industry insiders. From fashion and shopping to art and design, be led around the city by someone who really has a passion for their subject. Bespoke tours are also available.

## SPAS

Pity those poor Londoners. More specifically, those cash-rich, time-poor Londoners – so time-strapped are they that the trend now is to offer multiple pairs of hands to get hands, feet, hair and face sparkling at once, carwash style (try Groom, 49 Beauchamp Place, SW3; 020 7581 1248, www.groomlondon.com, and Cowshed, 119 Portland Road, W11; 020 7078 1944, www.cowshedonline.com). There are still relatively few true spas combining therapeutic treatments with wet spa facilities (steam, Jacuzzi, sauna, pool) – we believe Mandarin Oriental's E'SPA and the new Ushvani spa are among the nicest places to lose a day.

## Bliss Spa, 60 Sloane Avenue, Knightsbridge, SW3
Tel: 020 7584 3888   www.blisslondon.com
Open: 9.30am–8pm Mon–Fri; 9.30am–6.30pm Sat; noon–6pm Sun

Bliss's tongue-in-cheek treatment names (The Upper Hand, Foot Patrol, Homme Improvements, etc) belie its high-tech, no-nonsense standard of procedure. Decorated in a clean signature palette of white and aqua, the ground floor of Bliss London (the UK outpost of the cult New York spa) houses a row of nail stations where well-heeled locals and day-trippers indulge in manicures and pedicures (so rated are their therapists that they're often dispatched to tend to high-maintenance celebrities who might have chipped a nail). Downstairs, beyond the suede banquette-lined relaxation room are private treatment rooms for all face and body services – including the Quadruple Thighpass and the Betweeny Wax.

## Elemis Day Spa, 2–3 Lancashire Court, Mayfair, W1
Tel: 020 7499 4995   www.elemis.com
Open: 9am–9pm Mon–Thurs; 9am–8pm Fri–Sat; 10am–6pm Sun

This exotic spa off Bond Street can get so oversubscribed that flying to the

Far East seems easier than getting an appointment. However, once in the incense-infused, silk-clad, Buddha-guarded confines, you'll see that those far-flung destinations have been brought to you. The mosaic-ed Moroccan Rasul (or steam chamber) is fit for an Arabian king and starts with a slathering of medicinal chakra mud and a recline in a heated throne to allow its detoxifying properties to take hold, followed by a rain shower. By the time the Tibetan chimes signal the end of your treatment you may well feel you have spent a week in a tropical idyll (NB: serious skincare is also available with facials for every complaint). Privacy-seeking Elemis fans may prefer Intercontinental Hotel's VIP spa suite (Park Lane; 020 7318 8691) with its secret entrance for A-list guests.

## Spa Illuminata, 63 South Audley Street, Mayfair, W1

Tel: 020 7499 7777  www.spailluminata.com
Open: 10am–8pm Mon–Fri; 10am–6pm Sat

Classicists will appreciate the décor of Spa Illuminata whose marble pillars, mosaic floors and mock gargoyle fountains lend it the feel of an ancient Greek or Roman bath. However, the emphasis of this women-only sanctuary is not traditional wet spa therapies but holistic skincare treatments courtesy of the sophisticated French botanical brands Decléor and Carita. Each treatment begins with a diagnostic back massage that eases you into a deeply relaxed state, laying bare any troublesome areas. The facials are some of the most thorough around, while the deeply relaxing four-hands massage is almost enough to persuade the imagination its mistress is a goddess being tended by her cherubs.

## The Spa at Mandarin Oriental, 66 Knightsbridge, SW1

Tel: 020 7838 9888  www.mandarinoriental.com
Open: daily, 7am–10pm

The cosseting starts before you have even changed thanks to soft spotlighting, dark granite flooring and black walnut wood fittings. Complete relaxation is promised with a dip in the Vitality Pool, while hydrotherapy jets give muscles a satisfying massage. Toxins are gently purged in the Amethyst Crystal Steam Room and Sanarium (cooler than a sauna), and in case of any residual stress, there's chill-out in the colour therapy relaxation area. Holistic massages, facials and body treatments (with E'SPA products) are East-meets-West in philosophy. Full- and half-day spa programmes are available and include use of the gym but recommended is the Advanced Time Ritual – a two-hour treatment (often Ayurvedic) matched to your specific needs on the day.

## Urban Retreat at Harrods, 5th Floor, Harrods, Knightsbridge, SW1

Tel: 020 7893 8333  www.urbanretreat.co.uk
Open: 10am–7pm Mon–Sat; noon–6pm Sun

The gargantuan proportions of Harrods' Urban Retreat (covering a whopping 2,320sq.m/25,000sq.ft) and its constant bustle may not make this the ultimate beauty utopia, but what it lacks in tranquillity it makes up for in choice. The Urban Retreat houses some of Britain's best beauty experts: there's a Shavata brow studio, a Leighton Denny nail salon, a Philip Kingsley trichology clinic and a Roja Dove bespoke perfumery. It is also the only place in the country where you can indulge in the deluxe Crème de la Mer facial, administered in a suite with exotic fish tanks for windows. Perfunctory beautifiers such as waxing, laser hair removal and endermology (cellulite-busting) are not forgotten.

## Ushvani, 1 Cadogen Gardens, Chelsea, SW3

Tel: 020 7730 2888  www.ushvani.com
Open: 10am–9pm Mon–Sat

Inspired by South East Asia, clients are greeted by an aquarium, considered by Malaysians to promote good fortune. Before treatments – scrubs, wraps, facials and Malay, Thai and Balinese massages – guests are encouraged to spend the first 20 minutes limbering up under the vitality pool's water jets, sweating it out in the steam room or indulging in a spot of colour therapy under the tropical rain shower. Like at all of the best spas, it is the attention to detail that makes the experience most magical. Here, tiny drawstring bags are provided for storing jewellery, flower features are set into the floor to amuse when face down on the couch and you can hook up your MP3 player if you would rather listen to something more inspiring than pan pipes.

## TENNIS

### All England Lawn Tennis Club, Church Road, Wimbledon, SW19
Tel: 020 8946 2244  www.wimbledon.org
Open: daily, 10.30am–5pm

For spectating, strawberries and cream, Wimbledon is the obvious venue (the fortnight-long championship starts in the last week of June). Access to Centre and Number One courts requires corporate clout or obsessive-compulsive organization; day tickets for the outer courts can be queued for on the day, though 'the day' for many starts the night before with sleeping bags and gritted determination. The museum, whose collection dates back to 1555, is open all year round.

### Regent's Park Golf and Tennis School, Outer Circle, Regent's Park, NW1
Tel: 020 7724 0643  www.rpgts.co.uk
Open: daily, 8am–9pm

Three floodlit outdoor tennis courts are available by the hour (booking essential). Professional tuition is available. There's also a nine-hole golf course and a driving range.

# info...

## DRIVING

'The man who is tired of London is tired of looking for a parking space,' said Paul Theroux, paraphrasing Dr Johnson (see PLAY). Add to that a weekday congestion charge (www.cclondon.com; 0845 900 1234), traffic that chugs along at 10mph, aggressive drivers (especially the notorious 'white van man') and a confusing road layout, and drivers are sure to knot their knickers. The undeterred should drive on the left and keep to 20–30mph in town – as if there's much chance of exceeding it. Many roads have bus lanes (the far left lane, clearly marked); you can incur a fine for driving in these at certain times, so check the road signs. Parking – if you can find it – is by the meter, Pay and Display or in car parks – and pricey.

## MONEY

Britain continues to resist the euro, and the proud pound lives on. The majority of British banknotes in circulation are issued by the Bank of England (in denominations of £5, £10, £20 and £50), but some Scottish banknotes can infiltrate London's system. If unfamiliar or uncertain, ask the cashier to swap them.

## NAVIGATION

No Londoner is without their A–Z map to get from A to B (see also www.streetmap.co.uk) but with medieval town planning, it's rarely straightforward. London's alphanumeric postcodes follow about as little logic as its street layout. The initial letters indicate the compass orientation (C=Central, NW=North West etc) but the numbers can seem meaningless, so SW1 is central while SW2 is Brixton in the south.

## PUBLIC HOLIDAYS

Public holidays, or bank holidays, land on 1 January, Good Friday, Easter Monday, the first and last Mondays in May, the last Monday in August, 25 and 26 December – many enterprises take this opportunity to close, so call ahead to check.

## PUBLIC TRANSPORT

Forever a source of anguish to Londoners, this includes the Underground, bus, overland trains and river transport. The Underground, or tube, is the most efficient (or the best of a bad bunch) but rush hour by any mode is grim. Fares vary depending on how many zones (some six concentric circles, where Zone 1 is the bull's-eye) are travelled through. Allow three minutes between each station and if making two or more journeys in a day, buy a Day Travelcard or Oystercard (which can be used on buses and trains). Tubes run 5.30am–12.30am Mon–Sat and 7am–11.30pm Sundays. London buses are good for getting your bearings but not so useful if you don't recognize your destination. London Transport's helpline is 020 7222 1234.

## SMOKING

Smoking is banned in all bars, restaurants and clubs. This has led to a spike in patio heater sales, pavement parties, and 'smirting' (smoking and flirting on the pavement).

## TAXIS

All black cab drivers have the 'knowledge' – a qualification that takes on average 34 months to memorize the streets of London. Cabbies can take up to five passengers and are usually up for sharing cabbie politics; empty cabs light up their yellow 'TAXI' light. Cheaper taxis can be booked through Addison Lee (020 7387 8888). If alone and in a hurry, call for their traffic-busting motorbike taxi (try also www.passengerbikes.com, 0700 596 3292, and www.virginlimobike.com, 020 7930 0814). Ignore approaches from unlicensed minicabs.

## TELEPHONES

The international dialling code for the UK is +44. The code for London is 020, followed two sets of four digits. Central London numbers start with 7, outer London numbers start with 8. If calling London from abroad, the code is +44 20.

## TIPPING

Taxis, restaurants and fancy bars expect a tip. For cabbies, it is polite to round up the fare (many Londoners don't tip any more than this since fares are so expensive). Bar tipping is discretionary, but expected with table service. Restaurants expect from 12.5%, but check it's not already included; tipping in cash gives it a better chance of staying out of management's hands.

# index

# Hg2 London

# index

# index